The Bones & Breath

The Bones & Breath

*A Man's Guide to Eros,
the Sacred Masculine,
and the Wild Soul*

L. R. HEARTSONG

WHITE CLOUD PRESS
ASHLAND, OREGON

White Cloud Press books may be purchased for educational, business, or sales promotional use. For information, please write:

Special Market Department
White Cloud Press
PO Box 3400, Ashland, OR 97520
Website: www.whitecloudpress.com

Cover image by Shutterstock
Cover and interior design by C Book Services
Author photo by Rae Huo

First edition: 2014

14 15 16 17 18   10 9 8 7 6 5 4 3 2 1
Printed in the United States of America

Library of Congress Cataloging–in–Publication Data

Heartsong, L. R.

The bones and breath : a man's guide to eros, the sacred masculine, and the wild soul / L.R. Heartsong.

    pages cm

  Includes bibliographical references and index.

  ISBN 978-1-940468-16-7 (paperback)

1. Spiritual life. 2. Soul. 3. Sensuality--Religious aspects. 4. Masculinity--Religious aspects.

I. Title.

BL624.H38155 2014

155.3'32--dc23

2014030084

For Kuʻuipo—cleverly disguised teacher, mirror, best friend and beloved. This work would not have been possible without your enduring and unwavering support. I go on choosing you.

For Suzanne, Celeste and Katherine . . . guardian angels, all.

And for Madame Pele, fiery but loving embodiment of the Divine Feminine.

ACKNOWLEDGMENTS

I remain humbly and gratefully indebted to the many wise and awakened ones who have influenced and guided me along this mysterious journey. A few particularly luminous souls warrant particular mention:

Erika Luckett, *hermana de alma*, the heart of kindness and inspiration. Your passionate song uplifts the Soul of the World. I owe much to your astute and highly conscious insights.

Sara Rowan, good witch of Kent and brilliant artist, for being a true and spooky friend when I most needed one. You remain the very best that England has to offer.

Author and visionary, Bill Plotkin, whose words and teachings offered a cornerstone for my working consciously with soul. Thank you, Weaver.

Wise mentor, the lovely Annie Bloom, my Kinswoman of the Healing Hands. You embody Mystery so eloquently in your wild, compassionate heart. I am honored to call you *friend*.

Underworld guide, Peter Scanlan, who first gave me the words, *the Sacred Masculine*. You are a wise embodiment of that beautiful energy.

My wild kindred, "Shaper" and "Temple," for tending the heart fires and sharing your beautiful sanctuary with me while I penned the final chapter of this book. Honeysluts, unite.

Steve Scholl, publisher at White Cloud Press, for enthusiastically welcoming this book, believing in its merit, and guiding it into the world as an offering to humanity's collective evolution.

To the many unsung heroes—clients, workshop and men's group participants, teachers, authors, friends, lovers, and strangers—bless you for all that you bring to the "other-than-human" world.

For every being—human and *other*—who has stirred me to wake from the trance of daily existence to the sensuous dream of life.

Gaia and the Wild Beloved, manifested in all the places I have lived and where this dream of earth has emerged *through* me.

If we are not in awe, we are not paying attention.
~ Erika Luckett, singer/songwriter

What if we discover that our present way of life is irreconcilable
with our vocation to become fully human?
~ Paulo Freire

CONTENTS

AUTHOR'S NOTE

Throughout this text, I have routinely employed the differing capitalization of *nature* and *Nature*. The noncapitalized noun stands for the various wild organisms, creatures, and ecosystems of our terrestrial globe, while the capitalized represents a spiritual force and collective entity.

In a similar vein, eschewing the current minimalistic style popular in American publishing, I have deliberately chosen to capitalize specific words—not merely for emphasis but to further acknowledge their distinct identity as a spiritual force, mythic experience, or archetype (i.e , the Sacred Other, Dreamtime, the Larger Story, Death, etc.), or to denote a Native American-type of recognition and honoring (i.e., The Old Ones (elders and ancients), Standing Ones (trees) etc.).

PREFACE

This isn't the book I originally set out to write. As often happens in the creative process, what was intended to be one thing became something else entirely. My initial intention and words focused around soul and the body but, somewhere along the mysterious road, I ended up being seduced and drawn in by alluring hands of shadow and light. I found myself writing about the elemental energy of Eros.

For a good portion of the writing, the working title of this book was *The Erotic Warrior*. Despite the word *erotic*, this is not a book about sex. Not directly, anyway. It is, however, a book about heart and soul and how these elements underpin our sensual connection with life. Like dappled sunlight amid leafy trees on a summer afternoon, it's an invitation into the senses—an offering of how our innate creativity and sensory nature can guide us in a tangible, body-centered way to an existence of deep meaning and connection. What you hold in your hands is an embodied approach to the soul's longing for authenticity in life: vital and visceral connection with nature, work, community, relationships . . . and sex.

A river whose swirling currents shift along the course of its journey, the manuscript for this book morphed repeatedly. Originating with a series of essays about soul and the senses, I found myself writing about the spark of creativity as the embodiment and energy of Eros. As the focus evolved, it became clear that what I was writing (or what was being written *through* me, rather) was a man's book. Written by a man and directed to men, heart to heart, with nothing held back. In rough terms, what was evolving was a sort of field guide for full-spectrum living.

Initially I thought that I was writing from a fairly embodied place—feet on the floor, upright posture, comfortable in my body, breath open and full—but I realized that I was mainly composing from my cognitive faculties (not an unusual trait for a writer) and that something much deeper was seeking its way through. I struggled to set aside what I thought I knew or should tell and began to listen more keenly. More and more insisted on coming forward concerning the Sacred Masculine and Eros until it became the very heart of the book. I grasped that I was no longer the one steering the boat. Rather than struggling to contain the writing in a direction in which it no longer wanted to flow, in order to keep my vessel upright I simply needed to let the river run and trust in its guidance.

It was the breath and body that led me to a deeper place, guiding me to undiscovered levels of embodiment, where I encountered a significantly different vision of the soul than I had held previously. The initial outline for this book quickly landed in the recycling bin, and each chapter has emerged organically in a curious, nonlinear fashion and in an order different from that of the finished chapters (thus the reader may note that the cycle of seasons as narrated seems out of order or lacks continuity). As the process has spiraled me along a journey of discovery and expansion I have spent hours simply living the questions. Walking with them, dancing with them (literally), and breathing into them, I listened for what then arose: a quiet truth ringing like a bell in my body and an accompanying sense of expansion in my core.

More than once I threw my hands up in desperation and went for a long walk through the green fields and whispering woods of England, feeling overwhelmed by the task at hand. The storyteller in me longed to sit down and weave a fantastic tale, a soulful novel, but this strange work held me firmly in its grasp. Like a stubborn terrier with his ball, it simply refused to let go. I became a reluctant messenger; drawing a deep breath, I endeavored to open more fully to the flow.

In a spiral-like process, this book emerged through dreams, walking in Nature, creative movement, breath, listening, and being fully in my body. As I surrendered to the process, the manuscript's evolution changed not only *me* but also my very notions of soul and embodiment. Cooperating with this expansion, yielding to the power of it, I found myself catapulted forward on my own journey of transformation.

Much has been written about heart and soul over the ages, a theme nearly as timeless as the myths of mankind. More than a fair number of words have been printed about living a path with heart, choosing a road less traveled, and being in the moment. However, it seems that less has been set forth about *embodying* heart and soul—that is, the body as primary referent for engaging a soul-infused life.

The printed words slow to a mere trickle when they address men seeking an embodied life of authentic, creative meaning. Yet surely there is something worthwhile to say about a man's spirit, heart, and flesh as the wellspring for a soulcentric life. Our bones and breath form a miraculous framework from which to engage the world with imagination, dreams, power, and passion—the way of the wild soul.

Currently on our planet there is a Great Work at hand and men play an essential role in it. Indeed, the male principle of action will prove indispensable in setting things right in a world very out of balance. However, it will take a new sort of man, a multidimensional and soulfully embodied one, to counterbalance our destructive patterns and embrace a more relational nature with the earth and her denizens, human and not.

As I look over this book, the heart of it now rests in the connection between Eros, "bodysoul," (our embodied, authentic essence), and the creative union of the Sacred Masculine and the Divine Feminine within all of us. I would say it is an evolution from our stale, limiting notions of manhood. It's a journey to wholeness and healing—really, an expansion past restrictive patterns and an awakening of the heart. Embodying the soul is as much an adventure as sailing to the edge of the world . . . and then beyond.

My own experiences and stories are interspersed throughout the book, mostly as connections with nature and the "other-than-human" world. As I gaze over my shoulder and look back at the curiously twisting road that I have traveled in life, perhaps it isn't so strange that I would end up here with this offering in hand and bring the Erotic Warrior to life.

I certainly never intended to be writing a book about Eros or the Sacred Masculine, but I can now see how my love of writing and a career in the healing arts have dovetailed mysteriously together. Through twenty years of working with clients—integrative bodywork, counseling, "Soul Embodiment" coaching, men's groups, workshops, rites-of-passage work, and wilderness retreats—I have come to understand a fair amount about the bodymind, healing, creativity, and the soul's journey. Like a harvester among the leafy vines with his wicker basket of sweet, sun-ripened grapes, I carry a wealth of stories, both others' and my own, and I want to share them with you.

My hope for this book is that it finds and fills a niche, sending tendrils into the hearts of men and cracking them open as a growing tree can shatter stone with its probing roots. In regard to the Sacred Masculine and the Erotic Warrior, I offer that it doesn't matter whether you identify as straight, bisexual, or gay. Soul-centered, embodied manhood has nothing to do with one's sexual orientation; Eros unites the broad spectrum, embracing all our various and infinitely creative approaches to sexual expression. There's something here for every man. Women, too.

Actually, I hope this book finds its way into the hands of countless women, perhaps as an unexpected token from a lover, partner, or friend. A gift of Eros and the Mystery. Regardless of one's physical gender or sexuality, the Sacred Masculine exists as consort to the Divine Feminine, and this hallowed union is the source and spark of creativity throughout the cosmos, from atoms to artwork.

My prayer is that something in these pages and chapters stirs your soul, like a sunrise flashing with luminous fire across hushed fields at dawn, offering a pause to ponder something hitherto unconsidered. There are questions that cannot be answered—ones that can only be lived with an open mind and heart—and this book is full of them.

What does it mean to be an authentic, heart-centered man who owns and wields his true power? How does a man integrate the disparate parts of his self, both light and shadow, to embody his creative soul? And what does it mean to be in expansive, sensuous connection with the other-than-human world, the Sacred Other, and our human beloved? How does the body guide us? Can we have a truly wild soul in the modern world?

The book you're holding (or reading on a tablet) is the first of two books, each roughly half of the original, much larger manuscript. Though I felt the information was important and the gestalt of it complete, I decided that it was simply too long. Less is more. In an attempt to make the work even more accessible, I have added a section titled "Embodying the Erotic Warrior" at the terminus of each chapter, where I highlight an essential Soul Skill and outline an embodiment exercise. The intention behind these offerings is to firmly anchor some of the key messages, as well as to offer practical tools for the soulful journey. In their own way, each of the skills and exercises invites you to step outside your gate, shift from your well-worn groove, and expand your worldview. Myriad "soul skills" exist beyond the few I have outlined (seven more follow in the next book). Individually or together they help build a bodysoul practice— opening the senses and heart; building authentic power; descending fully into the body; joining in communion with the other-than-human world.

The unique Soul Skills require no particular setting or environment; they work whether you live in Savannah, Santa Fe, Santiago, or the Seychelles. However, it can be very useful (and evocative) to explore the embodiment exercises while outdoors in a semiwild, natural environment where your senses dilate in a different way. An inviting park or garden makes a good option if "nature" seems far away or difficult to reach. Even a backyard or outside on a fire escape can offer the soul a welcome getaway from the four walls (ceiling and floor, as well) that typically contain you. Anywhere you can find some quiet, uninterrupted space will suffice for most of the exercises dotted throughout the book. For a deeper excavation of psyche and soul, explore the additional bodysoul insights offered for each Soul Skill and embodiment exercise.

Essentially, this is a book about wholeness, authenticity, healing, personal evolution, and being connected to something larger . . . *much larger*. If we open our hearts, senses, and minds, we begin to detect a cosmic story unfolding everywhere around us. Something is seeking expression *through* us, nudging us further in a soulful evolution, both personal and transpersonal. Our mission is to wake up, pay attention, and engage that Larger Story in a meaningful manner that embodies our soul and resonates in our bones with authentic power.

A new voice speaks in the gathering, powerful wind. Like a noble stag that emerges from the dark wood to stand at the edge of a clearing, the Sacred Masculine returns. Mighty Eros is his herald and Gaia, with a welcoming heart, celebrates his very timely arrival. Our mission as conscious men is to embody this archetype in our bones, breath, and compassionate heart and to evolve to a higher ideal of manhood.

Brother, in the pages ahead we will descend into the bodysoul and explore a different vision of masculinity, one that is steeped in the soul's authentic power. I hope this book will help guide you in discovering an answer to the questions I repeatedly ask: *What is your gift to the other-than-human world, and what does it mean to be a wild soul?*

L. R. Heartsong

INTRODUCTION
THE EROTIC WARRIOR

Revelation strikes in the midst of an English field at twilight as I am walking alone with my thoughts. Below me, the Weald of Kent stretches and rolls away towards the South Downs and the English Channel, the vista trembling in the soft light of a May evening. Stopping at a weathered, wooden fence post, as I gaze towards the setting sun a silver bell rings out within my chest, scattering my thoughts with its crystalline tone.

For an exquisitely shining moment lasting less than a minute, the veil falls away and I behold this small facet of the world as more than a picturesque, painted landscape of dusky light and shadow. Instead, it is a living miracle beyond comprehension. Each blade of grass, every purple clover flower, each buzzing insect, the noble trees dancing in unseen currents of conscious air, the living soil and microbes; everything is alive and spinning with infinite, cosmic intelligence. Each molecule communicates and hums in harmonic relationship with everything around it. Our planet is the ultimate symphony of consciousness.

Though I have understood it as a concept and held it as a belief, in this illuminated moment gazing across the painted fields at sunset, I literally *see* and comprehend the Unified Field of energy. Despite the distinctly unique and separate objects that form the ecosystem around me, from English oak to ring-neck pheasant to wriggling pond newt, this entire existence is one seamless conversation. Everything coexists in a sphere of incomprehensible, interdependent relationship and harmony, existing both in form and nonform.

Standing on the edge of the grassy hill, my own life seems insignificant, as passing as a noisy bumblebee. Yet I, too, am composed of the same elemental intelligence that breathes in blazing stars and sighs in the terrible beauty of galaxies. With each breath, I draw in that living intelligence, suffusing my cells and blood with far more than mere oxygen. Inspiration. With every inhalation, I am filled with more than air; I am permeated and alive with the creative intelligence and breath of the Divine.

For a few glimmering moments, the hazy curtain of perception rises and I truly *see* in a way that I never have before. There is no burning bush, no numinous illumination from the trees or grass to knock me breathless. Instead, I can see inside everything: simultaneous light and shadow, fathomless intelligence, harmonic frequencies, and a mind-shattering complexity of relationship. Visible and invisible. Sound and silence. Form and nonform.

Awesome is far too clunky and meager a word to describe the moment. *Sublime, revelatory, rapture* . . . all words fail and fall short. How does one capture the Infinite when it reveals itself?

Instead, every cell of my body sings itself alive to join the cosmic chorus. I tremble as the bell in my chest again rings out with its clear, high tone across the fields, calling all beings to prayer and celebration.

WALKING IN BEAUTY

Before this moment of revelation, I was out walking a dirt footpath through familiar fields and orchards, marveling at the exquisitely rich illumination of the late May evening and the way it coaxed forth the utmost splendor of everything it touched. Every whispering field stood forth to become a luminous Impressionist painting. Each tree, crowned in leafy glory, transformed into a dancer on stage in a golden spotlight. I, lucky soul, sat spellbound in the front row of the audience, dazzled as the spectacle unfolds before me, unsure of where to turn my head or look next because *everything* was surreal in its illuminated beauty.

At this hour of the evening, the wild rabbits in the fields were thick as thieves. They were everywhere, alarmed at my hulking approach, some of them preciously small and scarcely larger than my fist, all of them bounding quickly into the safety of underground warrens and thickly green hedgerows.

The air smelled of dry earth, heady grass, and sweet flowers. As I passed a darkly alluring burrow beneath tree roots, a cozy den for some wild creature, I caught the unmistakable whiff of acrid fox urine.

Hello, clever fox, I smiled, walking on. *It's been awhile since I've seen you on my doorstep or in the lane. Are you watching me now from some sheltered spot?*

It was my third day of fasting; a conscious abstinence from food as part of a ten day, internal cleansing program that I learned years ago from Auntie Margaret Machado in Hawai'i. My body felt light as air, my senses keen and unusually sharp. I was in a split mode of consciousness as I wandered, like dolphins who sleep and dream in the dark sea while half their brain stays awake to remind them to surface and breathe. My mind mused on sleep and waking as a metaphor for consciousness, while my physical senses absorbed with rapturous delight the sights, sounds, and smells around me as I walked, gathering them up as sensual treasures of the temple of my soul. The sensation of wind on my face and stirring my unruly hair; the audible, textural crunch of earth beneath my feet; the way my breath felt in the hollows of my legs; the way the swaying movement of the trees sent subtle ripples through my own body and sensations; the flow of vitality, energy, and passion in my core like a current of aliveness and power.

Feeling energetic despite the evening hour and my abstinence from food, my body was a chorus of muscles, sinews, and bones humming together in harmonious resonance. Walking brings me alive, calls me into the sensory experience of my body as nothing else does but dance. If I don't walk a few miles every day, I quickly begin to feel restless and agitated, a host of carpenter ants swarming under the soft, elastic bark of my skin. Or I slip gently but steadily into a malaise that clouds my spirit, weighing me down with invisible gray rain. The body aches to be played like the instrument that it is; muscles as notes waiting to be plucked from a grand piano that sits in an empty hall, yearning to be brought alive into somatic music. The body wants to *move*, to tell its bound and hidden stories, and to find delight and freedom in that motion. It yearns to expand outward through the senses in communion. To dance with the soul and the natural world brings the bodymind alive and singing.

So I walk. Wherever I live, wandering gypsy that I am, I head out on foot. There is beauty and mystery to be discovered everywhere, from the wild places of the earth to the bustling streets of urban cities. With senses cast open wide, there is a feast to be savored in a multisensory connection with the moment . . . a wild soul, awake in the world.

It was a Technicolor sunset, one to take your breath away, and I imagined that even the rabbits were sitting up to notice. As I passed through an apple orchard, I noted the dramatic increase in the size of the leaves since I had passed this way a week ago, alongside the swelling polyps with faded remnants of blossoms attached. I love this old orchard with its straight, quiet rows of gnarled soldiers, soon to bear sweet fruit rather than guns or swords. I sensed that I, too, in this season of growth was quietly and irrepressibly blossoming forth into some new creation to offer the world.

Alas, I didn't yet know what that might be.

NAKED TO THE GODS

And so it was that threading along the skirt of the hill and savoring a quiet countryside evening, I rounded a bend and came face-to-face with the Universe shimmering with numinous light and reverberating through the English fields. The Unified Field, indeed.

When I finally move on from my stunned moments of revelation, an airy lightness animates my body, as if someone has stripped off the heavy outer layers; ones that I never realized were leaden and dead. Though the mystical union of the higher, transpersonal state has already retreated behind the veil, I move through the whispering and waving wheat field in an altered awareness, sensitive to my own energy in a way that I'm not accustomed to. I feel as exposed as a tender mollusk with its protective, lacquered shell pried open. Will something vast and dark now snatch me up and swallow me whole?

Yes, I accept. I will not resist. I surrender to the Mystery that is unfolding.

Long ago I realized that it is only by fully embracing our mortality, the sure inevitability of our death, that one appreciates the preciousness of life. As we engage life with sensory awareness and soul, choosing to consciously inhabit this temple of body and breath, our days echo with the voice of the sacred. We are only passing through. How will we live and savor this day, this moment . . . ?

From the hill, I descend across the open field of emerald at twilight, an apple orchard to my left. Still in an altered state, I feel as if my body is woven of some light mesh rather than flesh and bone, that I am open and porous to the pulsing web of life around me. A voice whispers in my mind.

Go naked to the gods.

In a flash, I remember my dream of the previous night. In the mystical Dreamtime, I am walking naked down a country dirt road alongside an orchard to my left. I see a woman approaching and, feeling suddenly embarrassed for my nudity, I step into the orchard to hide, hoping that she won't see me.

Go naked to the gods.

More than just a mishmash of neural firings, our dreams—both sleeping and waking—carry important invitations and messages from the soul. Remembering this dream and seeing the orchard now on my left, I sense an upwelling of energy in my core, something like a trembling. I'm gripped with the nearly overwhelming desire to strip off my clothes and walk naked through the field; to expand in bodymind rather than contract in fear. There is a somatic sense of urgency to be essentially and unutterably myself—naked—and to reenact my dream.

I feel the cool swirl of fear in my gut, whirling and mixing with a rising core of energy. My eyes scan the surrounding fields of rippling green wheat and the edge of the hill hemmed in dusky ribbons of rose-infused light. The nearest farmhouse is more than a half-mile distant and I see no one about.

This is crazy, I think. *I'll be arrested in a foreign country for public nudity in a wheat field.*

The electric vibration streaming up in my core feels like a scream waiting to explode and my body trembles visibly with both fear and anticipation. I stand in the evening breeze, internally wrestling with myself, sensing how fear constricts the energy that seeks expansion.

Just do it. Take off your clothes.

Slowly I strip off my shirt, the evening air cool enough on my skin that my brown nipples contract and stand up perkily. I stand for a minute, hesitating. Trembling, I slip out of my shoes, peel off my socks, and then step out of my old, faded jeans.

I will not limit myself in fear. I will go naked before the gods.

Stripped bare, I stand in the field, arms outstretched to the fading, periwinkle sky and gentle breeze. The wind moves around me, appraising my offering with soft fingers that measure and whisper.

Slowly I walk, carrying my clothes in one hand and my shoes in the other. My tender, bare feet explode with the sensations of direct contact with crunchy soil, prickly grasses, and jagged rock. Manroot hanging freely, bouncing lightly from side to side as I walk, I savor being unbound and exposed. Authentically free.

Step by tender step, I follow the worn footpath across the field of knee-high wheat, parting a grassy sea of green like some wild, naked prophet. Tremblingly alive and awake with every sense heightened, I cross the rough ground, wondering who can see me and laughing at myself for my self-conscious fears, imagining dialogues between my potential observers, human and otherwise. Only the humans would be fussed.

How tightly shame keeps us bound, I muse.

As I walk the rough earth, my fear seems to fall away. My shoulders roll back a bit, opening my chest. I breathe fully into my entire torso, letting my belly expand and soften. I feel my entire being expanding, senses wide open in communion with the evening sky above me, the air that dances round, and Mother Earth underfoot.

When I reach the far side of the wide field, nearly a five-minute walk, I stop at the fence post and pull my clothes back over my body, grateful for their familiar warmth on a cool evening. I step back into my shoes, offering a sheath for my tenderized feet, and then continue walking across the two remaining wheat fields that stretch between me and the narrow lane that leads home.

I feel as if I have just passed some strange initiation, an opportunity to let go of fear and shame while trusting a deeper energy that brings expansion. A dramatic emergence from the shell rather than continued containment in old patterns. Also, there is the overwhelming sense that everything I once knew (or thought I knew)—including the vision I held for my life and work—is now far too small. My body feels light as a thin cloud, as if I were nothing more than a wisp of intention and blue smoke rising from a smoldering stick of sandalwood incense on the altar of a shrine. I am a humble, trembling prayer. Nothing more.

We must all go naked before the gods. Perhaps not literally nude but vulnerable, willing to be exposed to all our perceived flaws as we walk towards a shimmering, elusive dream. We must be willing to face our shame, wrestle with our fears and doubts, and risk following our deepest longing on a mysterious journey. There is a much larger purpose to life that reveals itself only when we leave our comfort zone, expanding and crossing the open field of possibility. Following the path of the wild soul.

Destiny looks different from inside the Mystery, especially when the door is open and we are willing to say *yes*.

THE EROTIC WARRIOR

Arriving back at the old brick farmhouse, I step inside the heavy wooden front door, and the quiet house welcomes me home with its familiar scents of wood, dried sage, and lavender. An effervescent energy continues to well up in my core like a bubbling spring, and though I don't generally write in the evenings, I know that I *must* put words to paper. Right now. Write now. Beyond the mystical experience in the field, apart from the nearly unbearable lightness of my being, something else is arriving *through* me . . . a gray dove of inspiration or a whirling storm of lightning bolts, I don't yet know.

I slip off my shoes and leave them at the door. Barefoot on the cool wooden floors, I walk to the large, farmhouse kitchen to put on the kettle for tea, desiring something light and aromatic such as jasmine pearls. My body continues to feel light as air and expansive as a supernova, exploding out in rings of a shock wave. A few minutes later, seated at the broad table with my notepad and favorite fountain pen, the small ceramic teapot steaming fragrantly and an empty porcelain cup beside me, I begin to write. In the evening stillness of the empty house, the gold nib of my pen glides across the page with a scratching sound, trailing a jumble of black letters and insights in its wake.

◆　◆　◆

Who is the Erotic Warrior?

The Erotic Warrior is the embodied agent of soul, his realm the deep imagination, creativity, and the sensual world. Open to his senses, he is intrinsically connected to his "life force," to Nature and the great Mystery. He exists as potential within every man, waiting to emerge from patterns of containment into authentic possibility and action.

The Erotic Warrior is a multidimensional and sensual being. He is a man enraptured with the world as it blossoms, unfolds, crumbles, and dies before his wonderstruck eyes. He howls for the beauty of a moonlit night, reaching for the great luminous pearl that can be found only in darkness. He dances naked in his inner-city apartment or on a windswept beach. His great heart weeps for the cruel injustice and lonely terrors of humanity, the dark shadows of man, for the shame and aggression that stalk like hungry wolves. He trembles at his own possibility, both light and shadow, at what he might bring or withhold from the world.

The Erotic Warrior serves Eros, variously described as both the oldest and the youngest of the gods. It matters not the Warrior's religion or absence of one: Eros beckons all, whispering of beauty and stirring deep longing in the soul. The deity of desire, the god of lust and love and longing, Eros embodies connection.

The most powerful force in the universe is allurement, the power of gravitation, binding everything from atoms to chemical compounds, from planets to spiral galaxies, together in an invisible dance. Eros is attraction, not in the physical, superficial sense but in this deeply dynamic, energetic longing and connection.

When Eros beckons, worlds collide and cohere.

The Erotic Warrior is alive with his soul's passion. No matter his career or work in the world, the Erotic Warrior is an artist, a builder, and an explorer of possibility. He is a voyager and a sensual visionary. A wild soul. He apprentices to his own embodiment as one who seeks conscious connection with the world around him, as related to honeybee, grove of aspens, and every facet of earth as he is to humankind.

The Erotic Warrior senses that life on this planet is one of communion and interconnected relationship. The more he opens and expands through his sensory body, heart, and imagination, the deeper he is drawn into that mysterious web. He is awake as a fully sensory, sensual being; alive to his senses, to the breath that animates his body, to all that inspires. Inspiration, literally, is breath. The senses lure him outward into communion, deepening his connection with the "other-than-human" world.

Irrespective of its current shape or limitations, the Erotic Warrior perceives that his body is created as a place of power and grace, a vessel of potential and vital passion. He cultivates somatic sensitivity and mindfulness, seeking to discover the ways that he unconsciously restricts himself in life and how such limitation manifests in the bodymind. He allows himself to experience the full range of his emotions, tending to what is buried and blooms in the sensory garden of his body. Where in his bones and breath has he locked away anger, grief, power, or elusive dreams?

The Erotic Warrior understands that the collective darkness of humanity runs deep and that he is a manifestation of light and shadow, both. He seeks to bring a healing light to his wounds, integrating them within himself to become a soulfully embodied and conscious lover, partner, husband, father, teacher, and wise elder. He will claim and honor his anger, beating his jagged sword into a plough, and use his energy to cultivate growth, healing, and wholeness. He allows himself to be broken open, for only then might he be wholly changed and strangely free. Whole.

The Erotic Warrior is a man who understands that life is a continual invitation to open to something far larger than what he has imagined. Only his own patterns of containment—etched and embedded into the bodymind like curious runes that predict his fate—hold him back. Through allurement, passion, and connection, Eros draws him outward from his shell into a deeply embodied journey of emergence, expression, and eventually, elderhood.

Such a man finds wonder and awe in the most ordinary things, from dew-drop prisms sparkling on the grass to the spider devouring her prey in a shimmering web. Whether through the ever-unfolding mystery of his beloved or the sight of his children playing in an open field, he seeks to savor the stream of moments that constantly flow over him. As he passes through the world, alone or in the warm arms of a lover, he savors the fleeting beauty that constantly surrounds him. Where there is beauty, there is love, expansion, and evolution of heart and mind.

As Eros beckons him onwards with a strange music, he glimpses that to live fully from soul is to hold a sacred conversation with the other-than-human world. Such a conversation demands deep listening—to himself, to others, and to the unfolding Mystery—and what emerges will not only enliven his soul with passion but also transform him in the process. He deepens into conscious relationship with the place he dwells, becoming ever more aware of his own connectedness in the web and deep ecology and ever more mindful of his choices. Eros and the Earth conspire through the power of place to aid his evolution and soul journey.

The Erotic Warrior celebrates that the creative, sexual, and spiritual energies are all streams of the same river of consciousness. With its erotic light and shadow, sex holds a key to profound integration and transformation. Sacred and profane are simply two sides of the same coin. Through mindful awareness, he seeks to understand and transform his patterns around pleasure, power, and sexuality. Alive with breath and heightened sensation, his body becomes a temple of pleasure, a sensual terrain that offers a portal to the Divine.

The Erotic Warrior acknowledges the sensual connection with everything around him and the mysterious spirit-stream in which we all live. He trusts that he has something vital and precious to offer the world, and in his journey to discover that gift, Eros is always his guide. Allurement, passion, and a felt sense of aliveness draw him on. He may be a warrior but it is of a spiritual sort, and he views the world through a lover's eyes. The Holy is everywhere. Through each and every being, through the wild soul, the Universe celebrates its own imagination and grandeur.

I am. Not because I think but because I feel, and because all the world exists as one entwined web of relationship.

As the song of the earth and stars embodied, he sings the deep music that he hears in his soul and that resonates in his bones. He moves through his days and challenges with a fluency of presence. He journeys to the edge of the world and back—or beyond—navigating with his heart, trusting in body as vessel and in his soul for the sail.

REVELATION, ENCORE

I look up from my writing. Beyond the leaded-glass windows and their framework of hundred-year-old, diamond-shaped panes, the soft hands of evening have drawn a hazy indigo curtain across the English countryside. In the thick quiet of the old farmhouse, I lay my fountain pen aside, hushing the steady scratching of its tip across the paper. Deep, velvety silence settles over the room. I draw in an expansive breath and push the pages of scrawled script away from myself.

My hand is tired and cramped from the steady stream of inspired writing, but my body feels open and peaceful, tingling softly with an easy current of energy. It is as if a sudden storm has blown through, leaving a sense of rearranged calm in its wake.

Rearranged, indeed.

My revelation in the upper field still reverberates through my body-mind like the roar of silence after a great bronze bell has been rung. I know that I cannot adequately describe what has happened nor what I have seen as the world's veil lifted away. All words fail. Mystic revelations are always ineffable. Yet in the quantum shift occurring within me at this moment, an expansion in my core and breath, I understand this:

Animated by a song of Divine intelligence in form and nonform, everything is relationship and harmonic resonance.

I sit quietly, breathing into the softness of my body, staring at the scrawled pages of words that have come through. In this moment, I don't yet fully grasp my own writing on the Erotic Warrior, yet I sense that everything is about to change and that my life has just veered unexpectedly in a different direction.

So be it.

Somehow I am charged with bringing this revelation into words and action, though I do not comprehend fully how this evening's experience weaves together with my current work with the soul. I doubt that I have the skill or vision to manifest it in adequate form. Surely it should fall to one more qualified than I. Yet I know that we must all go naked and vulnerable to the gods, insecurities in hand. I accept the challenge that has been thrown down at my feet and which invites me to choose something different, something much larger than I have previously imagined possible.

Who is the Erotic Warrior? He is something more than a metaphor or mental abstract; he is the multidimensional potential for every man. As the embodied agent of Eros, he is a living and breathing example of the Sacred Masculine, one who lives in a soul-centered manner and celebrates his wild soul. He is part of the awakening and healing of both humanity and earth.

Like a shockwave of consciousness rippling around the globe, an evolution is at hand. As humanity struggles with the chaos and implications of its material and exploitive existence on our planet, the Great Work of cultural transformation is decidedly underway. Looking around at our current state of affairs, from rampant consumerism and mounting violence to environmental destruction and climate change, there is serious cause for concern. Yet as much as there is to grieve, there is also much to celebrate. And there is always hope.

The Soul of the World is singing itself awake through each of us. Some are listening and some are not, but all are essential. The Sacred Masculine is slowly and surely reemerging as a keeper of consciousness, a timely and essential response to the crisis and changes at hand. From the Green Man to the Erotic Warrior, he takes many forms, but the Sacred Masculine is *always* an embodiment of conscious relationship and the appropriate use of creative power. In every guise, he is hand in hand with environmental, cultural, and sacred activism, while teaching about conscious relationship, the authentic, soulful use of personal power, and spiritual ecology.

Welcome, my unmet friend, to your soul quest. It is a man's journey to soulful embodiment, passion, power, and personal authenticity through his breath and unfurled senses. Do you feel the sense of personal calling, tugging at you in dreams and strange longing? It's the reason you are alive—an invitation to come into the body to *feel* . . . deeply. Discovering the Sacred Masculine is a descent into the sensuous, an opening and expansion that never ends but spirals steadily into realms of untapped creativity, deep imagination, earth and body wisdom, and the Mystery. This is the way of the wild soul.

The time has come to reimagine what it means to be fully human, to descend into the bones and breath. Join me, brother, on a journey to discover the awakened heart of the Erotic Warrior and the Sacred Masculine—a transformation and evolution as men—that we all might stream together in the conscious, soulful wave rising up to change the world.

1 Eros, Passion, and Soul

The old English farmhouse still feels unfamiliar in the dark, the creak of the floors a language different from others I have learned and since forgotten. Outside, the tranquil, green countryside of Kent stirs to its daily waking in a manner far different from the buzzing urban congestion of London. Rather than cars and the hum of the city, the sounds of suited and booted heels clicking on pavement, here the dawn chorus of birds awakens me each morning. I've not heard such a jubilant avian celebration since I dwelt in the windward rainforest of the Big Island of Hawai'i.

After a long night of mysterious dreams, the animated conversations of the neighbor's flock of tawny chickens and the insistence of a full bladder conspire to wake me. Groggily, I throw back the fluffy bulk of feather comforter, slide from the warm bed, and stumble naked into the bathroom. I'm not yet thinking clearly, and without eyeglasses, I am nearly blind. Habitual senses impaired, I remain at the threshold between worlds, a stranger who hovers between waking and dreaming, wondering what is real and not.

Thirteenth-century poet and Sufi mystic Jelaluddin Rumi reaches out to me through time and space in a whisper:

> The breeze at dawn has secrets to tell you.
> > Don't go back to sleep.
> You must ask for what you really want.
> > Don't go back to sleep.
> People are going back and forth across the doorsill
> > where the two worlds touch.
> The door is round and open.
> > Don't go back to sleep.

1

I feel the Dreamtime still pulling me as surely as heavy hands on my shoulders, and fragments of dreams illuminate my mind like streaming meteors. As I turn away from the toilet to return to bed, my blurry eyes gaze briefly though the diamond-shaped, leaded glass windows. In the pale gray light, a peach-colored mist drifts across the fields. Beyond the front lawn and along the narrow country lane, the great bare trees, as naked in their winter dreaming as I, stand silhouetted against the slowly lightening sky. All that I can perceive of the hazy dawn world seems draped in an apricot-hued prayer shawl, woven of misty threads of dreams and birdsong.

The bare sentinels stand silently, their branches reaching up into the sky, and I suddenly "see" the graceful beings as spirits cleverly disguised as trees. A thousand slender fingers fanning out to touch the heavens. In a flash of quiet revelation, I sense them letting go of the dreaming stars and joyfully celebrating the promise of the dawn.

They are *singing*.

The moment shivers with reverence, infused by a sense of wonder as palpable as the morning's glowing light. Everything is holy. As the Standing Ones sing their praise, I inhale a tremulous breath of awe and joy as my chest expands with gratitude. Am I dreaming or awake? It doesn't matter. May I, too, celebrate the promise of this new day as I strive to bring the best of myself to the world and offer something of tangible value.

Isn't this the challenge and the unwritten opportunity of each morning? Each moment? As the American poet Mary Oliver eloquently demands in her poem "The Summer Day," "Tell me, what is it you plan to do with your one wild and precious life?"

In my silent reverence, the muted, pastel dawn trembles with possibility and celebration. It is the moment when seeming opposites touch and unite to create something new, something greater than each of them. For a short time Night and Day are joined as lovers, cocreating a unique sense of possibility. The world glows, inspired with the numinous passion of darkness and light.

Dawn offers an aperture to the soul. Like the slight pause between an inhalation and exhalation, it is a space of potential. A place where disparate worlds, unspoken potential, and dreams all overlap in nonduality. Wholeness.

The door is round and open.

The soul speaks to us in dreams, sharing its own visions and curious images for the waking world, where it hopes to sing us awake. It whispers a longing to be embodied rather than denied, remembered rather than forgotten, sung and not silenced. Soul yearns to fulfill its unique role and destiny as creative human potential.

When the Dreamtime retreats and we move blearily and busily into our daylight hours, we either carry our dreams forward or lose and forget them in the mists. So, too, with the waking dream of our precious lives. Each day we have the opportunity to work towards embodying a dream—a life of authentic and soulful meaning—or set it aside amid the noise, distractions, and well-spun illusions of the world.

As I return to the warm comfort of my bed in the softly growing light, I reach back towards the already fleeting dream from which I awakened. It is a familiar one that regularly surfaces in slight modifications; sometimes involving a plane, other times it features a boat or train. In every version, however, I am departing to reside in a foreign country, but in my rush to board, I realize that I must leave my luggage behind. Checking that I have wallet and passport, I decide that these two items will suffice to see me through, and I choose to go on.

The door is round and open.

The dream's significance and repeated message are not lost on me. Awake to the morning, listening to the dawn chorus outside the old farmhouse, I won't be able to get back to sleep now. It doesn't matter. The day has arrived with a tremulous sense of magic, wonder, and awe. Once again I have heard the Song of the World and received a reminder to celebrate the beauty.

Don't go back to sleep.

EROS

In the beginning, only Chaos existed. The ancient Greeks tell us that from the primordial Chaos, five great powers sprang forth: Gaia, the earth; Tartarus, the Underworld; Erebus, the dark gloom of Tartarus; Nyx, the power of night; and Eros, the primeval power of love. In this primordial eruption of the cosmos, Eros was not a man but a four-headed, mighty, and mythic beast, double-sexed and bearing golden wings. Born of the stars, this powerful being embodied the creative force of Nature itself: the light and order of all things.

Eros as this multiheaded and dual-sexed creature is also said to have coupled with its daughter and consort, Nyx and spawned everything in the cosmos. Other pre-Olympian accounts claim that the mating of Chaos and Eros brought the world into being, and thus even the gods owed their existence to this mighty union of primal energies.

In later ages of antiquity as the deities morphed, evolved, and multiplied atop the cloudy heights of Mount Olympus, Eros came to be depicted as the son of beautiful Aphrodite. The goddess and feminine embodiment of love, she held many lovers in her shapely arms, both gods and men. In most Greek myths, Eros's father is Hermes, swift-footed messenger of the gods, but in others he is the son of Ares, vainglorious god of war. Eros, as a beautiful and alluring divinity, embodied the masculine aspect of love and became a powerful deity in his own right. Sometimes regarded as a male fertility icon, the god of desire personified the energies of lust and intercourse as well as beauty and love.

The conquering Romans, in their adoption of the Greek pantheon, diminished mighty Eros into a pint-sized, chubby cherub. The handsome and arousing god devolved into the mischievous Cupid, hiding behind clouds to dart unsuspecting souls with his arrows of desire. In this infantile guise, mischievous but charming, Love fades from an elemental force of the universe, deteriorating from one that can join or break apart the fiery stars to something of mere ego romance.

Further trivialized by our modern culture, Eros turned Cupid is now the stuff of candy valentines, hothouse-grown roses tied with satin ribbon, pop songs, and fluffy Hollywood movies.

A multifaceted and misunderstood energy, mighty Eros has been portrayed in many forms but routinely is whittled down to a notion of sexual love. The word *erotic*, which stems from *Eros* conjures the following definition:

> e·rot·ic (*adjective*)
> 1. arousing, or designed to arouse, feelings of sexual desire
> 2. characterized by or arising out of sexual desire[1]

Diverse, beautiful, and powerful as sexuality is, physical eroticism is but one expression of this magnetic force. In a fuller sense, Eros is energetic longing. As such, it is the gravitational allurement that holds the cosmos while it expands and collapses. The electrical charge that pulls subatomic particles together, it is the essential attraction that builds atoms and ants, molecules and microbes, bones and beasts, binary stars and burgeoning solar systems.

There is also a spiritual element to Eros's longing, a soulfully creative essence that mirrors and embodies the deep imagination and creative energy of the Cosmos. Indeed, the full, powerful nature of Eros embodies the entwined, golden energies of desire, creative passion, and spiritual force—the "erotic spiral"—and each of these energies is inherently imbued with movement. All energy is movement. Eros as energy unwinds with sensation and motion in the human body, either subtle or animating and forceful. The beckoning of Eros is a tangible, *felt* sense in the body.

The body is the temple of Eros.

More intrinsic than our rational mind, the energies, sensations, and movement of the body are the primal language of allurement, longing, and connection. Eros draws us further on the evolutionary journey through our senses, which play a vital role in unlocking us and opening us to a deeper sense of connection. Our physical senses are the doorway through which we greet the world, and the body is ultimately sensual.

Though the words are often used loosely as interchangeable, *sensual* is not the same as *sexual*. Consider that *sensual* is merely "of the senses": tactile and kinesthetic, visual, auditory, olfactory, and gustatory. It is predominantly through these senses and the nervous system that we experience our material reality. The senses bestow a wealth of stimulation, from pain to pleasure, and because sex tends to be so pleasurable—not to mention intrinsically stimulating to the senses—we have come to equate *sensual* with *sexual*.

Embodied, we are deeply sensual. Far more than merely sexual, Eros is a *felt* connection to the life force and passion that arises from the soul. It is movement and sensation, ranging from subtle ripples to powerful waves that can literally rock the body. It is a somatic experience of aliveness and vitality when we are in alignment with our authentic, sensual nature.

Through our senses we know beauty and the soul. We emerge into a multifaceted and deeply layered sense of communion. Belonging. Meaning.

Let us expand the commonly narrow definition of *erotic* to include something of these embodied creative, sensual, and spiritual energies of mighty Eros. If we seek vitality, soulful passion, wholeness, and healing in our lives, the body is a sure guide, for these energies of Eros can be experienced somatically. Sensual, creative, and expansive in bodymind and spirit: these are a few of the determining qualities of the soul on its human adventure.

EROS AS LIFE FORCE

Understand that Eros and any talk of "gods" is merely metaphor, a colorful way of describing the powerful forces that animate the universe. Present since the dawn of time, these dramatic and creative energies still propel us today, regardless of our belief systems. The gods *do* exist, if only as archetypal energies that blaze like comets through the collective conscious (or unconscious), still driving us blindly to lust, greed, anger, revenge, low treachery, and grief. Also from our uncharted depths arise noble deeds, goodness, and heroism, alongside art and beauty. Destruction and love *both* embody our primal, elemental nature. By their nature, these energies of Eros and Chaos are larger than life. They are cosmic forces of attraction and obliteration, stellar light and impossible darkness that collide in endless lovemaking and creative transformation. From a cellular level of protein bonding to the building of chapels and skyscrapers to touch the distant skies, energetic allurement and spiritual longing shape our worlds.

The ages slip past into mist and myths, yet Eros remains an undeniable energy that flows through our lives as the desire for connection. Omnipresent and elemental, Eros is a primal force seeking expression in the world *through* us, perhaps even to serve its own mysterious ends as destiny. In the words of noted Jungian analyst and author James Hollis, "Eros is the 'life force'—*desire* that wishes most to connect, to build, to combine, to fuse, to generate with the other." [2]

Eros is desire in the truest sense, that which goes beyond merely sexual energy and embraces the spiritual yearning for union and wholeness. It is a psychic energy, not merely a sexual one. It is the longing that arises in the body, heart, and soul to connect with the Other in a deeply meaningful and *felt* way: somatic and embodied. Without our longing, Mystery cannot meet us. Indeed, our longing is the entry point for the larger life that awaits us.

An exquisite god with his lover, Eros kindles a fire in our bodymind and core. Desire stirs in the soul, bubbling up from a mystic wellspring with movement and sensation, seeking creative expression through the body. A man most deeply experiences this erotic force when following and expressing his energetic allurement. Body and senses come alive. In a curious dance, longing invites us home to the body, where we are twirled further into the soul's dream for life, thus led deeper into our passion, longing, and felt sense of aliveness.

In all its many forms, Eros is the creative force that pulls us into conscious relationship with life. The natural world—the human body included—is the sensuous (often sexual) manifestation of Eros on this planet. If our senses and hearts are open, longing draws us into the beauty and mystery of the sensual world as a lover, seducing us, stoking the slumbering passion in our core.

Having worked therapeutically with men for twenty years, I believe that what most of us are truly seeking is a sense of connection: with Self; with lover, partner, or spouse; with family and work; with community and the world. We feel the sense of urgency rising in the body—a silent cry of despair and desperation, even—yet remain unclear on how to take the next step. Few of us know how to make that meaningful connection we seek. Instead we are blindly groping and grasping in misguided and frustrated attempts.

Whether in our dreams or our waking daylight hours, it is the longing for an authentic sense of aliveness that holds a key to the soul's purpose. If we begin to pay attention to the hidden realm under our skin or locked within armored hearts, when Eros beckons, we sense it in our core. When awakened, the soul rises up in a wave of sensation and personal power. We *feel* it.

I ask, brother, what arouses, draws, and moves you? What is your deepest longing? What stirs a sense of creative energy within you? Where do you feel that in the body? I'll invite you into these and similar questions at the end of this chapter, in the section, "Embodying the Erotic Warrior."

EROS AND SOUL

Beyond the celebrated Muses, the force that inspires painters and poets, lovers, and legends is Eros. It is the power of myth and song of heroes. More than inspiration, this elemental energy is our deepest longing, embodied. One experiences it in the body as swirls of emotion, currents of sensation, and a shift in the tides of breath. When we track and follow this quickening of desire, stepping towards our dreams, we begin to embody the soul.

In many ways, Eros is our longing for passion. Not simply for sexual union or a mate but as a sense of intrinsic connection to the life force, an energy greater than that we normally perceive in our daily routine.

Passion is the felt sense of being truly alive, connected, and ignited by an internal flame. It animates with energy, breath, and sensation, expanding us past familiar boundaries. Aroused from the soul-numbing stupor and endless, trivial distractions of modern life, the body trembles and hums with the vibrant current of the life force. We feel awakened and powerful. Yet passion far exceeds mere arousal or sexual stimulation; like joy, it brings us alive with an energizing sense of somatic resonance and connection. Arising from a union between opposites—self and other, inner and outer, masculine and feminine—passion is wholeness and a harmonic convergence with the Cosmos, a palpable sense of energetic connection and relationship.

Soul is the union of the Sacred Masculine and the Divine Feminine within each of us, embodied as the creative life force.

In the "wholing" of the Sacred Masculine and the Divine Feminine, the union of opposites within us, the creative spark seeds the womb of possibility. Body and soul become lovers, moving effortlessly and joyously together in bliss and cocreation. Awakened and entwined they are one, and Eros's longing becomes the embodied passion of soul.

When we connect with the soul, we sense our essential wholeness; we literally *feel* the possibility of it. Our boundaries expand. The body feels open, energized, and alive, either with joy or with great yearning.

The soul's longing lights up the bodymind in a myriad of ways, but subtle clues to this integration include a rush of sensation (either powerful or subdued), movement (active or restrained), perhaps a surge of emotion, and a change in respiration. Whether inspired by nature, beauty, music, dreams, dance, rhythm, or any artistic and creative harmony, when the soul sings forth, the bodymind and breath resonate, and something in our core expands. At an early level of somatic awareness, we may perceive this expansion and movement of the soul as the quickening of excitement, more like an emotion than a keenly kinesthetic experience. Yet it is a distinctly *felt* event.

In the erotic union of the soul—when Eros draws us to connect—the life force flares up and passion ignites, offering a beacon in the dark night. As with the dawn, a portal between worlds opens and possibility beckons. When we embody the soul, healing happens. The formerly divided and separate now becomes unified as one. We glimpse our unrestrained, powerful potential, and the body hums like that of an athlete in exercise. We become the wheel that spins from its own center, and in following our longing we are carried forward to a life beyond imagining, for the soul itself is power, energy, and movement.

STEPPING OUTSIDE

Outside my windows, a soft rain washes the gray flagstones and splashes in a rippled, chaotic symphony on the small fishpond of the terrace. I am seated at the broad rectangle of dining room table, gazing out through the old, leaded glass windows of this small cottage where I currently reside in southeastern England. It is a place that I never expected to be, and a strange and circuitous journey has led me here.

I've spent my life working with my hands, heart, and soul. At the age of twenty-one, with the loss of my mother to cancer, I was catapulted into a life of exploring the realms of healing and seeking to help others. Primarily my work has unfolded through roles as a body-centered therapist and practitioner of various healing arts, but also a few years of working as a private chef, fusing the healing element of food with beautiful, fresh cuisine. Before I departed America, my vocational roles expanded to include facilitating men's groups and workshops and developing something I call

Soul Embodiment coaching—roughly, a somatic approach to eco-depth psychology.

Like a wandering gypsy, I've rolled through many places on this journey with my colorful painted wagon. From a childhood and adolescence in sunny Southern California, I spent many years in the cool Pacific Northwest, followed by Colorado, New Mexico, and Hawai'i. In my thirties, I traveled to Paris, France, for a year of culinary school and then returned to the misty dreamworld of the North Shore of Kaua'i. Repeatedly, I have heeded the longings and whisperings that called me, both geographically and within the landscape of my own psyche. I've never chosen any path or career for the sake of earning money but followed that which genuinely drew me from a deeper place: a somatic place of energy, longing, and connection. Thus my life has unfurled as a continued and mysterious adventure—a soul quest—while I have embraced the understanding that the only constant is change.

Still, I never expected to end up residing in England. Or writing this book.

The creative energy of Eros has percolated inside me through curious dreams, my revelation in the field at twilight, walking the land, and a strangely pressing, somatic need to give voice to this book—all beckoning me to undertake a challenge significantly larger than any I have previously imagined for my life.

Despite the nectar that writing offers my soul, I've routinely relegated it to the secondary role of hobby. A "closet writer," I frequently joked of myself. Circumstances have conspired to bring me to this unexpected venture, however. Mystery unfolds. Heeding Eros, I must open and listen to this new voice of the deep imagination, trusting that it will lead me somewhere worthwhile and wondrous—overwhelming or impossible as it may seem from where I stand now. As in my recurring dream, I must also trust that the basics I carry—a fountain pen and notebook, in this instance—will suffice to see me through this adventure as I leave the familiar behind.

As this work aims to illustrate, one of the primary routes to soul is through the body and breath. It is here in our warm, sensual flesh that we learn to recognize the bodily sensations of our longing and allurement. The dense web of bodymind is where we expand or constrict in familiar patterns. To that end, I walk in nature to drink from the sensory well that inspires my writing, to awaken my "bodysoul" through movement and conscious breath, and to emerge as my most creative being. Nature stirs the elemental waters of my psyche and reconnects me in a tangible way to the endless, interwoven relationship of the Larger Story that surrounds and enfolds me. When I am outdoors amid the forms and forces of the natural world, my open senses draw me into sweet, sacred communion with both visible and invisible. Connecting with Nature ignites the passion in my core, and my body hums with energy and vitality. My wild soul takes flight and soars, or slinks on its belly through the tall grass. In that sensual, connected, embodied place, I feel wholeness and am often flooded with insights and creative ideas.

Yes, this *is who I am. I'm awake and listening.*

We must all ask, where is Eros in our lives? What beckons to us with mysterious allurement? What stirs ripples in the body and the soul? How often do we pay attention and heed the somatic energy we feel in our core, our muscles, or tightly held breath?

For my own evolution, I step outside and walk the landscape in which I live, wherever that may be on the planet as my strange journey continues to unfold. I embody my soul and dreams by descending fully into the body, speaking the primal nonverbal languages of movement, breath, dance, sound, and sensory engagement. Walking (preferably somewhere semiwild) is one of the primary ways that I rouse from inertia, bring movement to my bodysoul, and unlock inspiration. Indeed, it was largely through my wandering in nature that this book emerged. Movement always reawakens a sense of my own power and energy; I feel my true creativity unbound and my soul's frequency as harmony. It is only then that I truly resonate as a voice in the chorus of the world's soul and can offer my unique gift forward as an offering. Ultimately, this is the purpose for each of us: to uncover our soul's authenticity and to offer something of our creative essence to the other-than-human world, as guided by Eros.

EROS AND LOST DREAMS

Longing stirs us to wake from our slumber, called by some restless desire to rouse from the numbing stupor of our small daily lives. We begin by seeking Eros, the mysterious force that beckons us, but how does one touch a god or an elemental energy?

He begins to discover Eros by listening. Not with the ears or even the brain, but the other senses and *sensation*, itself: the cool fear in the belly; the tingle of excitement in the gut; the way the heart skips a beat at the mention or thought of sailing a boat or trekking in Nepal. He listens to his soul's longing the way an owl, perched high in a tree in total darkness, hears the timid gray mouse shuffling through leaves hundreds of yards away.

The body yields clues and tells the truth in all sorts of ways: the sudden lurch of longing in the chest; a shortness, shallowness, or increased rate of breath; a building of nervous tension like a swarm of termites under the skin; the tight fist of fear punching home that we are near something important, however frightening it may seem to the ego and our dayworld persona. Our sensations belie the soul's desire as surely as the giddiness of madly falling in love.

Eros dwells in the body . . . and loves the body.

We track the elusive Eros—our desire for connection, our longing for passion and life force—through the jumble of our dreams each night, untangling the mysterious images and characters that beckon us. Beguilingly masked actors always seeking to drag us onstage into the play, the Dreamtime uncovers our buried longing in surprising, sometimes uncomfortable ways. Daydreams, too.

We follow the trail of Eros through the books and stories that inspire us, noting what moves our heart, bodymind, and soul. We note our hobbies and fancies, from doodling characters to collecting model trains to gardening or hiking outdoors.

Eventually, if we follow long enough, Eros leads us to the overgrown bramble patch that hides the garden of childhood dreams. Approaching this site deep within our psyche, we are certain to feel the grip of both fear and excitement, pulse racing, once again young boys sneaking into some forbidden place.

This is not a book about recapturing the lost dreams of childhood. Far from it. Yet those early wounds and lessons, the first messages of shame, and our lack of models for authentic and balanced manhood, formed the dark wood in which we eventually wander. Childhood, that often-painful place we've struggled so hard to leave behind, often holds the keys to our deepest imagination and soul's gift.

As boys and young men, few of us are fully encouraged to follow our creative inclinations. Our childhood dreams are displaced by a myriad of factors: from economic hardship to parents who knew only the options that they themselves had followed; our own fears of failure or success; the initially convincing messages of society about money and security; or notions about *right* or *wrong* for a man to pursue. Far and large, we are directed to set imaginal and soulful creativity aside, follow a prescribed course of education or work, join the working masses, and perhaps start a family.

It is still too rare that someone whispered in a young ear, *You can do anything in this world. Reach for your dreams. Don't let them go.*

Imagination is the unique and priceless gift of humanity. It is the soul's primary language, spoken fluently in dialogue with the creative Cosmos.

Yet imagination is something we're generally encouraged—even forced—to grow out of, sometimes early in our lives. Amid the toil and hard work of previous generations, imagination seemed largely a luxury, certainly not within the realm of men who needed to provide for hungry mouths at the table. Few were the "artists" who could afford to indulge their imagination and soulful creativity, such privilege largely the province of the wealthy.

Even if encouraged to follow our creative dreams as we grew, many of us have lost hold of the golden thread as we have searched for answers as to what it means to be a man. Perhaps as early as adolescence, heavy burdens of responsibility pressed down on our shoulders or we took them up willingly, ourselves. As we awkwardly carved out a viable social identity, we found ourselves juggling rent or mortgage, providing for mate or family, paying bills and car payments, all while being told that this is what it means to be an adult. For most, imagination dims until it becomes merely the realm of daydreams and sci-fi novels.

Yet the window to the soul remains open, a magic portal into the creative world of possibility. Each of us has a dream that beckons us. Perhaps it seems as impossible to reach as the distant stars, but it exists regardless.

Not the ego's ambition or desire for escape, it is born of youthful, creative longing. It may be long buried, like pirate's gold on a forgotten beach, or submerged in the body, held deeply in bones and breath. The soul speaks through our dreams, both waking and sleeping; like Eros, it beckons. We may hear it sung in jubilation on a mountaintop or whispering or weeping in the lonely, desolate places of our lives.

The ancient Greeks spoke of one's *daemon*, a guiding spirit or inner deity closely tied to one's fortune and fate. Knowing this invisible guide meant discovering one's unique talent or genius. I think of the daemon as a personal guide with a mission closely allied with that of Eros: to lead us to our personal passion as an expression of our authentic self and soul.

It was claimed that if a man followed his daemon, it became his guiding spirit or guardian. If, however, a man heard but failed to heed his daemon, then it transformed into a demon instead: tormenting him with self-destruction rather than expressing his innate, divine creativity. Daemons versus demons. Dreams and possibility versus doubt and limitation. To which do you answer, brother?

When we open to possibility, possibility opens.

I ask, what stirs your imagination and the soul? What draws you forward from the protective shell? If you knew you could not fail, what would you pursue? What is the buried dream that whispers truth in your body like a fingertip tracing up your spine?

PASSION AND SOUL

The noted mythologist Joseph Campbell is often quoted for his famous encouragement, "Follow your bliss." Rather than *bliss*, I'm inclined to agree with Jungian scholar, author, and therapist James Hollis and instead use the word *passion*, for it is passion that burns in the heart of Eros. Passion evokes a sense of fire and longing that mirrors the elemental forces that move, inspire, and ignite the soul.

It is true that bliss does often arise when one follows one's soul longing or embodies the deep imagination and creativity. Engaged in our soul's creative expression, time and space can disappear; we experience timelessness and flow, a felt sense of alignment, energy and ease in the body. We're writing, painting, singing, working on a sketch or project and suddenly two hours flash by like sunlight glistening on a passing crow's wing.

Much of the time, however, a soulful pursuit is other than blissful. Sometimes it proves distinctly challenging and frustrating. Heartbreaking, even. Yet still there is the desire and longing—a physical need, even—to continue to see one's vision through for the sense of aliveness, truth, and authenticity it brings. This is truly following one's passion, something deeper than merely chasing bliss or elusive happiness.

Along with dreams, our passions are a compass with which to navigate the soul's uncharted waters. I'm speaking of deeper, creative passions here as opposed to the love of new cars, playing rugby, or card games and gambling, sex, or whatnot. The passion of the soul is something more vital than those pursuits that we enjoy but that serve mainly to distract us from the mundane existence of work and daily life. Soulful passion stirs our creative life force and power. We feel it. Our senses open and engage as something in us expands and resonates.

As men, we're often so disconnected from any genuine sense of our deeper selves that trying to discover what we're authentically passionate about may prove challenging. To that end, anything that one considers to be a true passion is worth investigating, as it may offer clues to where Eros resides, hiding out like a watchful red fox in the sheltering thickets.

I recently visited with a young politician whose promising career had just been unexpectedly derailed by an unfortunate incident in his youth, exploited by some rather slanted, sensationalist journalism. As I asked him about his journey ahead and what direction he might take (with politics now mostly off the radar), he rather dispiritedly rattled off several possibilities for work that he might pursue. His eyes were flat blue stones devoid of any spark or life. Offhandedly, he added, "This is crazy but actually I've always wanted to pursue filmmaking . . ."

For the briefest second a light flashed in his eyes. His energy shifted along with his posture, and he stopped fiddling with his mobile phone. Tracking the subtle shift, I sensed that Eros hovered near. Then, as if a cloud passed in front of the sun, the light disappeared and he began rattling off the many reasons why he couldn't possibly pursue this dream.

I had witnessed something in his heart, however, a creative impulse waiting to be explored. A brief flare against the overcast gloom. I let him go on for a minute and then, like a scent hound, I circled back around. Having glimpsed the flash of a golden thread, I intended to help him follow it out of the labyrinth and home to his own heart. At the very least, I hoped to open a window of possibility.

I offered him several reasons why he *could* pursue filmmaking, and why it might prove deeply rewarding. As we spoke further about the resources and personal connections that might perhaps open a door, his energy shifted once again. He sat upright and his shoulders opened as he set his phone aside. Leaning forward with elbows on the table, he made an energetic connection with me for the first time. He looked me directly in the eye and held my gaze. I smiled to myself, for merely the touch of Eros brought this man's bodymind alive.

Brother, what stirs you? What is your deepest longing? One's childhood fantasies are relevant here. As a boy or young adult, what did you dream of doing and becoming? Close your eyes, take a deep breath, and then listen and *feel*. What happens in your bodymind as you recall that longing?

Most of us are firmly rooted in inertia, safely ensconced inside walls of our own making. Longing and dreaming mark the call of the soul: the summons of Eros to a larger, authentic life.

There are a million seemingly good reasons to not heed the soul's whispers, not to shake off our containment and inertia. Whether those reasons include the responsibilities that we have shouldered or the internal messages in our heads that keep us shackled, it seems easiest to remain a part of the "chain gang," toiling away on the railway. *Best not to rock the boat*, a warning voice says. Childhood dreams may be breezily dismissed as flights of fancy for someone else to follow but they do not entirely disappear. No, the quiet longing still follows like a homeless dog whose dark, glassy eyes are a plea of tired hunger.

Eros beckons. The soul whispers its steady longing, urging you to life beyond the small, domesticated one you only half inhabit. If you could do anything, what would it be?

To seek out Eros, one need simply begin paying attention to the clues of one's body, allurements, and curious passions. It may be a challenging and circuitous journey, like trudging uphill in the dark. Surprisingly or not, most often the footsteps lead back to the secret boneyard of dreams.

It is entirely possible to discover one's passion later in life, and it's al-most never too late to begin searching. Years ago, while living in Portland, Oregon, I took a weekly wine tasting class at a local wine shop taught by an engaging older man. Over the months, a friendship grew out of those Wednesday night classes and this man later joined a couple of the men's groups that I facilitated. My friend's knowledge of wine is nearly encyclopedic but he also possesses a keen eye for design and aesthetic beauty; his condominium always impressed me as a stylish sanctuary for the soul. Along with various forms of art and creativity, time outdoors and working in the garden has long served a hobby for him; overall, I would say that a strong sense of Eros is present in his life.

After several years without significant contact, I recently reconnected with this man on a visit to Portland. As we sat with cups of jasmine green tea at a popular enclave in the renovated, hip Pearl District, I learned that at fifty-five, he left the wine industry and went back to school to study landscape design. He graduated with honors four years later and success-fully launched his own business designing alluring gardens and outdoor spaces. Turning sixty, this sprightly and energetic man now followed his passion in a way that he never had previously, offering something of him-self forward in a new, dynamic manner that helped others enjoy beauty in their world. As he spoke of his freshly created life, his energy and excite-ment felt palpable, while the gleam in his eyes revealed that he had found his soul work.

Containment and Inertia

Despite the frenetic busyness of our lives, most of us are held in a state of containment and inertia. It is a sticky place of nonmovement and relative safety, where life is mostly predictable and homogenized. We are numbed to the deeper messages of the body, deaf to our soul's whispered longing, and mutely dumb to the power of our authentic voice. Inertia holds us all on some level, whether it is simply an early morning grogginess and lethargy from which we must wake, or a sense of dull routine that blurs our days into fog. It is also the passively drugged state of television watch-ing and Internet addictions, or the haze of drugs and alcohol as an escape from the pressures or doldrums of life (or our own demons). Inertia is the stale relationship or career we've outgrown but are too afraid to leave.

Our containment is a place of stagnation in body, and soul where we remain comfortably rooted in our familiar patterns. Psyche, body and soul are stuck in a sedentary, domesticated rhythm of well-patterned grooves and restriction of vital energy. It's a state in which most of us live and die.

As a basic level, containment and inertia constitute the lowest common denominator of energy in body and mind. It's an unconscious realm of unquestioned beliefs, unexamined values, rigid attitudes, and accepting the status quo. Shifts of expansion and movement may be perceived as uncomfortable or even threatening. Indeed, there is a seductive, sedentary pull of inertia; our containment is effortless, easy, and nondemanding. Newton's first law of motion—that a body at rest tends to remain at rest—is essentially the law of inertia.

Containment can feel natural, but such restriction isn't our natural state at all. The soul is expansive and the body is designed to move. A tremendous amount of energy is required to remain frozen in inertia, yet we have little to show for this daily expenditure other than a rigid holding in the bodymind and a perceived safety in life.

In the containment of our modern, disconnected lives, the soul's creative impulses remain largely ignored, existing merely as potential rather than power. To wake up and embrace a meaningful, authentic life, we must recognize and loosen inertia's grip on us. We confront our ways of being lackadaisical procrastinators, avoiding or simply drifting along, or surfing one wave of drama to the next. Dare to step out of familiar, habitual roles and move, stretch, expand, improvise, and discover.

Yes, it takes effort to rouse from inertia. There's always a reason not to break out of our containment, a million tempting reasons to stay right where we are. Complacency wears many clever disguises. If you are inactive for an extended period and start exercising again, you know that the activity may seem difficult—even uncomfortable—at first but then it gets easier. The stiffness, aches and pains diminish and we rediscover the ease, power and grace of our stride or activity. Movement guru Gabrielle Roth says, "the simplest way out of inertia is to start moving." [3]

The way we move, allow ourselves to be moved, or resist movement reveals much about us. Movement is the opposite of holding; it offers the antidote to inertia. When we begin to free the body, we simultaneously open the heart, emotions, and mind. And the soul. Only when you begin to fully inhabit your body will you unleash your core, authentic power. Even if he is not an athlete or dancer, a man who fully embodies his soul radiates energy with a similar prowess, energy, and vitality.

For us as men, one of our primary soul lessons is to learn that the body is the teacher, healer, and guide. As you begin to reinhabit and awaken your bodysoul, you will discover not only courage but also an enticing new world of possibility. Muscles, bones, and breath launch us from a lazy comfort zone into a state of grace, potency, energy, and alignment. The body is the temple of Eros and the treasury of our soul's power.

I ask, have you stopped dancing in life? When did you lose the joy of moving? Singing? What are you afraid of? We are yearning for a larger life and yet shrinking back from it at the same time, fearful and unsure. When we resist the summons of Eros, the soul remains trapped in inertia and containment like a graceful wildcat behind iron bars.

Inhale a deep breath. Move your body. Discover your untamed animal energy. A wild soul lumbers restlessly within.

Don't go back to sleep.

A Soul Quest

In the classic myths of history, the forces of destiny (gods, fate, adventure, etc.) issue a summons on an unsuspecting individual. Often this initial call is refused but ultimately the soon-to-be hero emerges from the containment of his quiet life and goes off on his great adventure. Despite the mundane details of our modern, seemingly soulless world, our own lives are no less mythic. Our summons may be a dramatic event like an earthquake in life, persistent dreams, or the quiet, steady hunger somewhere deep inside. It is through our yearning that the soul awakens and a warrior/hero/poet/artist is born. We must each rouse from inertia and heed the strange call of our longing, even if we're not clear where it will lead us. In daring to follow Eros, more will be revealed and our lives transformed.

Seeking our authentic passion and following Eros to a life of meaningful connection is a soul quest. Few of the standard accomplishments in modern society—earning large sums of money, gaining fame or celebrity status, or simply a good pension—could possibly outweigh the deeply compelling reason for engaging in the soul's evolutionary journey. When we pursue our innate longing, when we begin to live from a place of deep creativity and embodied imagination, not only do we ignite our passion but we birth something vital into the world.

Rather than being divided, we come into alignment, wholeness, and power. We create something that is much larger than any small sense of self (job, title, income, car, etc.); it emerges from the soul's taproot: the wellspring of Mystery, the core frequency, and the creative union within the Self. In such authentic expression, an individual finds and *feels* a connection to something larger. A resonance hums like music in our cellular tissues. Synchronistic opportunities begin to manifest. From a place of soul, one delivers to his community (both human and "other") and the world something more than simply ego and surface conversations.

Most of us feel trapped in lives of dull routine that offer no expansion or nourishment for the soul, treading aimlessly like a hamster on a wheel in its cage. Inertia hides behind many masks. We rely on packaged entertainment to distract us from the banality of daily existence, for if we truly tuned in to how we feel and the disparaging lack of meaning in our jobs—perhaps even our relationships—most men would be faced with crossing a desolate wasteland. To numb the quiet, gnawing despair inside, we employ a million distractions, from surfing the Internet to getting lost in our work, drugs, or alcohol. Even our "adventure" tends to be prepackaged. Whether actively searching or simply daydreaming, we seek passion in our lives because we're desperate to *feel* alive. Typically, this search tends to focus on a superficial level: sports, sex, cars, travel, and other alluring escapes that never truly satisfy in the way we hope they will. Such trivial forms of passion fade as surely as any flower, so we either rush to the next passing object of desire and distraction or begin to dig for something deeper.

Go deeper, unmet friend.

From the soul's point of view, the average person is living life completely backwards: we seek passion as an escape from the doldrums of daily life. Yet if we embody our soul's longing with movement, breath, and authentic action, passion arises spontaneously as a result. We are animated from *within* rather than stimulated by what is *without*. In this place of core authenticity—a realm of both shadow and light, open and connected to our sensations, breath, and life force—a vitality energizes us as little else can but love. This is the realm of the wild soul where, as men, we discover the core connection we long for. We meet Eros and begin to engage life in a powerful, meaningful manner.

Your longing is the departure point for your soul quest, from whence you step across the threshold into something larger. As the poet William Stafford wrote in "The Way It Is," it is a glimmering golden thread to follow:

> There's a thread you follow. It goes among
> Things that change. But it doesn't change.
> People wonder about what you're pursuing.
> You have to explain about the thread.
> But it is hard for others to see.
> While you hold it you can't get lost.
> Tragedies happen; people get hurt
> or die; and you suffer and get old.
> Nothing you do can stop time's unfolding.
> You don't ever let go of the thread.

BIRTH OF A DREAM

Most of us spend the first half of life creating an identity: an ego-based persona fashioned through family, education, work, social and peer groups, and religious affiliation. It is also woven from our inner wounds and workings, and is decorated with external objects such as job title, style of clothing, car, and house. Yet this persona projected at work to the outside world is not fully who we are. Below the superficial façade—clever, flashy, and appealing as it may be—waits a hidden and secret part of the self. Unclear of its shape or true desire, a man may not fully grasp exactly what this deeper part of his self is, but he senses its presence like a shadowy figure standing behind or beside him.

Even if we have accumulated the trappings of material success, beneath our carefully fashioned day-world identity an uncomfortable sense of disconnection exists. Usually, we unconsciously project onto the outer world what we feel is lacking or missing in our lives, thinking that what is not *in here* must be *out there*. Thus we go chasing after superficial forms of Eros: physical connection, new lovers and egocentric romance, sports cars, exotic travel. Alas, these brightly flaming stars always burn up as they fall towards the atmosphere and gravity of our patterns, becoming only shards of cosmic rock and handfuls of dust.

One senses a disconcerting possibility like a wind whispering with strange voices as it swirls around the cozy confines of our house: to find what we truly seek, we must unlock the door and step outside our four walls. We must risk dismantling the self so carefully constructed over the years. We have to step outside the narrow grid of our modern world and veer into unknown territory, following only a winding path that doesn't appear on any map. To encounter the wild soul, we have to leave the village and venture into a dark wood alone—but first we have to rouse from inertia and containment.

Inside, something waits to be born. Something vital and secret, tender and powerful. The divine Cosmos unfolds within us, solar systems of possibility dreaming awake in our own cells and imagination. For a chick in the dim confines of its shell, the space grows too small. At a mysterious moment, something stirs it to wake up and begin pecking with its beak against the wall. It doesn't know what waits beyond the small, dark world of its existence, only that it must break free. Tightly folded up, it hasn't yet discovered its own wings. Yet it risks its entire existence, the only space that it has ever known, to struggle forth into what it is meant to become.

How many of us listen to our own innate intelligence in such fashion? Offering a million distractions but little of true grace, the false gods of Money and Machine have seduced most of our world. The inside of the modern shell is lined with television and computer screens, lulling the restless quietly back to sleep. In their troubled inertia, the masses are frantically numb, anaesthetized to soul, and busily waiting to die.

As a man, are you willing to crack your protective shell that you might emerge into a much larger and unimagined version of your self? How much longer will you remain tightly curled up in close, familiar confines, chanting to yourself all the convincing reasons why you must not risk breaking free?

To emerge from the shell you needn't quit your job, leave an intimate relationship, take a year off, live in a mountain cabin, move to a foreign country, begin psychotherapy, or undertake a wilderness "vision quest." Granted, these may all be perfectly relevant and worthwhile things to do at some point along a soulful journey, but they are not necessarily required for you to begin emerging into a soulful, authentic existence as an Erotic Warrior.

Only the Mystery knows where your longing will take you.

Your deepest, creative yearning for connection and passion is the call of the soul seeking to expand within you, ready to emerge in conscious relationship with the other-than-human world. Eros beckons, urging you to step outside what you know of the world and go in search of the secret, essential parts of your self. Emerge from the shell. It's time to wake up. Remember your forgotten dreams, the precious ones wrapped in tattered silk. Rouse from inertia. Listen to your body and begin to learn its pulsing somatic languages of energy, movement, emotion, and breath. In the union of the Sacred Masculine and the Divine Feminine within us, there is wholeness. And power.

Heeding the summons of Eros and allurement doesn't necessarily mean you will switch your job or career (though you well might). It guarantees, however, that you will change your life. Significantly. Your soul carries a unique gift that *only you* can bring to the planet, and there are myriad ways it can manifest apart from an actual career, such as being a supportive and compassionate father; a defender of the environment and an advocate for sustainability; starting a "green" business; assisting underprivileged youth; becoming a cultural visionary.

Brother, who are you and what do you bring? I ask, what is the part of you that is holding back? What are the ways that you remain secure in your inertia? What will you gain—and what will you lose—if you risk the secret dream in your heart?

PROMISE OF THE DAWN

The world remains cloaked in velvety winter darkness, the horizon sky only a glowing ribbon of satin stretched across distant hills of shadow. I stand outside in the frosty air, breathing deeply of the stillness, my nostrils and lungs crackling with the chill. In the glimmering blueness, the frozen lawn twinkles with the light of stars and diamonds. The luminous pearl of moon has disappeared and I gaze up at the elegant and shapely trees. How is it that I cannot hear the Standing Ones singing? With no movement or breath of wind, there is only stillness. The moment throbs with the existential silence found between heartbeats and arcing between stars.

As with dusk, the gift of dawn is union, a place where worlds touch briefly and entwine as mythic lovers. Father Sky and Mother Earth. Eros and Psyche. The Sacred Masculine and the Divine Feminine. Body and Soul.

These early hours are always dear to me, a time when the unspoken promise of the day seems close at hand and easily heard. Tangible as my own breath. The divine imagination suffuses me with inspiration on each inhalation. As the graceful shapes of the naked trees reach up to kiss the fleeting stars goodbye, I am reminded of the interweaving of the everyday and the sacred. They are not separate. Through my breath, awareness, and open senses, I can access the magical realms that, even if mostly forgotten and ignored, still lie closely entwined with our everyday reality.

My body is still and quiet as a deep pool of clear water, while my dreams still hover close and near at hand. How will I carry them into the day? How much of my soul will I bring to the world? Or will I hold back, stuck in inertia, lost in the busyness of daily business and distraction? No, I choose otherwise.

Nothing opens us like inspiration.

Breathe.

The beckoning day ahead—with all its tasks, trials, and triumphs—offers a unique wrinkle in the Mystery. May I fully and consciously engage the hours that remain to me before nightfall, though only the Fates know if I should be graced to live that long. In this moment—and the next, and the one that follows that—may I move with an awareness of bodysoul, cognizant through my senses of the larger story unfolding around me. Each moment flows over another as a living stream of impressions and possibility, a continuous invitation to be present to the awe and wonder of it all.

Everything is relationship.

Like a fiery phoenix, dawn arrives with promise and potential as dreams reach out and the soul beckons. Will you choose a life of passion and adventure, sailing beyond the protective barrier reef? Or remain on the familiar shoreline with the crowds, gazing out longingly at the sea but not setting sail, never risking to set foot beyond our smugly troubled and noisy existence. In the vessel of your body, push off from shore into the deep blue waters of possibility and imagination to discover the wild soul.

The door is round and open.

Brother, step outside your door. Escape the four walls that confine you. Unlock the gate and walk beyond the fence into the open field of possibility. Take off your shoes and stand barefoot on the earth. Unfurl your senses like brilliantly feathered wings. The soul is calling you to wake up, to expand rather than constrict, and to risk your significance to the other-than-human world. You have your passport and wallet, now board the plane and embark on a compelling, unfamiliar, and foreign adventure to discover your soul's gift. A spiritual ecology and a sacred activism beckon, calling you as a catalyst of change and cultural renaissance.

Don't go back to sleep.

The sharp needles of the frozen dawn bring my body intensely alive. The quiet calm is peppered with the voices of little birds in the bare trees, now celebrating the arrival of daylight after clutching to their perches through a long, cold night. The small Winged Ones twitter with excitement in the early light, eager for another day to be alive. As an Erotic Warrior, may I be inspired by their example and do the same. Life is precious. I will celebrate the deep imagination expressing itself through creation. I will walk a path of power this day, nourishing the four aspects of my being—body, mind, spirit, and soul—and I will channel that energy into my soul's work. May I hold nothing back and expand into the most authentic version of myself possible as an embodiment of the Sacred Masculine. A wild soul.

Don't go back to sleep.

◆　◆　◆

Embodying the Erotic Warrior

A man who embodies the Erotic Warrior heeds his allurement and sense of passion while seeking his soul's gift to offer to the world. He knows that to pursue the call of his soul is to risk his own significance and a life less ordinary, and he chooses to cultivate his personal life force. He recognizes his habits of inertia and containment and understands that he can shift his patterns by opening to other sensory channels. Whether in the buzzing concrete hive of the city, the manicured suburbs, or living in a rural homestead, he opens his senses to the beauty and wonders around him. He honors that his body is the temple of Eros and that his wild soul is housed in bones and breath. Movement, authentic action, and soulful skills will unlock the door to true potential and embodied purpose.

The Erotic Warrior walks a path of power, seeking to be fully "awake." He also recognizes that his deepest, creative longing is the call of the soul seeking to expand into meaningful communion with the world.

Everything is relationship.

SOUL SKILLS

The yearning for an authentic, meaningful, powerful life is a valuable first step; it signals the entry point to our larger life. Yet we also need practical skills for the soulful journey, for Eros and passion on their own will rarely carry us all the way through. The skills and exercises outlined here and at the end of each chapter provide you with practical tools for your soul quest. Soul Skills form rungs on the ladder by which we climb to our higher purpose and/or descend into the mysterious, sacred *kiva*—an underground ceremonial chamber—of the bodysoul. For a deeper exploration of psyche and soul, pair them with the accompanying insights.

SOUL SKILL #1: ROUSE FROM INERTIA

As surely as gravity, containment holds us rooted in place. The first challenge we face on the quest for a soulful, meaningful life is to shift the habitual patterns that have lulled our domesticated souls into uneasy sleep. We must step out from narrow roles of limited movement and expression. When we recognize the body as the soul's vessel and the starting point for our awakening, we emerge from the murky pool of stagnation. Now is the time to shake off the status quo, bring movement into the bodymind, and get "unstuck." Once you are moving, if you heed the body's messages of sensation and energy, you'll find the path forward to your soul's gift and authentic power.

EMBODYING SOUL SKILL #1: A WANDERING WALK

The ideal setting for this exercise would be a naturally wild or semiwild place where elemental beauty enfolds your senses. Given that a less domesticated place may not be easily accessible, a good alternative would be an inviting city park or perhaps a pleasant backyard or garden. One of the many benefits of nature is that it opens and draws us outward into communion and relationship while inviting us to rediscover a different, slower rhythm in bodysoul. Ultimately, even an urban neighborhood will suffice for this walk. Don't let perfect get in the way of good enough. Grow where you're planted.

Walk without the intention of "exercise" or going somewhere. Instead, allow yourself to casually wander. You have no destination other than to eventually come home. Turn off your phone. Don't text message or check your emails. Don't take your dog along or anyone else: this is a solo time. Give your attention totally to your surroundings, following a curious innocence and your soul's promptings rather than your head. Give yourself at least an hour on the land (park, bike path, sidewalk, etc.) to explore, meander, and sit.

Follow your allurement.

Allow yourself to be drawn to what interests your sight and senses. An example might be a curious cluster of strikingly different trees in close relationship, or a dramatic jumble of granite boulders. You might heed the beckons of the wooden bench at the water's edge or an inviting cobblestone alley filled with small, funky shops and the scents of warm food. An unexplored trail might tempt you, or a wall of colored posters and rain-stained notices might pull you closer for inspection. Meander like a lazy river on a summer's day, letting your senses and intuitive, nonverbal summons in your bodymind steer you with their subtle currents. Willingly be seduced by the blood-red rose, the hulking wreck of an abandoned, wrecked, and rusted car, or the clog of trash in the river. Notice what beckons and take time to explore that and then discover something unique about what you're drawn to.

Observe what it's like to be alone and on your own. You might notice difficulty with or resistance to not having a specific goal or purpose in mind. Is it challenging to be non-goal-oriented? If you can set aside the serious adult and explore with childlike, unhurried wonder, you will begin a reenchantment with the sensual world and reencounter your wild soul.

BODYSOUL INSIGHTS

Either during or after the embodiment exercise #1, reflect on the following insight queries and unfinished sentences. Of course you can simply explore these insights without doing the exercise, *but the point is to combine the two*: you'll receive deeper and more authentic answers if you answer the questions after doing the exercise. Trust me. Muse on the answers in your head, speak them aloud, or journal them. Writing is very effective and revealing but you might also want to draw, sketch, color, or paint your responses (doing your best to let go of any need to create "art"). The soul often reveals itself more readily through nonverbal expression such as image, sound, movement, posture, and art.

Address a few of the Insights or all of them. Pay attention to your resistance and note which ones you skip over or avoid. Dare to explore, risk and be vulnerable with the truth. With mindful awareness of your sensations, notice what happens in your body as a response to the questions and statements. Does your belly constrict, or does it soften with a gentle openness? Does your breathing stop or get shallow? Perhaps your jaw tenses suddenly, or your neck, shoulders, or back suddenly begins to hurt. Sensations in your body offer meaningful clues: they reveal the subterranean waters of psyche and soul.

- What is my deepest longing or yearning?
- What dream have I abandoned as impossible or unrealistic?
- Something I have always wanted to try is . . . (finish this sentence).
- If I could create anything, what would it be? (let this be something other than simply "money")
- What are the ways I remain stuck in inertia?
- What is the sense of passion in my life? Creativity?
- What do I feel connected to in a meaningful way in my life?
- I am most creative when I . . .
- What do I gain from remaining in my shell?
- If I had a wild soul, I would . . .

2 THE SACRED MASCULINE

A cloudy morning has evaporated as I've spent the hours attempting to upload a new website, running into one challenge after another. My frustrations are exacerbated by the fact that I'm not technologically savvy and I have to spend additional time figuring things out. Here at the cottage, the broadband Internet connection keeps failing as I attempt to upload files, and my agitation grows steadily. The hours before lunch are normally the ones I spend writing. This morning, as I tinker with publishing the site, I tell myself that I'm working but I know that it's a convenient and comforting lie. In truth, I'm actually avoiding facing up to a challenging chapter in the manuscript.

Something glimmers in my intuition like darkly polished glass. Rather than procrastinate, what I really need to do is go for a walk to clear my head and connect to the earth. The elusive words and inspiration I seek to write about the Sacred Masculine won't be found by puttering with online tasks; they will, however, surely arise as I traipse across soggy fields beneath an autumnal blue sky.

I shut down my Mac with a disgruntled sigh, change into a pair of worn and faded trousers, and pull on my high rubber Wellingtons for a wet and muddy walk. The past few days have witnessed some of the worst storms in England's recent history, complete with massive flooding across the country and gale winds that toss shingles like toys and lift entire roofs. I wrap a light scarf around my neck, step out the door and glance up at the bright blue sky. A few thin clouds hover at the edge of distant hills, sulking teenagers at the schoolyard gate, but I decide that rain is unlikely.

Opening the gate in the high deer fence, I step through into the squelchy field with its newly sprouted carpet of vividly green wheat. The sky shimmers with its welcome illusion of blue, and a sheer, golden quality

29

to the thin light illuminates the bare trees and the rolling South Downs in the distance. I head south from the cottage, my rubber Wellies squashing noisily through the sodden grass and mud at the edge of the field. I've no clear intention of where I'll walk, but I want to avoid any roads and to keep only soft, wet earth underfoot, so I'll wander footpaths that weave like waterlogged, bedraggled ribbons over wooded hill and dale.

As I stride along in my high boots, I sense a softly humming content-edness in my leg muscles and the pumping of blood and breath animates my body. My senses are open and engaged like a somatic radar, bringing me into connection with the earth and landscape around me. I am hap-pily at home in the natural world, moving through the interwoven and multisensory web, both visible and not.

I'm on this walk not to think but to listen. Observe. Feel. To pay atten-tion to what presents itself to my senses and awareness. I settle the noisy thoughts in my head and return to the easy and full breath in my belly, offering up a silent prayer for inspiration.

Everywhere around me I see and sense Mother Earth, the collective forms that we refer to in a feminine gender. Indeed, the luscious and sensually soft curves of the landscape seem decidedly female. I muse for a bit about the associated and complementary metaphor of Father Sky, carrying the stars on his broad back and arching protectively above his wild and sensuous lover, Gaia. Together, they form a sacred marriage that constitutes the sum of our worldly existence.

Walking on, I ponder the word *husband*, reflecting less on it as "the male partner in a marriage" than on its expanded definitions "to man-age prudently and economically" and "steward or manager." These other definitions rest closer to *husbandman*, "one that plows or cultivates land," or *husbandry*, "the judicious use of resources,"[1] yet neither of these quite captures the essence of sacred masculinity.

Perhaps the word that best fits what I'm considering and sensing is *stewardship*, the careful and responsible management of something en-trusted to one's care. The idea of stewarding "natural resources" springs to mind and, as I walk, I quickly spiral down to the root of the Sacred Masculine: a respectful and conscious connection with Nature and Earth, particularly as a model for interconnected relationship.

Tromping along the muddy trail, I find myself dimly aware of the faint presence of the Green Man, an ancient pagan archetype of masculine connection with Nature. Depicted in image and stone with his beard and hair growing (or formed of) leaves, vines and boughs, the Green Man is the steward of the forests and the land. He is "husband" to the plants and trees, animals, and the feminine Gaia. An enlightened being who exists in conscious relationship and harmony with the living energies of Earth and the cosmos, the Green Man embodies a silent, gentle wisdom through his respect of all living things. Bearded and inherently masculine, he offers a different model of manhood and strength: one based on relationship, caring, and true husbandry or stewardship.

Far older than Christianity, the Green Man reemerged powerfully in the twelfth century alongside the Goddess as embodied by the Holy Mother, Mary. His bearded image can be found carved into stone pillars in cathedrals throughout Europe. At the sacred site of Chartres, France, the Green Man can be found at least seventy-two times within the great cathedral, and reputedly over a hundred of his stone faces can be found in Rosslyn Chapel in Scotland.

As an embodiment of the Sacred Masculine, the Green Man understands the hidden laws of nature and interconnected relationship. In a modern incarnation, he stands for environmental awareness and action, symbolizing cooperation with Nature rather than dominion over it for resources, wealth, and power.

Living here in the Old World, particularly when I am wandering through whispering woods or less domesticated places, the gentle Green Man often enters my consciousness. On some subtle level, his energy is still present in these verdant isles, both as an energetic presence in the wilder places and as a reemerging part of the regional folklore. For men today, there is much of value in this ancient, archetypal energy as a representation of the Sacred Masculine—an image of malehood entwined with Nature and mystery. He offers a signpost for a different way forward, a path of balance and wholeness through conscious relationship and harmony. The way of the wild soul.

I pass the strangely quiet stables of the landlord's farm, which normally is a hub of activity, following the muddy track along the uppermost of the large ponds, bordered with tall reeds and grassy banks. Inundated by the storms, the brownish water is higher than I've ever seen it. Even the broad lily pads are submerged, transformed into large and flatly round ingredients floating in a murky soup.

At the edge of the pond, amid a cluster of giant, chanterelle-look-alike mushrooms, I note a very large mussel shell. It is roughly six inches long, and its shiny, charcoal exterior is splayed open to reveal the smooth emptiness of its pearly white interior. How curious, I think, and I wonder briefly if a heron has fished it from the depths. Another ingredient of the pond soup. I walk on, wondering about the shell and how it came to be there in the mud and nestled amid the enormous, pale yellow mushrooms. I wouldn't have expected mussels to be in the pond, though I know they are common enough in rivers and canals throughout Europe, and I consider what sort of creature has dragged the shell up to the bank and consumed the contents. A water vole, perhaps. There are otters in this part of the country, now making a comeback after being driven nearly to extinction, but they prefer fresh, moving water.

At the far end of the small reservoir, where the path veers away towards the open field, I note another open mussel shell on the muddy bank. As I muse about this different sort of mussel, one that lives in freshwater, my mind makes the short leap from *mussel* to *muscle*. It occurs to me that the Sacred Masculine embodies a different sort of muscle.

A balanced, healthy masculinity is less about force or brute strength, the hypermasculine that our society currently regards as "manly." Instead, it's more about flexibility and flow. The Sacred Masculine is akin to a dancer's lithe strength as opposed to the inflexible mass of a bodybuilder. It's a different sort of muscle, a different way of being in the world.

As with *desire* versus *ambition*, or *cooperation* as opposed to *force*, there are effective and ineffective ways to pursue a goal or reach a destination. Few things in the known world are more powerful than water, that adaptable and life-giving element that shapes both outer and inner landscapes. Consider a river, a force mighty enough to carve canyons from granite. Powerful as it is, water never flows uphill; instead it finds the path of least resistance and flows around the obstacle, pulled ever onwards by the invisible hands of gravity. As men, how different our lives would be if we learned to flow like water, surrendering to the beckons of Eros and allurement, trusting a different sort of muscle and strength, rather than pushing on with sheer ego force and will.

Heeding some inner whisper, I leave the public footpath as it cuts across the lower hem of a grassy pasture and veer to the left to follow the field's border of tall, nearly nude trees. I'm heading towards the upper reaches of the field, where another trail ascends the forested hill. Passing alongside the narrow band of woods that fills a small ravine, I note a faint semblance of trail that leads beguilingly down into the hollow. I pause for a moment, unsure about changing my trajectory and the route I seemed be following, but then follow my intuition and plunge down the slippery slope into the thicket of tall trees.

I've passed this particular copse of oak, birch, chestnut, and holly a dozen times before but always kept to the field as I headed up or down the hill. Now I find myself in a wet and mossy dell, alive with the laughter of water splashing in two small streams that join together at the foot of a mighty tree. Like a pagan spirit, a strange and mythic face from another world peers out from the massive tree base. The visage is bearded with moss, and four separate, mature trunks rise from his head like antlers or a crown, each twisted round with the brown coils of vines and leafy green ivy.

As my boots sink into the bed of decaying leaves and mud, I stand quietly before this unique Standing One, transfixed by the mystical face while simultaneously absorbing the sights, sounds, and smells around me. After a week of fierce storms, all the tall trees stand nearly bare of leaves, their naked forms starkly elegant and shapely. The air tingles with the crisp flintiness of fresh rain while aromatic bass notes linger of the earthy muskiness of decaying leaves, mushrooms, and soil. A mossy odor, oddly reminiscent of green tea, flavors and scents the damp air.

An almost palpable sense of subtle magic radiates here. Given a per-functory sweep of the eyes, this sheltered glade seems an ordinary enough patch of woods, but somehow the two gurgling streams and the mighty grandfather tree cast a unique spell. I'm swept up in a curious sense of timelessness as if I've stumbled into a secret wonderland or a different world. Something in my core expands, like a door opening. My senses feel heightened and my body tingles softly as if drawn gently outwards by ten thousand invisible spider webs.

In my muddy boots, I crouch down in a squat beside the Standing One, its cragged, gray bark thickly covered in emerald moss, and I peer at the strange spirit face in the tree's wide base. He looks more ferocious than the gentle Green Man but the resemblance brings the King of the Wood to mind once more. If only through my own projections and presence, the Sacred Masculine is present here.

A branch fallen long ago lies crusted with dark, round fungoids shaped like glistening, black chestnuts. Another fallen log nearby has cracked and tapered to form an obvious raven's head, dark beak and eye. I'm at the threshold between worlds, it seems. The two serpentine waterways, gurgling noisily as they splash down the opposing hillsides in gentle cascades and moss-lined channels, join near my feet in a confluence of elemental energy and harmonious voices.

As I sit silently with my heart and senses wide open, I realize that mirrored and manifested in this glade is another essential characteristic of the Sacred Masculine: the understanding and appreciation of interdependence. As the Green Man understands, *everything is relationship*. What we have come to view, label, and categorize as an "ecosystem" is an incomprehensibly complex web of relationships, each dependent on and benefiting another. It is communion of the visible and invisible. Interconnected relationship is probably nature's first law. As a part of nature, a healthy, balanced masculinity is more about cooperative relationship than about "going it alone."

American culture abounds with images and characters that embody the self-reliant "I don't need anyone else but me" approach to manhood. Consider the solitary cowboy, the classic John Wayne westerns, and the Lone Ranger. From Superman to hypermacho Hollywood action heroes, overtly independent characters are venerated and celebrated in our society and deeply imprinted into the collective conscious. Furthermore, in nearly all these cultural icons and heroes, violence is an acceptable—indeed, primary—expression of strength.

Yet when one gazes into the mirror of Nature, the blueprint from which we developed as a species, one can see a more profound evolutionary strategy than "survival of the fittest." Certainly there is violence in nature, but even the fittest and fiercest remain enmeshed in the web of interdependence. More than competition, cooperation makes life possible. Where there is taking, there is also giving. Only humans in their cultural disconnection and mental arrogance believe that they can exist independent of the natural forms and forces that surround them. As a result, we are now faced with a crisis of global scale, one that will require cooperation and imagination to successfully resolve for the greatest, collective good.

From corporate boardrooms to bedrooms, from farms to factories, golf courses to greenhouses, we exist always and each moment only *in relationship*. Our eyes tell us that we are separate, noting the differences and space between things, but we are in constant connection: molecules of air surrounding us and filling our lungs; a steady exchange with viruses, bacteria and millions of microbes (the majority of which are "foreign" to us); a trillion chemical messages and reactions occurring within our bodies every minute; constant interaction with the energetic fields of plants, animals, and humans around us and with the physical spaces in which we dwell and work; contact with the earth or concrete underfoot, from which we push off with each step as we walk. Everything is relationship. Atoms bond together with gravitational force to form elements, which then form further, more complex relationships; larger molecules form cells and organs in the body or seemingly solid matter in the "external" material world. Thus the very elements of our being exist in innumerable cooperative relationships and a conspiracy of life. The power of Eros and allurement is everywhere and inescapable.

The Sacred Masculine understands and embraces the fundamental fact that everything is relationship, a "mutually interdependent co-arising." Our daily life and presence affects untold others from blue jay to businessman, like tiny gears turning other connected wheels around us within an impossibly complex biomachine. From the microcosm to the macrocosm, we exist solely within the Unified Field of intelligence and possibility, continuously immersed in a sea of energy.

I hear it first, the soft tapping of rain on the few remaining leaves high above, and I look up to see a heavy gray sky. Seconds later, my eyes sweep back down to the flowing ribbons of water, noting the expanding crystalline rings on the surface as the falling droplets complete their gravitational plunge to earth.

It was sunny when I set out from the cottage; now, less than twenty minutes later, the sky is made of gray, hammered tin and falls towards me. In an unusual twist for this time of year, I'm not wearing a raincoat and I have no umbrella, only a light scarf. I glance around for some place to take refuge but the trees are bare and there is no adequate shelter. The sound of ten thousand drumming fingers grows louder as the rain increases its volume, and I realize that I'm about to be drenched by this unexpected deluge. So be it. I haven't spent nearly the time that I wish to linger in this special hollow but I rise from my squat to begin walking home in the surprise shower. Discovering this dell, I know I'll soon be back, for there is something here that pulls me and whispers with a soft, secretive, and alluring voice. Many voices, actually, all calling my wild soul by a secret name.

As I stride across the sodden green field, the phantom clouds that appeared from nowhere let loose with unexpected vigor. Silvery rain begins to pour with driving, diagonal force and the distant horses in the field lower their noble heads and turn away. I squint into curtains of rain sweeping across the landscape, water running from my unruly hair into my eyes, and I suddenly laugh out loud. How crazy this is! There is no point running for home or trying to find shelter, so I simply surrender to the celestial baptism and give myself fully to the experience of walking in a downpour.

The unexpected squall lasts only ten minutes, leaving me soaked to the bone and looking like a two-legged, wet muskrat. Entwine some ivy in my hair and brown beard, and I could be a very soggy Green Man. Only my feet remain dry, tucked snugly into high rubber boots. As I cross the last flooded field to open the high deer gate and set foot in my garden, the sky is a brilliant powdery blue. Everywhere shines the same golden light that graced the world when I set out on this jaunt, lending a shimmering luminescence to everything it touches. Not a single cloud obscures the sky except over the far Downs. It is a stunning autumn day, one fit to inspire painters to rush for their brushes and easels in an attempt to capture the radiant splendor. Almost impossible.

I'm soaked and chilled but I feel fully and gratefully alive, my body coursing with a subtle current of electricity. Nature's torrential cloudburst has washed me clean and I'm now inspired to sit and engage the work I had been avoiding. As always, time spent amid the forms and forces of nature has brought me home to myself, drawing me out of the small world of mind into the larger web of interconnected relationship. I feel open and expanded, connected by invisible but luminous strands to everything around me.

Inside the cottage, I strip down for a brief but steaming shower, thankful for the everyday gift of plumbing and hot water on my naked body. Dressed again, I put the blue enameled kettle on the stove to heat for tea and then settle in to write with notebook and fountain pen. The flashing light on the router tells me that the broadband still isn't working but it doesn't matter. Rebuilding the website can wait. In my walking, as always, I have come home again to my body. Energized. Reconnected. Bearing the words and inspiration like crisp, harvest-ripe apples in a woven basket.

A DIFFERENT KIND OF MUSCLE

Mulling over the wander in my memory and making some notes, I return to the image of the open shells along the water's edge and the notion of *a different kind of muscle*. Men need something more than sculpted pectorals, bulging biceps, and washboard stomachs, however attractive those may be. Too, we need a sort of brawn different from our mental, cognitive, and rational skills. Something more than the ability to thrust, dominate, seek progress, strategize, and compete is required for balanced, healthy manhood. Men must discover a different kind of strength and still perceive themselves as *strong*.

Pioneer of psychology and the subconscious, Carl Jung notably championed the idea of *archetypes* as universal symbols and energies that channel experience and emotion. These forms exist as something beyond a mere model of a person, behavior, or personality; they invoke a shared imagery that can be found across diverse cultures and eras of human evolution. Archetypes are eternal, powerful forces that emerge from a mysterious place within the collective psyche. A few of the classic and well-known archetypes include the Child, the Hero, the Great Mother, the Crone, the Wise Man, the Warrior, and the Trickster. Like facets of our own soul, all archetypes are available to and inside each of us. Male archetypes are not solely about men nor are female archetypes solely the province of women; instead they illustrate and embody multifold elements of being human.

At different times in history, energies and archetypes surge forward to manifest their presence in the collective consciousness. Jung offered that archetypes emerge and reappear in new and different forms to assist in shifting imbalances on a societal level. Currently, as men seek a more balanced way of being—one no longer out of touch with Nature and self—some notable and powerful archetypes are emerging that embody the Sacred Masculine.

In his insightful book, *The Hidden Spirituality of Men: Ten Metaphors to Awaken the Sacred Masculine*, theologian Matthew Fox beautifully explores many of these archetypes now reappearing.[2] He explores not only the Green Man but the Spiritual Warrior, Father Sky, the Blue Man, the Earth Father, Grandfather Sky, and others. He writes compellingly about men's struggles with shame and aggression, and also of the healing union of the masculine and feminine within each of us. Each of the archetypes and metaphors he offers for the Sacred Masculine reflects a different sort of muscle; strength based on a wider scope of relationship and connection to self, community, planet, and cosmos.

It has been said that "what we seek is near and already coming to meet us."[3] On an archetypal level this rings especially true. A different mode for being, knowing, and "hearting" already exists in each of us and in the collective soul of the world. Through our conscious choices and personal evolution, we begin to embody what now seeks expression through us as a manifestation of universal energy, whether that be Green Man, Wanderer, Lover, Visionary, Wild Soul, or Erotic Warrior.

The Sacred Masculine is ready to reappear.

ADULTHOOD AND AUTHENTICITY

Recently, a friend in the UK who thought I'd be interested told me of an online "thread" he was following on a message board on a popular Internet chat site. The topic of this particular discussion was, "What is the definition of being a man?" Within a day of its posting on the site, dozens of men had weighed in with their various opinions and arguments, one fellow even including a dictionary definition to validate his words. Knowing the topic I was currently writing about, my friend wondered what I would say if I were to join the online discussion.

"Either too much or too little," I chuckled, as I typed my email response to him.

It is a topic far too broad and challenging to adequately address succinctly, more deserving of a book than a simplified answer or a tweet. Yet the fact that this question floated around as an Internet discussion with a diverse crowd of men logging in to share their thoughts underscores the deep ambivalence and uncertainty that we collectively carry about what manhood entails. Furthermore, the relative superficiality of all the posted online answers revealed how disconnected we are as a culture from any sense of deeper meaning around being a man.

At the risk of veering into *manhood* rather than *masculinity*, I offer that true manhood requires more than merely an accumulation of years or the passing of certain societal measurements—work and earning an income, sexual activity, independence from parents, marriage, fatherhood—to make one a man. Something more than a one-dimensional one, that is.

An authentic and meaningful sense of adulthood is seriously lacking in our modern, Western culture, partly because we have no real rites of passage or soulful initiations. Passing a driver's test, losing one's virginity, obtaining the legal age of accountability and buying a house are not rites of passage; they are achievements of an individual. *True rites of passage or initiatory processes abduct an individual into the mystery and creative core of who he is,* something much deeper than the ego, thus allowing him to better understand the unique inclinations and gifts of his soul. In illuminating the idea that the creative current of soul is our wellspring of personal power, such passages also help a person glimpse how he stands in integral relationship to the community and the other-than-human world around him. Personal evolves to transpersonal.

Lacking authentic rites and initiations that deliver deeper nourishment than merely ego achievement, men find themselves in a vacuum of meaning as to what true adulthood entails (women, too, though perhaps to a lesser extent due to their inclination for relationship). We exist in a cultural void where the only options offered are the largely superficial models of gender—firmly ensconced in the polar opposite roles of disconnected male and female—and a consumerist lifestyle that is invariably hollow at its core. Modern society remains psychologically immature. Few role models or roadmaps exist that illustrate how one's unnamed longing can serve as a guide to something larger or an embodied connection with life force, passion, and beauty of Eros.

A slightly expanded notion of adulthood, male or female, involves taking the risk to live on one's own inner authority and guidance and then accepting the consequences, for better or worse. On a developmental level, this autonomy entails the conviction and wherewithal to live from the center of one's being and follow one's guiding star, even when that means charting a course other than what our mainstream culture considers normal, appropriate, or successful. Further evolution into adulthood mandates embracing something larger than the ego and its notions of accomplishment and approval. At a highly conscious level comes the understanding that one must embody one's soul gifts and live in a manner that supports not only one's soul but also the larger web of relationship, from immediate family to human community, to the shared planet and all its denizens. Alas, such soulfully initiated adulthood is rare.

True adulthood is forged from exploring and *living* the questions that cannot easily be answered yet must be asked. Who am I? What or where is my place in the world? What do I most fear? And love? What am I willing (or afraid) to feel? What do I uniquely bring to the Larger Story that is unfolding, and what will I risk to bring that forward?

In living such existential questions, a man steps beyond social conformity and turns towards the elemental truths of his being, those that emerge from the soul with unique voices. He expands into personal authenticity, creative potential, and embodied power, a place of somatic resonance and vitality. Holding such questions as constellations guides us towards our destiny, leading us from the shallow waters of an imbalanced, stereotypical notion of masculinity into the depths of meaningful connection afforded by the Sacred Masculine. It is only through a personal soul quest—and being broken open to something much larger—that we emerge into truly authentic, soulcentric manhood.

OUTMODED PARADIGMS

We seem to have confused *male* with *masculine*. Our gender is largely determined at conception through the pairing of chromosomes. If we develop external gonads, we are male; later in life, we will develop other secondary characteristics particular to our sex, such as increased bone size and musculature, thickened vocal cords (which create a lower voice), and facial hair. Yet these features only make us male, not masculine.

Our expression of gender, either masculine or feminine, is a combination of anatomy, genetics and hormones, role models and parental influence, family dynamics, cultural customs, and social feedback.[4] The soul may play a curious role, as well. The definition we give to *masculinity* or *femininity* is a collection of traits typically associated with male or female gender, respectively. Within the broad and brilliant spectrum of expression there are feminine males and masculine females, but their personal traits do not define or change their gender, and they are still male and female.

Our current notion of masculinity (and by general association, maleness) is a construct based primarily on personality attributes that portray a more outward and probing orientation, as with the male genitals. The *masculine* is inclined towards qualities that display assertiveness and forward direction, seek linear locomotion and sense of progress, are competitive and/or territorial, frame challenges and opportunities outside oneself, and value rational thought and processes.

Our perceptions about femininity are mainly opposite, embodying a more receptive and inward orientation (as with the female genitalia). We associate the *feminine* with openness and inviting cooperation, relational orientation, intuition and awareness of what is present (though perhaps not always seen or named), and celebration of beauty.

The masculine tends towards sharper distinctions and more rigid, defined boundaries; for the feminine, boundaries tend to be more flexible and permeable, which in turn blurs distinctions and embraces similarities (in line with the overall tendency towards receptivity and communion). The so-called feminine traits are more attuned to relationship, process, and harmony. For men, as we cultivate more of these relational qualities, we then enhance our ability for resonance, feeling, cooperation and intimacy . . . and wholeness.

For much of humanity's recent evolution—the last several thousand years—the traits of the masculine have exerted a dominant, patriarchal control not only of women and other beings, but also of nature's resources. The problem lies not within masculinity itself but rather in the imbalanced, distorted embodiment of the masculine that is focused on dominance and power. Most of humanity suffers from a decided lack of harmony. Our current worldview and the powers that support it—industry, government, education, and religion—have been built and continue to be run by the one-dimensional aspect of the imbalanced masculine.

With the significant influence of Judeo-Christian religion on Western culture, God has been identified as male. These religions evolved in a time of severe patriarchal control of culture, and the notion of God in their sacred texts and teachings reflects the dominant, distorted qualities of the masculine. We are presented with a male deity, creator of a universe that is separate from him, who communicates his wishes for humanity largely through a select group of prophets, sacred texts, and believers. Though they have proved both damaging and destructive, these images of an imbalanced male godliness remain deeply ingrained in our society.

The emphasis on reason and intellect that evolved from the Western classical traditions, coupled with the rise of science, relegates the world of soul or spirit to an unreal, emotional, disenfranchised, or "airy-fairy" experience. Subjective and lacking tangible evidence, the ethereal and invisible wrestles with objective validity. Despite the fact that everything in the universe is held together by invisible bonds and relationships, the realm of the indiscernible or otherworldly seems to trouble our overly logical, rational brains. Westerners (men, especially) have developed an overvaluation of thinking and an undervaluation of feeling.

Historically, men have predominantly viewed *feminine* as something apart and "other," decidedly female, and generally weak. Too frequently overlooked in this assessment are the depth, determination, and fierceness that the feminine can embody. A woman protecting her children or mate is ferocious as a lioness. Rather than weakness, the feminine embodies a *different* sort of strength and muscle: flexible, tensile, and more relational. In mythological forms and archetypes, strong female images abound, such as the mighty warrior goddess, Athena, and the deft huntress, Artemis, who both embody a depth of fierceness and strength that rival that of any man. The Dark Mother, Kali, and the Hawaiʻian goddess of volcanoes, Pele, each embody a powerful, fiery energy of destruction but one that gives new life, as well.

Traditionally—and tragically—our imbalanced notions of gender shape a profoundly imbalanced individual, one who needs to attract his polar opposite to find any sort of equilibrium. Day and night, *yin* and *yang*, Mars and Venus. In this split duality, the energy or quality that offers wholeness or balance is something outside the self, leaving one seemingly incomplete on one's own or whole only in the context of external relationship.

It is a misguided and shortsighted notion that only *masculinity* makes a man. If one embraces solely the masculine aspects of one's gender, this does not make one a "real man"; it makes one a distorted and imbalanced man. A shallow and rigid man. Rejection of the feminine, either inside or outside us, is a sure sign of false masculinity, unhealthy maleness, and an immature sense of self. It also fundamentally undermines our ability to be in harmony, either within the self and soul, or with the world at large.

Embracing the feminine does not involve surrendering our inherent maleness or the positive aspects of masculinity (assertiveness, forward direction, etc.). It is not about becoming safe, subdued, passive, and overly gentle men. We are not looking to become women in men's bodies or to adopt only matriarchal forms of gods or leadership; such actions would only result in a backlash and a renewed resurgence into the imbalanced masculinity. Embracing the feminine is about a sense of wholeness and balance, not only within ourselves but also in the larger relationship of which we are a part.

FROM GENDER TO SOUL

One of the many ways that humans are unique is that we can embody both masculine and feminine traits and tendencies while retaining our physical gender. Our gender roles and expression develop as an integral part of our provisional identity, the early social persona of the ego.[5] Curiously, we learn these gender roles around the same time that we are generally being weaned off youthful creativity and imagination. Our initial, innocent expansion of soul is overlaid with cultural roles and patterns of containment, both emotional and physical.

Every stage of life has certain developmental tasks and challenges that must be successfully navigated. Failure to complete a task or stage results in an underdeveloped aspect of an individual's personality, one that will appear later in life as a deficit or stumbling block. Establishing a gender role and its appropriate expression is an earlier psychological developmental task than awakening to the mysteries of soul and one's deeper, authentic identity (rooted in a core sense of one's creative gifts rather than a provisional social identity). As we mature into puberty and adolescence—which for some continues most of their lives, at least in an emotional sense—an important task is to question the roles we've been handed. Yet even after passing through the shoals of puberty into so-called adulthood, a man may still find himself questioning what manhood really entails. In a healthy individual, the journey to an authentic sense of self and wholeness is an ongoing expansion and quest.

The fundamental query "What does it mean to be a man" rests inextricably linked with "Who am I?" and one's deeper purpose.

If we question what it means to be a man without also considering the essential, creative, and relational element of soul, we end up with only the flat, one-dimensional definition of manhood much like the cultural version currently in place. It lacks the key of interconnected relationship. Alternatively, if we consider what it means to be a man while *also* considering the soul—or what it is to be a soul while embodied as a man—the picture looks quite different: it now forms a double helix, a spiritual DNA. Our creative imperative to evolve to our full potential reveals the Universe's imagination.

You have a deeper purpose even if it is not yet clear what that may be.

A CRUMBLING CASTLE

Three now-classic books helped establish the mythopoetic Men's Movement in the early nineties: *Iron John: A Book About Men,* by Robert Bly (1991); *Fire In The Belly: On Being A Man,* by Sam Keen (1992); and *King, Warrior, Magician, Lover: Rediscovering the Archetypes of the Mature Masculine,* by Robert Moore (1991). Collectively, these books sold nearly two million copies. Yet one could argue that despite such phenomenal book sales and popular conferences, the early men's movement proved only modestly successful at shifting entrenched, mainstream notions of masculinity and manhood. An expanded, evolved definition of manhood remained largely on the fringes—though from an evolutionary standpoint, that is *always* where evolution begins, never in the status quo.

Rome wasn't built in a day. A mighty oak takes a very long time to grow from a small acorn. As with attitudes on racial or gender equality or sexual orientation, a meaningful shift in beliefs can take generations to occur. In considering the success—both immediate and long term—of the initial men's movement, there are many factors to consider. In part, the lack of a truly substantial, initial change reflects the media's trivializing of the men who, inspired by Bly, went off into the woods to discover their inner Wild Man, drumming, and male bonding. The initial absence of perceptible shift in cultural attitudes was also partly due to the differing ideas of masculinity among men, ranging from the stiff, hypermacho types to sensitive New Age guys ("SNAGs," as I once heard someone say derisively). Just as a backlash arose against feminism within the ranks of women, a tremendous resistance and fear exists among men around perceived threats to traditional manhood, whether from women or from men themselves.

In my early twenties, when I was first deeply questioning what it meant to be a man, I happened across a book called *Sacred Manhood, Sacred Earth: A Vision Quest into the Wilderness of a Man's Heart*, by Joseph Jastrab and Ron Schaumburg (1994).[6] The words and stories moved and inspired me, opening new doors of possibility for an authentic, heart-centered manhood. I eventually gifted my copy to a client who I thought would also find it relevant. What I remembered of the book seemed timely to the work coming through me with clients, workshops, and this writing, and recently I decided to attempt to locate another copy so that I might reread it.

Though the book is now out of print, I tracked down several copies through the Internet. Also while on Amazon.com, I read the original review and my heart sank under the words. The critic's patronizing assessment began, "A flaky journey into the heart of dimness that is the

Men's Movement..."[7] He then proceeded to ridicule not only the modern adaptation of the vision quest but the vulnerabilities and tender stories shared by the men who were participants.

The condescending remarks of the reviewer illuminated the underlying fear and insecurity lurking in the hearts of men about anything that potentially undermines their limited concept of manhood: a mode of containment, emotional restriction, and somatic contraction. Somewhere in the subconscious rumbles a defensive statement like *I may not know who I am but at least I'm a man.* Thus when a men's movement—or anyone, really—begins to dismantle and renovate the longstanding fortifications of traditional masculinity, the fear is that there may be nothing left to hide behind. To question the outmoded, imbalanced, and severely limited tenets of the entrenched masculinity is to risk opening to something much larger. We hazard lowering the castle drawbridge and becoming vulnerable, engaging in unarmed relationship with those who have gathered in the wide, grassy field.

Thick walls have been built with heavy stones of historical and cultural precedent, and most men remain hiding behind them. Protected with chest plates of armor and seemingly strong, we're frightened and unsure. Even among our comrades and colleagues, we are strangely alone and isolated. We face a host of emotions that we are told we're not supposed to feel as men, and in our shame around this, bodies and breath are tightly constricted in a collective, silent scream. *When we are closed in bodymind, senses, or heart, we cannot authentically engage in relationship.*

We all wrestle with demons of anger, shame, fear, grief, and despair, and each of us carries a deep and nameless longing in his bones. Yet risking creative evolution and heeding the mysterious call of the soul is not generally supported, popular, or understood in our society. Most men are imprisoned in a cage that is largely of their own making.

A healthy and balanced notion of manhood is not a castle or a prison cell, and it is something far more than a sports arena, a boardroom or private club, an office or a factory. Rather than a fortress, imagine an interconnected pavilion of colorful tents in a wild meadow among the noble trees and alongside the flowing river. A community sharing a wealth of ideas, emotions, stories, and creative innovation. It is a place of conscious relationship, one that supports a council of all beings. Relational interaction and intimacy require openness.

You have a deeper purpose, brother. Will you remain behind the walls or risk emerging into something much larger and far more powerful?

NEW FRONTIERS

Whether we define the early men's movement as success or failure, men are still seeking answers and inspiration regarding what it means to be a man. Beyond the therapist's couch, in every major city across the USA, small groups meet where men are questioning what it means to be an authentic and good man, seeking to embrace their shadows of shame, anger, and grief, to find support and camaraderie while opening to something much larger and affirming. A more relational approach.

In personal sessions, groups, and workshops I've led, I have repeatedly been moved and inspired by the bold and beautiful men daring to ask the biggest questions of their lives. On retreats, wilderness quests, and at larger conferences, I have been privileged to sit among soulful men engaging courageous conversations about work, family, love, and their general manner of being in the world. They are asking how to be open, how to awaken their hearts, and where to find support for such raw, vulnerable authenticity.

These are men searching for their purpose and passion, seeking to embody Eros and their soul's longing through new and creative avenues. Brave souls all, each heeds the call of archetypal energies of transformation and connection in his way. Each struggles to work the key in the lock that he might step outside into the bright sunshine and expand into a felt sense of power and connection. Each follows a glimmering golden thread into the darkness of the labyrinth.

Perhaps it grows from seeds planted in the earlier movement, or maybe those early trees are now beginning to bear fruit, but our ideas of what constitutes an acceptable masculinity are slowly changing. As evidenced by a burgeoning number of websites, initiation trainings, online magazines, and teleconferences, a men's neo-movement is quietly rising. A new generation of men looks to evolve in relationship and their sense of self, personal meaning, and genuine connectedness to the world. How will we make a difference? Each of these seekers understands that only through his personal work—integrating his own shadow and light—will he achieve satisfactory and nourishing relationships with others. Only then will he find the wholeness and healing he seeks.

Even if we allow ourselves to claim it, are we prepared to dance with true power? How do we develop a more mature ego that allows knowledge to arise from the body, the deep imagination, and currents of Mystery? What is our larger role at this time?

Evolution happens at the edges. In the States and abroad, I'm honored to know some admirable, wise, powerful, and soulful men—therapists, guides, healers, writers, businessmen—serving as "way-showers" on the path of awakening the soul. I respect them as compassionate, strong, flexible, tender, sensitive, intuitive, educated, ecological, and self-actualizing men who embody the Sacred Masculine. Wild souls. Daily they inspire me as they bring their soul gifts forward in word and meaningful action, heart-centered sharing and vulnerability.

We are shaped by our cultural roles and past experience, certainly. Yet at no other time in history has there been such fluidity and freedom in defining roles and expectations, not simply in terms of gender and sexual orientation but also with reinventing work, careers, and collective entities such as corporations. Among the younger generation, many are questioning and reinventing the old, stale social identities handed down to them. Organizations like the ManKind Project with their New Warrior Training, the Shift Men's Initiation, the Ultimate Men's Summit (teleconference), the Minnesota Men's Conference, the Redwood Men's Conference, and many others are gathering men together to ask the big questions about what it means to be a conscious man. It is a time of doubt and ambiguity for the future, but it is also a time of unbridled imagination as we collectively envision a new future for ourselves, the human race, and the planet.

Imagination is the great gift of humanity. We stand at a crossroads where it is possible—imperative, even—to reconsider and reimagine what it means to be fully human and connected to the world around us. A new cosmology is being birthed—a spirituality that isn't about religion, one that embraces the discoveries of science—where we understand that the Universe is within us. A Great Turning is at hand, a shift evidenced by cultural visionaries, ecologists and environmental activists, social entrepreneurs, "green" businesspeople, and other soulful agents of change working to collectively reinvent our world through their daily living. Cosmologist Brian Swimme, environmentalist/entrepreneur/author Paul Hawken, author/environmentalist Bill McKibben, biomimicry inventor Jay Harman, EnlightenNext Magazine, and the Bioneers Conference are just a few of the popular, noteworthy voices steering us towards a reimagined, integral future. Old social constructs are dissolving while new stories and archetypes seek to emerge. Business and commerce are changing. Despite the tide of disparaging news and melting ice caps, a change in consciousness is underway, rising up in a wave. A different wind is rippling through the grass. It may not yet be sweeping through at the level of national politics and leadership but it is moving across the globe.

Brother, you're not alone. We are changing and evolving.

I ask, what will you bring?

EVOLVING MASCULINITY

A reenvisioned masculinity is not about vision quests, rites of passage, or drumming circles beneath a full moon. It is not focused on a connection with nature as a quaint, old-fashioned notion or as a panacea for the cut and thrust of daily life. At its core, it serves something larger than saving a forest or an endangered species. Political and environmental activism holds an essential place for the "new man" but unless such action stems from a true understanding of our mutual interconnectedness, it remains something apart from the sacred activism that emerges from the soul.

An enlightened masculinity means that our self-worth comes from something *inside* rather than from external validation—the vehicle we drive or the size of our manroot. It grants us access to the full spectrum of emotions and their fair expressions and allows us to share them with other men. Simultaneously, it requires vulnerability and a willingness to descend into the bones and breath and discover our patterns and deep-rooted fears.

Soul is the guiding principle of unity in our psyche and a stream of potential and kinetic energy in our body. It is our life force and true, authentic power. Soul invites us to step from the small cage we have created; it even places the key in our palm. By its very nature, the creative essence of soul is enlarging. It seeks to expand from our core and join in conscious connection with the other-than-human world (of which it is an intrinsic part), yet most of us are firmly held in containment and inertia.

Brother, we must learn to be open, for only then will we discover our deeper purpose. Our body and senses play a pivotal role here. When we are expansive *and* receptive we experience connection, union, and wholeness. Opening in a polysensory way is a primary skill in developing our more relational, intuitive, and "feminine" nature. Expansive in senses and bodymind, we begin to shift habitual patterns. The deeper we descend into the bodysoul and begin to move and open, the more we rouse from inertia and *feel* something of the soul's somatic guidance.

The frenetic disharmony of modern life is not an easy or conducive environment in which to open our senses. It is far more challenging than a pine forest or some other natural, tranquil environment. In Distraction-ville, USA, we live in a world of noise and nearly constant stimulation. Amid the urban hum, our waking hours are repetitively bombarded with television, radio, phone calls, messages, and sonic beeping alerts. Activated in an ongoing "fight or flight" stress response, our nervous systems are simultaneously overstimulated and desensitized. Breath is shallow and restrained. Countless interruptions and electronic intrusions—most of which we feel compelled to acknowledge or respond to, at least briefly—effectively divert us from introspection, emotional processing, and the deeper journey of psyche and soul. Virtually glued to our "smart phones" and SMS texts, browsing Facebook, surfing the Internet for porn, or working late into the night via email, we are engaged primarily through our visual sense. Staring for extended periods at flat, two-dimensional screens, we are losing our sense of true depth, in more ways than one. Conspiring with our own patterns, technology has enabled us to become masters of avoidance. We are effectively disembodied from bodywisdom and natural rhythms while our powers of focused and sustained attention steadily dwindle. Most of us think all of this is *normal*.

You have a deeper purpose, and your body holds the key. We need to unplug and, even amid the noise, begin to listen. Not simply with ears but with our senses. Feeling. Intuition. We need to "tune in" rather than "tune out," and allow ourselves to be guided deeper into a tactile, sensual connection with life and the way of the wild soul.

THE SACRED MASCULINE

Each of us is the Cosmos embodied, a deeply creative and imaginative force in human form. There is something essential and long overdue about wrestling the idea of a "sacred" masculine away from our historical, Judeo-Christian religious interpretation. Scriptures and images of a jealous, angry, and patriarchal God have soured many of us on the possibility of a holy maleness. Too many wars and crimes of hate have been perpetrated in such a god's name. Religious intolerance is not spiritual.

The teachings and messages of the world's dominant religions retain value at their core, but the interpretation of those truths often becomes distorted and twisted. The one-dimensional, Biblical version of a male deity who communicates through chosen ones and a select sect of believers is no longer useful to our collective, conscious evolution with the planet and her denizens. It is time to widen the view.

Sacred need not mean *religious*. If we considered a "sacred" masculine as a heart-centered one, a different picture emerges, for no force exists more holy than love. In framing our concept of the Sacred Masculine, we would also be well served by restoring it to stand alongside the Divine Feminine as half of a balanced equation. No more, no less.

It doesn't matter whether your sexual orientation is straight, bisexual, or gay. A man who embodies the Sacred Masculine understands that embracing the "feminine" aspects of himself does not lessen his manhood. To the contrary, his ability to be in a conscious relationship with self, life partner, family, and the world at large is enhanced by cultivating the more receptive, life-enhancing qualities of empathy and compassion, intuition, body wisdom, tenderness, flexibility, respect, and cooperation.

This chapter began with a wander through fields and woods, musing on the Sacred Masculine as embodied by the Green Man, the Old World steward of the forests. As an overlighting energy and presence, the Sacred Masculine assumes myriad shapes and forms. Eros, as the life force and energy of connection, is one facet of the Sacred Masculine. So too is the Erotic Warrior: one who perceives the interfuseability between everyday life and the sacred, knowing that they are inseparable. No matter the archetype or metaphor, in all manifestations of the Sacred Masculine, a few key characteristics are omnipresent and interwoven:

- *The Sacred Masculine is a heart-centered manhood,* one that views the world through a lover's eyes rather than those of a conqueror or lone ranger. A spiritual seeker, soul agent, or sacred activist, he understands that more is ultimately achieved through collective sharing than through competition. He is compassionate, generative, and generous.

- *The Sacred Masculine honors bodymind as the sacred vessel of life.* The Universe (Cosmos, Holy, One, Source) experiences itself and the world *through* us with the body as its instrument. This changes a conscious man's view of exercise, food, nourishment, sex, work . . . everything. We exist only in relationship, and soul is drawn into communion with the other-than-human world via opened senses. Body, soul, and nature are inseparable.

- *The Sacred Masculine wields personal power in an appropriate and balanced manner.* In a material world we tend to perceive power as money and influence, but power exists in many forms. True power is a force of Nature. Authentic power is the life force that animates our breath and bones, carrying us through the day. Such vitality manifests in our creative, sexual, and spiritual energies, and the Sacred Masculine cultivates and builds this power through conscious living and bodysoul practices.

- *The Sacred Masculine is a wise father to deep creativity and imagination.* Even without children of one's own, there are a multitude of ways to embody the compassionate father energy of the Sacred Masculine, teaching skills that reach far beyond passing a football, driving a car, or shooting a gun. Whenever we foster creativity and dreams, or soul skills, or when we embody and display principles of stewardship, ecology, and interconnectedness, we hail this healing, archetypal energy.

◆ *The Sacred Masculine exemplifies a yielding energy while still moving forward with direction,* flowing more like a river than plowing ahead like a bulldozer. He demonstrates a willingness to be guided by the shifting currents of life and Mystery rather than seek to impose linear, forceful will on a perceived direction and destiny. Flexibility loosens our hardened plates of muscle and emotional steel and begins to unfasten the armor of the heart. He models a different kind of muscle, a tensile rather than rigid strength.

◆ *As a force of balance and harmony, the Sacred Masculine is always a life-enhancing component of the planet rather than a dominant, parasitic, or destructive one.* He respects that the world does not exist solely for the use and exploitation of humans, and that we are an integral part of the other-than-human community. Nature is not simply something *out there*; it is within us as well, and we are not separate from our environment. We depend on the earth, and we must care for it as stewards rather than exploiters or mindless consumers. The Sacred Masculine constructs bridges between people and builds community, cultivates gardens (both literal and figurative), and tends the earth as he husbands the other-than-human world. He knows where his water comes from and where it goes, and remains mindful of his personal impact on the planet. He makes conscious choices in his energy use, food selection, and consumerism.

◆ *The Sacred Masculine understands that everything has an entitlement to be here.* Such empathy and kinship with life is something that has to be *felt*. It arises through observing the interrelated nature of things, which happens only when our hearts, minds, and senses are open wide. Other times this knowing is experienced through a sense of wonder and awe. Salmon to sycamore trees, jellyfish to jungles, coyotes to coral reefs, rocks to rivers, each being holds its privilege to be here. Everything is sentient and part of the creative imagination. The Sacred Masculine respects that the nonhuman are not merely "things" that are not alive or are somehow inferior or simply here for our use. Nature's first law is connection and interdependence.

- ◆ *The Sacred Masculine is aware of his cosmological connection.* He is cognizant of the larger story emerging through him in the form of his imagination, creativity, and soul; his creative life force and passion have a higher purpose. Simultaneously, he recognizes that *everything is relationship* and that he is constantly interwoven with all that surrounds him. Conscious relationship exists on many levels. Life is a multisensory communion with the physical world and his community, from his human beloved to his children and family, to the place where he resides and his work in the world.

Humanity's impact on the web of life is staggering. Yet a shift is underway: an evolution in the understanding of who we are and our greater, interconnected role at this time. We see the first glimpses of a shifting worldview and changing agreements as a culture—what we might call *intersubjectivity*—a reimagining of what it means to be a man. Or a human. A larger story unfolds everywhere around us, and the Sacred Masculine plays an essential part in it. The new man who embodies the Sacred Masculine assumes many entwined roles: consciously loving mate and spouse, compassionate and protective father, patient teacher and mentor, challenging guide and wise elder, steward. All are timely and essential.

GOOD MEN AND THE GREAT WORK
We stand at a pivotal moment in our development. As has been described eloquently by the noted cultural historian and spiritual ecologist, Thomas Berry, the Great Work of our time is to reenvision humanity and carry out the urgent, essential transition from being the most destructive force on the planet to being a life-enhancing element. Despite the imbalanced, patriarchal cultures that have existed throughout our long evolution as humans, we have had relatively low impact on the larger web of relations that form our environment. We still lived largely in harmony with the natural world that surrounded us, subject as a species to the forces and

seasons of Nature. However, since the dawn of the industrial age, humanity has now quickly reached the level at which we significantly affect the planet directly, not only in our sheer numbers but also in our destructive, materialistic, and resource-hungry lifestyle. Humans now face a massive challenge, the scope of which dwarfs anything previously experienced in history. We are poisoned by a staggering array of toxins in our air, water, earth, and bodies, and an ever-increasing tide of chemicals. Systemic pesticides—now bred into GMO (genetically modified organism) crops—are killing off bees and beneficial insects worldwide while poisoning soil and groundwater water for decades (every repeated application or planting extends the death sentence). The delicate pH balance of the seas has been shifted, and the major oceans churn with floating plastic debris in massive patches larger than some countries and most US states. Simultaneously, a crisis of overpopulation strains the earth's ability to truly support humanity, and there is a steady depletion of natural resources. Climate change threatens to significantly alter our existence. From cultural breakdown and alienation from the natural world, to widespread damage to the planet and atmosphere, the extent of our disruption is nearly overwhelming. The collective state of dissonance has reached environmental cacophony.

Largely it is our secular and isolated mindset that contributes to the widespread destruction of our environment. It has been said that the clash between the industrial-commercial entrepreneur and the ecologist forms the central human issue (and the central Earth issue) of the twenty-first century.[8] Yet because the industrial establishment is the dramatic embodiment of a very destructive and dominant patriarchal mindset, one might also see this struggle as the fundamental quest for healing and equilibrium between an unhealthy, imbalanced masculine and a more relational, sustaining feminine.

There is hope, however. Dark ages of humanity have always given way to new thought and new ideas in a renaissance of rebirth and awakening. Just as the universe emerged and expanded through a series of irreversible transformations, so too has humankind evolved through cataclysmic and turbulent passages. We are made of the very components and elements of the intelligent Cosmos, and the universal story is embodied in humanity's journey. As a unique expression of the Universal mind, we will navigate this imperative evolution at hand with unguessed-at and never-before-imagined ingenuity.

Let's honor women. The importance of women in this Great Turning, with their increased intuitive connection of body wisdom to the mind and their more nurturing impetus to weave relationship through communion, cannot be overemphasized. However, the Great Work of our time will not be successfully accomplished without men who acknowledge and embody a different sort of masculinity: men who understand and value the interrelatedness of all things, rather than those who view the world solely as an asset to be capitalized and exploited. The Sacred Masculine must reemerge through men who embrace their more feminine qualities and the ability to be in harmonic relationship, while also cultivating their authentic and creative power. The male principle is one of action; certainly it is necessary for change and making things right again, but it also requires empathy, consciousness, and compassion.

As Einstein is often quoted, "No problem will be solved by the same level of consciousness that created it." We must thus rely on new ways of thinking, feeling, knowing and being; a more embodied, intuitive, and connected mode. The linear, mechanical, and disconnected mode of our current existence must shift. We must evolve past the "fight or flight" part of our reptilian, lower brains and unplug from our typical left-brain dominance as men. Our collective way through this essential and challenging time will be less about "figuring things out" through rational thought, scientific insight or progress, or even socioeconomic agreements—all of which tend to personify dominant, one-dimensional masculine thought process rather than a more evolved, wholistic (or feminine) relating—than it will be through each person beginning to live in a more conscious and connected way to the planet and each other, aware of the interconnectedness of all beings and the other-than-human world.

We all live downstream.

On many levels, we are faced with a crisis of imagination: both our cultural lack of it and the imperative that only our creativity will see us through the Great Work at hand. We will have to reimagine a way of being that does not view the earth as a commodity and resource but rather as an integral web of relationship of which we are only a (very significant) part. We must reenvision new modes of education, commerce, law and government, along with ways of developing a more integrated, respectful, and sustainable connection—sacred even—with Gaia. Nature, with her endless models of interwoven interdependence, points the way. When we collectively begin to perceive that we are each an interwoven embodiment of the Universe, a miraculous story that has evolved with creativity and intelligence, then there is hope for the seemingly impossible task at hand.

Absolutely essential to this Great Turning are soulfully awakened individuals, ones who understand the imperative for balance and harmony and who proceed forward with the sense of creative authenticity and power that emerges from the soul. These are the artistic visionaries who will lead the way in reimagining the future: the creative catalysts, sustainability advocates, biomimicry inventors, new paradigm business owners, ecowarriors, and soul artists. Wild souls.

On the global scale, the Great Work is about shifting our ecological role to one of harmony, primarily by evolving the masculine and embracing the feminine. For every man, this begins on the personal level through cultivation of our more intuitive, relational aspects by coming into our bodies and breath and opening our senses wide in communion with the other-than-human world. It means coming into harmonic resonance with the Soul of the World. We conspire with our soulful expansion rather than our patterns of competitiveness or aggression, containment, and protection. This inner work then spirals out to the larger stage in a collective shift.

In the evolution of humanity and the Great Work, a culturally viable masculinity must be one that embodies the Sacred Masculine. By heeding Eros and soul—following the golden threads of allurement—through our creative awakening and claiming authentic power, we each contribute to this great shift. No matter our vocation in the world, we can become agents of change and transformation as we evolve into our capacity for harmonious relationship. Our creative power grows, along with a deep sense of meaning, purpose, and interrelated communion. The personal becomes transpersonal, the microcosm the macrocosm, as we collectively weave the tapestry of the Great Work with hands connected to heart.

◆　◆　◆

Embodying the Erotic Warrior

The embodied agent of soul, the Erotic Warrior is one who consciously experiences the other-than-human world through his senses and somatic experience. In polysensory awakening and soulful expansion, he summons authentic power and weaves a connection with the planet and cosmos. He embraces a more receptive, intuitive way of knowing: honoring the wisdom of the body and heart while heeding the allurement of Eros.

The Erotic Warrior knows in his bones and breath that he is a sensual embodiment of the Universe—with all its intellect, creativity, aesthetic and intimate processes—a knowing that brings him ever more fully into himself as a unique and integral being who is intimately connected to all around him. The more he expands his senses, the more fully he opens himself to his authentic essence and soul.

Stewardship, tending to something entrusted to one's care, includes not only the earth but also the body. The hallmark of the Erotic Warrior is that he is fully ensconced in his bodymind as a means of creative, sensual, and sacred connection. The body is the trusted agent for the soul, thus he cares for it, listens to it, and learns from it. He is an embodied steward. The bodysoul is his primary referent and the means through which he engages the biospiritual world around him.

Ultimately, the Erotic Warrior serves Eros—the primal energy of connection—and seeks to offer something of value to the world. Yet it is a giveaway that can happen only from an open, compassionate, and generous heart.

SOUL SKILL #2: OPEN YOUR SENSES

Soul is the unique, creative essence of a life, ever seeking to be embodied in a conscious communion with the Soul of the World. This creative core is inherently expansive. Like a house with windows that open to the elements, the bodysoul interacts with the other-than-human world through our senses. Open wide in senses and soul, we begin to sense the web of life in a conscious, somatic way. *Everything is relationship.*

We cannot authentically engage in relationship or wield authentic power when closed in bodymind, senses, or heart. Dilating, we begin to emerge from our typical, familiar patterns of containment. When we become expansive and receptive *both*, as with the senses, we bridge opposites and embrace wholeness.

Opening through our senses is a key method for embracing the more receptive, feminine aspects of our being while allowing ourselves to be drawn deeper into somatic embodiment and the present moment.

We kindle and enliven our less dominant channels, facilitating a different kind of knowing and connection: visceral and kinesthetic, intuitive, relational. We are all Soul Artists waiting to emerge, and the more our senses open, the more we activate our latent creative ability, imagination, and authentic power.

EMBODYING SOUL SKILL #2: POLYSENSORY PRACTICE

Again, take yourself for a wandering walk. Somewhere semi-wild where you sense nature in a tangible way is ideal, because senses naturally tend to open (even if you are uncomfortable, nervous, or afraid of Nature). Ultimately, any place will do. As with the exercise for Soul Skill #1, give yourself an hour to wander alone, unplugged from phone, emails, and text messages. Disconnect from technology and distraction; reconnect with body and soul (this is actually a later Soul Skill).

Open your senses and expand into your body's awareness.

As you walk or sit in nature, observe the collective uniqueness of the trees, the shifting shapes of clouds, flowers; if you are in an urban setting, observe the colorful diversity of other pedestrians, the neighborhood park, and the tight cluster of rigid buildings. Observe what crosses your path or field of vision. Note the dancing details of sunlight and shadow, considering depth and texture as an artist would. Stop and pay attention to a purple wildflower or a clover blossom in an emerald lawn; get up close and personal with it: the pigmented petals, stamen, and pistil. Get down on your hands and knees. Fondle the fragrant rosemary bush and inhale its resinous oils. Marvel at the golden honeybee, her legs plump with yellow pollen as she penetrates an inviting flower in search of nectar. Hear the ongoing chorus of wind in the leaves, the cooing of pigeons, the harmonious tones of water, the passing hum of cars and the wail of sirens, barking dogs, children's voices, and passing conversations. Note the sound of your own movements, the scuff of your soles on pavement or crunching along the trail. Taste the warm air, the salty inside of your mouth, a cool sip of clear water. Smell the new rain, pine needles, decaying leaves, acrid exhaust, autumnal wood smoke, a passing whiff of perfume, cologne, or sweat, and the enticing aromas of food.

Scan your body as you walk, feeling the ebb and flow of your breath along with the endless tide of tiny, evolving sensations within you. Explore the tightness you feel in your lower back, neck, jaw, or chest, allowing those constricted areas to shift and open with gentle movement and stretching. Feel your soles on the softly yielding ground or rigid concrete. Weather allowing, shed your shoes and walk barefoot, savoring a direct, tactile connection with the earth. Wiggle your bare toes into the grass or chalky dirt.

Close your eyes and let your other senses come forward. Your body is a living antenna, receiving all manner of messages: communication from Nature; soul; human and other beings; intuitions, harmonies, and disruptions; even Earth itself.

Invariably you will find yourself in your head, thinking. Descend back; you're your breath, bones, and awakened senses. Open to the interwoven relationship and beauty around you. It doesn't matter where you live; beauty exists everywhere—you may simply have to search harder to find it or expand your dulled senses in new ways. A green blade of grass growing in the cracks of a dirty sidewalk is an inspiring miracle of life . . . and beautiful. One man's unwelcome weed is another's flower. Begin sensing and noting the relationship of things to each other. Let yourself to be lured into a conscious sensory relationship with what surrounds you—in nature, at home, walking, sitting at a café—and trust that you will discover more about the role of senses and soul as you progress through the chapters ahead.

As before, observe what it's like to be on your own and "unplugged," along with any difficulty or resistance to the exercise. If you can set aside the critic (or the confident "know-it-all" or any other naysayer in your personality), through your expanded senses you can enter a realm of sensual magic and quiet intuition where the soul dwells in possibility.

BODYSOUL INSIGHTS

As in the previous chapter, either during or after the Soul Skill exercise, reflect on the following insight queries and unfinished sentences. There are many valid and revealing ways to explore them: mental consideration; writing and journaling; musing aloud; drawing, sketching, or painting; singing and improvisational music; movement and dance.

Note any Insights you skip because they seem too easy, too challenging, or irrelevant. All dare you to dive into the naked, vulnerable truth under your skin. Observe what happens in your body with each question as you read it, contemplate, and answer.

When my senses open, what do I feel in my heart?

- Where is Eros in my life?
- What are the ways I remain closed in relationship? At work?
- What do I consider sacred?
- I feel a sense of power when I . . .
- As a man, my biggest challenge is . . .
- What do I consider "feminine"?
- Describe the feminine aspects of yourself, then describe the masculine side. How do these embrace and complement each other?
- My physical senses (visual, auditory, olfactory, gustatory, kinesthetic) in order of dominance are . . .

3 Ensouling the Body

A bullying zephyr hurls with feisty glee across the green English countryside. Trees bend in pummeled arcs like screaming dancers while the grassland crops bow and flex in shimmering waves of clacking, flapping sound. The wild tumult of wind seems bent on ripping up the sturdy tent pegs of humanity's slumbering soul, setting our consciousness alight, aflame, and aright. I spread my arms wide as I walk, clumsy wings that fail to carry me aloft as I lean into the storm, laughing aloud. In the sheer power and turbulence that buffets me, a great shout suddenly wells up from my belly and loins. I yell with all my might, not caring what puzzled sheep or solitary English farmer riding his diesel tractor may hear me across the fields. Surely such a bellow will echo back from the hillsides to greet me, but instead the wind snatches my voice and races with it across the rolling horizon, a playful dog with a sonic stick as it runs happy and disobedient into the distance.

I shout again simply for the irrepressible necessity of letting go in this mad afternoon storm in late spring. Such power and life! Exposed to the rattle and hum of the turbulent elements, every cell of my body sings itself alive with trembling joy.

Gazing across the acres of verdant fields, I am mesmerized by their transformation into a rippling, emerald sea of endless motion. The wildly invisible wind slices across and through the grassy landscape, trails of flashing pale silver amid the crops like great schools of sleek, migrating fish. The air tastes sweet and metallic, crisp as flint. Separate and distinct from the dull roar overhead, a hissing rustles through the slender stalks and green grasses around me like some giant and legendary serpent with a forked tongue drawing dangerously near. When it reaches me standing alone with outspread arms, the sound abruptly changes course and glides away with a smooth, extended hiss, moving on through the field in search of other prey.

The wildness of the air wakes some slumbering energy within me, a restlessness that mirrors the windstorm. As I walk, a sensation of urgency builds in my legs like two fleshy kettles building steam.

Faster, commands an urgent, somatic voice beneath my skin.

Obedient, I stride faster up the chalky hill, taking longer strides and sinking like an athlete into the solid musculature of hamstrings, quads, and buttocks.

Yes, my body shouts wordlessly. *Yes, yes, yes . . . !*

I want to push harder, meet my own resistance and throttle until I win through to my untapped power. I feel a sudden urge to plunge into a dead run, discharging this powerful energy that makes my skin feel a size too small. As I climb the hill, rocked by the wind like an aggressive wrestler, my muscles transform and growl. The domesticated inelasticity of muscle fibers too accustomed to sitting becomes the snarl of a caged tiger, his yellow fangs exposed.

Push harder, demands this unnamed energy, awake and straining in my body as a stream swollen within banks from a sudden, hard rain.

Yes . . .

I shake my mane of unruly hair like an untamed, two-legged beast and roar at the wind, emptying my belly of its quietly simmering rage and insidious fear. The tension in my jaw snaps loose, freed at last from rigid, polite restraints. Animated and fully charged, I swing my arms as I continue up the hill, loosening the restricting shell of tightness between my shoulder blades. The rigidity stretches loose, crumbles, and releases. Taut as a sinew bowstring, I am raw and fiercely alive. A naked lover trembling with passion and desire. Dangerous. I am a hard, deep kiss with a jagged bone knife pressed against the throat.

I lean into the wind and dance.

As the stubbornly solid musculature of my body releases through movement and exercise in nature, the chords of my soul reverberate as if strummed by the gods. In this moment I am a human thunderbolt. Electric. Unrestrained. I sense the unlimited, awesome, and terrifying vastness of my being, and the cellular expansion in my core reminds me that anything is possible. I am powerful. Erotic. Authentic and free.

The body holds the key. This framework of bones, breath, and blood harbors the life force, a sacred current of creative, sexual, and spiritual energy. No matter the size, shape, or age, whether it is sleek and toned as a Greek god or flabby and wrinkled as an old leather purse, this marvelous and holy vessel is the temple for one's soul.

We are spiritual energies grounded in the physical body to experience the world around us through the sensory bliss of connection. Eros.

At the top of the hill, I slow to a stop, again spreading my arms to the wind as it roars madly about the landscape. I am not far from the place where I was struck with revelation, the transcendental glimpse behind the curtain between worlds. Closing my eyes, I tune into the pounding drum of my heartbeat, the rapid cadence of my breath, and the hum of energy in my expansive body. Within me I feel the solidness of elemental earth, the powerful force of air, the heat of fire, and I am as much a part of the natural landscape as any creature, plant, or mineral matter around me.

Inhaling fully, exhaling slowly, I drink the experience of being authentically alive, unrestrained, and connected to all that surrounds. In this moment, I am the Erotic Warrior intimately connected through my senses to my life force and the other-than-human world, rippling with sensual power and grace. A wild soul.

What will I dare to bring to the world this day? What will I withhold? Into what venture and experience will I channel this sacred power?

Unleashed, I am.

SENSUALITY AND EMBODIMENT

Through the endless tides of breath and through the streams and rivers of senses and sensations, our bodies constantly steer us to consciousness. In each moment, a dizzying wealth of experience is gifted to us—the smooth glide of a silk shirt on skin, the ebb and flow of breath in the belly, the feel of soft earth or rigid pavement underfoot, the zesty citrus zing of peeling a tangerine, the pressing urge to stretch and move, the constriction of clammy fear in the gut—but to most of these we pay little more than a fleeting notice. We are caught instead in an endless current of thoughts, distraction, and busyness.

We are inherently sensual beings; our senses and nervous systems make it so. We are wired for stimulus and response, both pleasure and pain. Yet very few people inhabit their bodies or physical senses fully, and our bodies themselves have lost their inherent vitality. Ours is a largely "disembodied" culture, relying upon and celebrating the powers of intellect and cognitive functions rather than the instinctual, intuitive intelligence of the body. The senses are typically ranked as one of our basic functions, little more than a motor skill and something we share with animals, while our rational and transcendental abilities are elevated to the top of the enlightenment hierarchy. Intellectuals, philosophers, and spiritual seekers value "higher" states of expanded awareness more than the "lower" states of physical sensation and polythesia. Somatic wisdom is not something we've been taught to explore or cultivate, and few of us realize its true potential or value.

Already in these pages, I have many times used the word *embodiment*, but what exactly do I mean by that? In general terms, embodiment is the ongoing process of fully inhabiting the physical body through present-centered awareness of breath and sensation. On another level, it is attentiveness to the somatic messages of the senses and nervous system, with the ability to track and comprehend the mental and emotional messages that we attach to those stimuli. Conscious embodiment is the ability to live with the senses wide open, aware of the expansive and somatic energies of the soul, and an ongoing sensual communion with the other-than-human world.

We are far more than thinking machines or human "do-ings," occasionally distracted from our distractions and called to our senses through moments of pleasure and pain. Instead, we are graced with the wonder of this human body that allows us to fully savor the sensual experience of the soul's incarnated journey and the humming, vital power of our life force. Choosing to become more mindful of the sensations of our bodies—both in pleasurable ways and not—deepens our connection to the present moment and being alive. Like a glittering diamond, we begin to reflect the many brilliant facets of our current experience, along with the soul's messages encoded in sensation and breath. *Somatic awareness allows us to expand past our patterns of containment and to emerge into an authentic, powerful sense of self—the wild soul.*

Remember that *sensual* means simply "of the senses": tactile and kinesthetic, visual, auditory, olfactory, and gustatory. Consciously rediscovering and exploring our sensuality (including sexuality) moves us closer to authenticity and wholeness as we become expansive *and* receptive. A balancing of the masculine and feminine. The pleasure of the senses draws us not only into a felt sense of personal power—the erotic spiral of creative, sexual, and spiritual energies—but also into communion with the world and to expanded states of consciousness. In heeding the allurement of Eros and the soul's longing, we realize that there is sensation, emotion, and movement tangled in that yearning; we *feel* it in the body. When we track, allow, and follow those somatic currents and messages, we expand into an authentic possibility for life, one that is richly imbued with meaning, the soul's creative expression, visceral power, and attunement.

I want to invite you deeper into the body. I want you to discover your *bodysoul*.

In terms of human embodiment there is a general, descending order from superficial to profound, with what I perceive as four distinct stages. Few individuals, either men or women, progress past the first or second stage or level, because such awareness is not widely taught or valued in our society. Most individuals are content to function at the level of body as machine, with consciousness inhabiting only the head.

The initial level of embodiment encompasses basic body awareness that includes only a passing notice of physical sensations. There is little connection with breath other than an automatic process that oxygenates the body, and no significant correlation of psychological or emotional processes to sensation.

The second stage of embodiment is often initiated by bodywork, somatic therapy, martial arts or movement arts, or spiritual or meditative practices (including yoga) and requires not only conscious choice but also practice. This level includes the rudimentary somatic awareness of the earlier phase while cultivating a mindfulness of the breath, movement and holding patterns, emotions and their corresponding sensations in the body. It is here that we may also begin to discover the *kinesthetic body*, a nonphysical, "subtle" body or form, which can be visualized, connected to, and worked with to increase our physical body's capacity and capabilities. Many athletes utilize this kinesthetic body to visualize motions and improve their actual physical performance.

If we descend deeper into somatic awareness, we reach the third stage: early soul embodiment. Incorporating all the insights and sensory skills of the two earlier stages, it also includes the first awareness of the movement and sensation of the soul's energy as it seeks elemental connection with the natural world *through* the body. It is here that we glimpse the amazing and terrifying potential of being fully human and soulfully embodied: realms of authentic power, vital life force, deep imagination, and sex as portal to higher consciousness. Even for somatic pilgrims, this is new wilderness for most. The body begins to awaken from its modern stupor, to come more fully alive. Vital. Wild. We begin to *feel* our true sensual nature as a creative embodiment of the Cosmos, connected to our place in nature. We literally feel when our soul is in attunement (work, environment, relationship, etc.) as a harmonic resonance in bones and breath or a discord when in disharmony or misalignment. Learning to follow the body's clues guides us along the soul's invisible path.

The deepest level of embodiment remains mostly uncharted. True wilderness explored by few, it is here that an individual becomes fully ensconced as an authentic, soulcentric human being—a significant and rare occurrence. This is a conscious navigation of the somatic currents of soul in one's daily life, an attunement to frequency and harmony, and a cultivation of the bioelectric life force, or *mana*, through deliberate bodysoul practices. With soulful fluency of presence, at this stage we come to know and understand our place in the world at a core visceral and energetic level. Here the grace of the bodysoul is fully manifested and ensouled. One's unique, essential nature becomes more distilled, clearly expressed, and utterly distinct—the wild soul, fully embodied.

As our creative essence, soul is embodied through conscious breath, primal sound, authentic movement, sensory and intuitive connection, and meaningful, heartfelt action in the world. *The passion of the soul, both its longing and its expression, is a somatic experience in the body.* Expansive, it spirals from the center of our being like a radiant sphere of conscious energy. It emanates from us like a dancer's grace or an athlete's power.

Alive it burns like a mystic, golden flame in the heart and glows like fiery embers deep in our eyes.

I once heard it said that the body is "the angel of the soul." Most exquisite. Certainly, the body is the divine vessel for mind, heart, soul, and spirit; without it, we would not be having this human experience. The body is our touchstone and the primary referent for our connection with the biosphere that enfolds us. Full, sensual embodiment is the deep imagination and dream of the human soul.

The bodysoul is beautiful, intelligent, creative, sensual, and sacred. Yet few of us are at home in it. One of our primary tasks as evolving men is learning to fully inhabit our breath, sensations, and energy and to care for—and celebrate—our human form and frame.

In the past two decades, I've done a fair bit of therapeutic work, writing, and coaching about embodying the creative essence through the body: grounding the soul's experience through sensations and breath. Lately, however, I find myself thinking about it in reverse: *ensouling* the body. If we celebrate the body as the agent—or angel—of the soul, then *ensouled* and *deeply embodied* must be nearly synonymous.

This I know beyond a doubt: when we pay attention to breath, sensation, and senses, we begin to hear the whispers of our forgotten, wild nature and the secret language of the soul. We discover that the body is the map to discovering, remembering, and reclaiming not only our passion and power but also our capacity for authentic, meaningful relationship with the Larger Story. Movement and sound arise like sandalwood smoke from a temple of prayer, animating us with elemental energy and sensual delight.

Both ancient and modern, other cultures understand better than does our own that the connection between body and soul is embodied through breath, voice in song or chant, rhythm, and dance or movement. The body is the vessel of the soul *and* the primal path of power. Like our imagination, bodymind is a realm of unlimited possibility. Will we embrace our passion and life force—the erotic spiral of creative, sexual, and spiritual energies? Or will we continue to bury these treasures in tightly held knots of tension and shame?

Brother, I'm inviting you deeper.

The Roots of Disconnection

If we consider that everything is relationship, what is the relationship we have with our body? Most men live as severed from a conscious aware-ness of their bodies as they are from the natural world. Few of us pay much attention to what happens in our bodymind during the day other than elimination or passing discomforts, and even these many of us try to ignore. Our bodies, even their organs and systems, remain numb and mostly unconscious. Only fleetingly aware of tastes, smells, sounds, and sensations, we perceive the world through our dominant visual sense. We engage on a mental level with what surrounds us—usually perceived as "objects" rather than living systems—wrapped in our thoughts, plans, and projections, rational or otherwise. Partly to keep us from being overwhelmed by minutiae, our brain filters out millions of the stimuli we receive. Yet even what still registers we largely ignore. Culturally, we have exalted thinking above feelings and sensations and have unconsciously numbed ourselves to a significant portion of our actual experience in the world. The soul's somatic messages, too.

For us as men, our sensual connection with the body centers on taste, touch, exercise, our genitals, and sexual activity. When we're not feeding, fucking, fighting, on the field, or feeling pleasure or pain in some part of the body, we're holed up in our heads, fretting or figuring things out. Being physical, however, whether in bed, at work, or "working out," is not the same as being consciously *embodied*. The seemingly simple act of present-centered awareness of breath and sensation—tightness in the jaw, the way one stands and holds oneself at attention (or lack thereof), the constriction of shoulders or tightening of the belly under stress or in challenging situations—remains anything but ordinary consciousness. Instead, we are spinning around in our heads, distracted by thoughts, details, drama, media, and endless machinations.

Our severance from the sensual *terra firma* begins early. When we are children, our natural curiosity and connection to our bodies is innate, but from a very early age we are taught to disconnect from the primal ground of our being.

"Don't touch yourself." "Sit still!" "Stand up straight." "Stop jumping around!"

Children love to move and dance as an instinctual expression of the expansive movement and energy of the soul. Yet frequently in our youth, our wild and naturally ebullient energies land us into trouble. Educational systems tend to require children to sit at small, cramped desks and memorize lifeless information (seldom with regard to individual learning styles), when what a young body teeming with energy and curiosity wants and needs is to *move*. We must stretch, wriggle, and hop as we explore the world through all the physical senses; instead, we are commanded to be still or even to sit on our hands. Behave. Control the impulses of the body. Disconnect from natural movement and energy. While truncating the urge to move may make for more disciplined and obedient students—this is highly doubtful—it also teaches us to split off from the messages and natural expressions of our body.

Like a sculpted ceramic jar filled with multihued butterflies, the body holds and carries our emotions. Indeed, to speak of body and mind separately makes very little sense, because they are seamlessly fused. The brain is the recognized seat of cognitive function and rational intellect but *mind* exists everywhere in the body. All the messages we have received in our lives remain embedded in the pulsing web of cellular memory, guarded like precious jewels and terrible secrets. And for every emotional thought, there is an accompanying impulse in the nervous system and musculature, like a shadow twin.

Try this simple exercise: Think of the happiest thought that you can, one that brings you all the unspeakable joy of an oasis in the desert, but *do not allow yourself to smile*. Not even a little. Focus on the image or memory while feeling the joyous emotion but not smiling at all. Notice how flat the affect remains. Go on, try it. Alternatively, think of something that sparks anger for you—an argument with your lover, a sharp injustice by your employer, or any smoldering resentment whose coals remain hot—and notice the sensation in your chest and belly (or wherever it may be). As with the previous experiment, attempt to access your anger and not have the accompanying sensation; you'll find it's impossible.

Feelings are energy. For many men taught to disconnect from, ignore, or bury their emotions, the only successful way to accomplish that is to also disengage from the body. In our attempts at being *strong*, we unconsciously constrict on a muscular level to close off the emotion. We control our feeling experience through patterns of containment and pulling in, evidenced by a lack of movement and breath, like wearing a suit of invisible armor. In doing so, we transform into tightly held bundles of restricted emotion and further estrange ourselves from the soul's expansive creative energy.

The soul longs to be free. Wild.

Our innate wildness and power are also locked in the living maze of connective tissue. Nondomesticated, disorderly, irreverent. Slightly dangerous. Whatever the "adult" role you have assumed in life (or continue to resist), for every one of us there is an authentically sensual, playful, unbound, and freed aspect of our being that we squeeze into submission and silence. Whether in childhood or adolescence, the Wild Child is usually shut away, bound in chains of shame, judgment, or developing adult responsibility; the message from our adult ego is clear: *no place exists for you here.*

Emotions and natural wildness are not all that we hold in our muscles, bones, blood, and restricted breath. Our deepest longings, heavily guarded secrets, silent prayers, unrealized tears, trembling raw power, forgotten dreams, and luminous joy all haunt the darkly tangled wood of body and psyche. Each waits to be discovered and released from containment through authentic expression. Each asks, *why do you fear me?*

We constrict these energies, emotions, and impulses in a mostly unconscious manner: tightening the body and breath to contain and suppress them. Simultaneously, we divert our attention through distraction and addictions. Some of us, rather than restrict and dull our vital energies, habitually discharge them through movement, exercise, emotional outbursts, work, or sex (or all of these). Yet whether we contain or deplete our primal energies, we are still unconsciously seeking to smother our fire, to limit our core of personal power, a sabotaging pattern explored in the later chapter "Pleasure, Power, Sex, and Eros."

Other dark agents have aided the somatic conspiracy of bodymind disconnection. Christianity has long condemned the body as an agent of sin and filth, its lusty impulses to be repressed and denied. Sex with all its gloriously juicy, sticky wetness is not the only offense; the body bleeds, defecates, urinates, expels gases, and perspires. It quickly becomes oily and muskily pungent, even odiferous. This earthly carnality is easily labeled *dirty*, a judgment that goes hand in hand with *bad*. Murmuring in low tones alongside religion's condemnations, the psyche casts the body further into a pit of shadows. From sexual hunger to murderous rage, our forbidden desires still percolate up from the body's depths. Shame wraps us in a heavy cloak of haunting thoughts and questions. *Is my cock too small? Am I too hairy? Is my body too fat? I'm too short. Am I perverted for fantasizing about this sexual act? Freak, I'm a freak.*

You're not a freak. And you're not alone.

In the West, we suffer from long-standing body hatred while being simultaneously obsessed with body image. We are fixated on a youthful appearance of health and beauty—a lean and idealized body—one that bears little resemblance to the actual, everyday man as he passes through the shapes and stages of life. From superfit Hollywood stars to underwear packaging, from health and fitness magazines to television commercials, the cultural ideal of the body besieges us at nearly every turn. We celebrate the body only as an attractive shell for the ego; as a frumpy, unshaved, and slightly out of tune musician of the soul, it is not nearly so welcome.

The narcissistic cult of the sculpted male physique has widely abducted urban gay men, in particular, though their straight and bisexual brothers are also enlisting in growing numbers. The human body is beautiful and a well-toned male figure is a sensuous marvel of nature, but we have become overly fixated on external, superficial standards of beauty that are fleeting; ones that require massive amounts of energy and denial (ignoring the demands, processes and tendencies of the "real" body) to retain. Throughout nature, the males of a species are often more vibrantly colored and ornamented to help attract a mate; pumping up the body at the gym may be our own egocentric version. Yet only humans are afflicted with the challenge of attempting to become (and maintain) something that we are not. Physical beauty and sexual energy fade; thus any meaningful relationship must ultimately be founded on something deeper and invisible.

Understandably, many of us feel betrayed by the body: its impulses and urges; the way it looks or the manner in which it breaks down; the sure descent into frailty and old age. "Meat is messy," as the transhumanists like to say. As surely as we attempt to avoid death, we also seek to escape the discomforts and demands of being alive—an ongoing production of tears, blood, sweat, semen, piss, and shit—for other more elevated, idealized and out-of-body realities, even virtual ones.

The popular mindset is a Newtonian, reductionist view of the body, considering it merely a brilliant machine whose parts wear out with time and use. For most men, the body is little more than a fleshy framework that carries around the brain's precious vault. The simplistic operating formula reads: if it feels good, keep doing it until you can't do it anymore; if it doesn't feel good, fix it—i.e., treat the symptom—or ignore it. Too simplistic, really, especially for a design imbued with all of Nature's creativity, imagination, and genius.

Our body's intelligence is cosmic and endlessly creative but we live largely disconnected from it. We're not listening or paying attention (an observation made repeatedly throughout this book). We're fixated on television while the house burns down around us. Many of us fail to make even the most rudimentary bodymind connections, such as "When I eat beef, I feel sluggish," "If I exercise daily, I feel better and less depressed," or "My shoulders are wired up to my ears with work stress."

Among men, few consider the body sacred. Largely we recruit the body to conspire in our own limitation. Through unconscious choices, whether of restriction, numbing out, or discharge, we repeatedly truncate our creative power and life force; we block and withhold the soul's expansive impulse. Over time, our bodies become painful, tight places constricted by injury, trauma, and somato-emotional patterns. Who wants to live in such a house? Our well-worn answer is to retreat to the familiar and falsely expansive confines of the mind. Rather than risk listening to the body's messages and attempting to understand them, we disengage and further our disconnection. Why risk venturing into the strange and largely foreign country of the body, where we often feel like a helpless stranger? The answer is simple:

The body is the soul's prayer.

Like the famous Rosetta Stone with its multilanguage inscriptions unearthed from Egyptian sands, the physical body offers a translation tool for the experience of being alive and the soul's journey. Our sensations and breath yield constant clues for following Eros in our lives: our bodies tell us when we are on track. Allurement, passion, and power are embodied sensations as surely as fulfillment, love, and joy. Have you ever considered or paid attention to what allurement *feels* like in the body? When you reflect on a dream or a longing, what happens beneath your skin? What do you feel and where do you detect it?

Can you imagine what might happen if you learned to notice, heed, and act on that sensation as a decision-making factor in your life, following the body's wisdom?

Reconnecting to the body is to uncover the rage, shame, fear, and dreams that we buried. Yet as surely as the flesh holds our secrets and shadow wrapped tightly in muscular tension and shallow breath, it emanates light as well. An expansive, creative, luminous energy and frequency smolders in our core, waiting to be rekindled with breath. To live fully and authentically in our own skin is to reclaim the radiant brilliance that is our birthright, releasing the shackles of fear and shame, channeling anger and aggression into energy for transformation. The deeper we descend into the body, the more easily we recognize our core, authentic power and the ways that we block, discharge, and sabotage that energy.

The disconnection is not your fault. It's not a failure. It is an opportunity. No one is born knowing how to play the violin; one must learn. To speak the lost language of soul, to become fluent in "soulspeak" and discover your authentic power, you need only to listen to your body. Tap into the wellspring deep inside.

Will you dare to risk it?

To become consciously embodied is to awaken the wild soul that sleeps within you and to evolve into higher states of consciousness and expanded worldviews. It means exploring nonhabitual rhythms and ways of moving and responding. No matter where you dwell in the world, you must discover and liberate the wild, erotic stranger that is your body: the sensual, passionate soul that moves freely, sings loudly, and dances naked in thunderstorms. The one you are afraid to meet . . . but secretly hope to.

THE LANGUAGE OF THE BODY

Just as we have forgotten (or never learned) how to speak the languages of animals, rivers, trees, and stars, so too are we at a loss in speaking the language of the body. If we can begin to reconnect, to notice and decode the sensations, our body serves as a powerful ally that guides us towards a balanced, meaningful life of connection with Eros and life.

Partly due to a more inward, receptive frame of reference—including the inner nature of their sexual organs—women tend to be better connected to a sense of their bodies than men are. Personal traumas, patterns, and disconnection aside, *in general* they possess a truer sense of the body's intelligence and intuition. One of the traits that men must develop is a similar, reflective listening to our body's signals, whispers and knowing. As we hone this skill, we develop an intimate relationship with our own bodysoul, with positive implications for our own well-being and transformation. Each one of us that awakens aids the planet and humanity's evolution; we begin to heal the Western schism between body and nature, a division that has had global impact and disastrous effects on the world. It is a healing that begins with our bones and breath.

Beyond the sensual and sensory experience that feeds the soul, when we fully inhabit our bodies we also begin to decipher the somatic code of our experience. Every aspect of our life is imprinted into the cellular memory of our tissues. Scientific studies on the brain and its dizzying array of functions and untapped potential reveal ever more clearly that the notion of *mind* as seated in the brain is entirely false. Rational, cerebral thought may be focused in the cortex of the brain but intelligence exists *everywhere* in the body. Each cell pulses with knowing, selective choice and memory, containing not only its unique genetic sequence stretching back through millions of years of evolution but also the singular and collective experiences of this lifetime.

On and under its remarkable skin, the body bears the anthology of all our stories like a library of ancient parchment scrolls. Every trauma, every limiting mental script, every patterned behavior, and every repressed response exists timelessly. These memories of trauma and restricting psychological beliefs, often unconscious, are held as tension in the muscular and connective tissues. Also contained in the bodymind are our daily thoughts and energies, particularly the ones we hold back or feel we cannot express for risk of being inappropriate, foolish, rude, hurtful, insubordinate, or truthful.

These buried stories and traumas, limiting beliefs, and brilliant luminosities we carry are largely encoded in sensation. Just as image is a primary language of the soul, sensation is the language of the physical body. Attempting to accurately describe a physical sensation proves challenging, for we have few words in our somatic repertoire. *Prickly, sharp, hot, cold, tingly, buzzy* are a few of the more common descriptors that one might use for sensation, but finding more often eludes us. Most individuals are far more adept at describing their emotional states—sad, unhappy, joyous, angry—than what is actually happening in the body. Yet each emotional state has a unique somatic experience that corresponds to it, and often a focused area of concentration in the body, as well.

Somatic words that accurately describe the sensation of joy might include *expansive, warm, bubbly*. Yet more important than describing the particular quality of a sensation is the ability to simply notice and monitor it mindfully. Like noting the ebb and flow of the breath, one needs only to bring one's awareness to the pain in one's shoulder or restriction in one's abdomen. Observing the experience of a particular sensation, sinking into the experience and qualities of it as if carefully listening, an individual begins to stitch together the pattern of somatic responses and one's emotional counterparts. A large number of movement therapies, along with a growing contingency of approaches for resolving emotional trauma (such as post-traumatic stress disorder), focus nearly exclusively on sensation and its role in repatterning the nervous system. From tiny, preparatory micro-movements to gross motor movement, a client's awareness is guided to stay with sensation (and movement) as it unfolds. In this manner, patterns, beliefs, and traumas arise and unfurl slowly (or rapidly) in authentic movement. From their truncated, frozen state they then sequence through to completion and resolution, accompanied by a decrease in symptoms.

In the early stages of embodiment and awareness, we struggle with learning the body's somatic language. It doesn't speak in clearly formed words such as "I am tight here because I'm afraid of my lover's possible rejection of me." Instead, we note merely the sensation of squeezed, restricted tension. Yet as we begin to observe what certain emotions and experiences actually *feel* like in the physical body, we begin to recognize and translate a few sensations and emotions.

What does longing *feel* like? What are the sensations of it? In my own body, as I consider the longing I feel in this moment, I detect a swirling, streaming outwards from my core like an energetic sandstorm reaching out into the open space in front of me. Though it is difficult to describe, there is also a subtle, inaudible frequency or sound like a cry of anguish that I can "hear" with some inner ear.

What does anger *feel* like in the body? Or inspiration? Grief? Fulfillment? Shame slithers and curls around our bones, haunting the hollows and heart. Where is it concentrated? Belly? Pelvis? Breathe into your abdomen. Ask yourself, *where in my body do I hide my deepest secrets?*

LEARNING TO FEEL

Men are well familiar with the general somatic messages of arousal and erection that accompany sexual desire. Yet these erotic energies and emotions do more than trigger hormones and engorge the manroot with blood; they circulate and flow through the body in an animating song of power and sonic electricity. We feel alive under our skin with a sense of animation and virility, buzzing with a hum. Sexual energy is one stream or current of our life force—the erotic spiral of sexuality, creativity, and spirituality—and this arousal offers a clue as to what aliveness, passion, and power feel like in the body.

In a nonsexual context, it may take some time and mindfulness to discern what one's vital energy feels like. It is not dissimilar to the sense of vitality and energy that one feels during or after exercise, when muscles and breath are engaged and our channels are open. A purring or streaming of energy enlivens our tissues along with a sense of expansion, movement, loosening, or being "unstuck." Notice your subsequent response to that rising sense of power: is it comfortable, or does it make you restless? Do you restrict it and close it down through limited breath, muscular contraction, or general distraction? Do you quickly seek to discharge it through familiar patterns of movement, distraction, work, activity, or ejaculation?

Our musculature and patterns of movement develop around our core psychological beliefs, thus making them also physiological or somato-emotional. Closed-in and rounded shoulders, a puffed-up chest, clenched buttocks, a forward head posture, or any number of structural holding patterns reveal our developmental character strategies and subconscious stories. If, for example, we believe that we are small and unworthy in life or that we are not essentially free to be who we wish or to pursue what we want, that limitation manifests as a restrictive holding someplace—or many places—in the physical body. It will be evident even in the way we stand, walk, move, and express ourselves. The way we move reveals who we are.

Our body language—the turn of our head as we speak, the way we fiddle with our hands, the tilt of the chin, the shrug of our shoulders—speaks volumes more than what we verbally communicate with words. Most of the time we are unaware of the messages that we are projecting or how those messages may be at odds with our spoken words. The gestures and expressions we use when communicating reveal far more than does our flimsy verbiage—and far more accurately. Words are merely kites in the wind while the body harbors and reveals the gathering storm. Researchers tell us that up to 70 percent of communication is actually nonverbal. If we became aware of even a small part of that communication, our gestures and unconscious holding patterns would reveal a great deal about our psychic landscape.

The relevance of all this is that the body is a map and guide. It offers a wealth of clues that lead us not only to our core psychological material but to our soul gifts, as well. When an individual becomes mindful of his somatic signals, he moves deeper into the untamed forests of authentic living. He gains awareness of how the body conspires in either limitation or expansion, and of the powerful three-way alliance between body, mind, and soul. He evolves to a higher level of embodied awareness in which he begins to release what is held—exploring avenues such as breathwork, sound, movement, bodywork, and creative expression. He recognizes his patterns regarding power and vulnerability and thus gains options for change and transformation. Learning the language of bodysoul, he emerges from a self-created shell, moving closer to something authentic. Closer to the wild soul.

Soul arises as a sensation of authentic core movement, either a subtle ripple or a powerful wave. This is the call of Eros in the body. When we heed the somatic cues, we can loosen our holding patterns, in turn facilitating expansion and evolution. What wants to move? To be freed? Noticing, following, and exploring authentic movement, we align with the soul's unfolding and further unfasten our restrictive patterns of containment. When we consciously follow sensation and movement in our body we invite transformation. We turn towards healing and touch on our power.

Brother, when you reflect on your deepest longing, what happens in your body?

The Body Knows

its way
surefooted among the rocks and deadfalls
with an instinct for edges, directions — trust it
in any forest, though the strong horse of the mind shies
at owl sounds, a raccoon's chuckle, the scent
of a bear now four days' foraging distant.
The horse wants the traveled path, daylight,
the gregarious corral, glad to take you
anywhere you've been. But the body
is its own animal, trail wise in spite of you,
sensing destinations beyond the dreams
of horses. Don't ask it why. It's told you
often, but you were never listening.

When you get there, you will understand.

~John Haags

SOMATIC MESSAGES

As a longtime bodyworker and somatic therapist, I certainly understand the impact of injury on a physical level. Yet I have also come to realize that our bodies are far more than merely physical machines with parts that get injured and wear out. Even seemingly random injuries or physical symptoms often point to something deeper, mysterious, and soulful. Our bodies are constantly conspiring to wake us into our soul's powerful, embodied expression and conversation with the other-than-human world.

The body bears our scars like cryptic hieroglyphics of past pain etched into our skin and memory, but it also offers a wayfarer's map to the treasure of soul. A commonly shared truism in bodywork, somatic psychology, and healing circles is that "the body does not lie." From limiting self-beliefs to the shattering traumas of abuse, rape, and war, it whispers—or silently screams—the stories of our past experience. Simultaneously, it hums and radiates with an expansive openness when we know the truth of something or are near to our soul's joy. More times than I can possibly count or remember, when I have encouraged a client to gently tune in to an injured or constricted part of their body, not only do they gain an insight but also they are often quite surprised at the content of the message.

I recall a fellow who came for a session early in my bodywork years when I was doing Hakomi-style work (a form of body-centered psychotherapy). A middle-aged man, he drove a nice car and worked at a professional desk job. I recall little of his features other than a sense of energetic heaviness about him as though he wore a leaden jacket. Old and burdened before his time, I thought: a man who knows intimately that shadows bear weight. His primary complaint was severe tension in his neck that he thought might be the cause of his recurring headaches. As I scanned his body and noted his posture and movements, it was clear to me that his neck was fairly rigid, but I also noted his jaw and the curious, restrained way that he spoke. It seemed to me that he was wearing an invisible, energetic gag.

His neck felt like cool, solid concrete beneath my hands. During the session, I worked using a combination of physical touch, mindful awareness, and visualization and soon guided his awareness to his jaw—the image in my mind was of an iron trap firmly closed. I invited him to note any connection between neck and jaw as my hands worked, offering a few verbal cues to facilitate awareness.

Eyes closed, in his muffled manner of speaking he said softly, "I'm holding back everything that I can't say in life . . . at work, to my wife, my kids. It's like this trapped scream that I'm holding onto."

When I asked him what it might be like to scream and let it out, he snorted with a dull, derisive laugh.

"Impossible."

Still working on his jaw, I enquired if he would be willing to try a little experiment. I invited him to scream into a pillow, suggesting that the padding would muffle the noise and allow him to be more uninhibited. For a minute, he mulled my suggestion silently and then reluctantly agreed. I fetched a cushion from my office couch and offered it to him where he lay on the massage table, and gave a few instructions for the experiment. I wasn't looking simply to guide him into catharsis (freeing as that might feel) but to guide him deeper into his somatic experience, to stay with it rather than split off.

Timid at first, he gave up a muffled, inhibited shout into the pillow. With a bit of encouragement, he managed to let loose. He shouted and roared into the muffled sound barrier of the pillow, each new explosion releasing more of his body into motion. His knees and shoulders rocked up with movement as he lay on the bodywork table.

When the tempest subsided, his face revealed a different man. He looked five years younger: color in his cheeks; eyes bright; his entire energy field had shifted. When I again made contact with his jaw and neck, I was struck by the difference; tightness remained but no longer did he feel like a construction of plaster and steel.

"I had no idea that was in there," he said in a quietly hoarse voice.

HOLDING BACK

In our own way, each of us is like that man. Between my shoulder blades I carry a chronic "knot." A contracted bundle of tissue along the medial border of my right scapula, it literally exerts a tug on my collective back musculature. The discomfort acts up when I haven't been taking adequate care of myself through stretching, movement, yoga, and bodywork. At the risk of being overly simplistic, the knot in my back *holds me back*. More precisely, it is the primary spot in my body where I hold myself back; a place where I am particularly inflexible.

We all carry and distribute tension throughout our bodies, and most of us hold a fair amount between our shoulders. In my case, when I'm sitting too long at the computer, not engaging my core muscles or allowing movement to unwind, the contracted tissues in my back begin to throb and burn. There's a chronic trigger point embedded in my rhomboid muscle that lights up like a red beacon; at times, it sears like a hot poker embedded in the flesh along my right shoulder blade.

The larger story and surprising gift of this chronic muscular contraction is that it *reminds me*. I'm aware that I've gotten lazy with my self-care lately, shortening my yoga practice and general stretching, and sporadic in my movement practice. Admittedly, I'm seriously overdue for a good massage but I have not found a therapist in this area of England whose work I truly enjoy or whose skills meet my needs. Yet these are only the superficial, physical elements of my discomfort and containment, and on a deeper level I must ask, *in what other ways do I hold myself back?* As I write, is there something I want or need to say but am unwilling or afraid to share? In daily life, am I holding back from my soul's dream, remaining static rather than open and flowing? Am I contained or expansive? What are the ways that I limit, discharge or sabotage my personal power? How do I squeeze myself into a smaller version of myself so that others will feel comfortable, rather than fully embodying my soul powers as a personal catalyst? If my contraction could speak (to me or others), what would it say?

Tightly held bodies reveal tightly held beliefs and attitudes, as well as powerful emotions locked away. I suspect (okay, know) that much of the anger I feel towards myself for seeming failures—in conviction, in discipline—gathers tightly in this spot, gnawing and festering until I release it with authentic movement, sound, breath, and creative expression. Movement is the antidote to holding. Don't hold back. When I forget or falter again, my body will remind me. Aches and pains are somatic messages that something is awry in the bodymind, one's well-being, or the soul's journey.

Over time, physical rigidity in the body slowly solidifies a man into fleshy stone. There is more at work here than simply the advancement of age or a person's inactivity. Like a steadily numbing poison, our restriction is distilled as much from the daily stress of a job and family as from subconsciously holding oneself back from dreams and whispers of the soul. The web of pliable fascia that encases our bundles of muscles slowly solidifies, further inhibiting our movements. Shortened tissues pull us into hunched, imbalanced postures and holding patterns become even more rigidly maintained. Eventually, it becomes nearly impossible to shift this bodily imprisonment without the assistance of bodywork and movement therapies, and then it can be done only to limited avail.

Are we listening to what our body is saying through our symptoms?

Carrying too much weight insulates us from the world, provides a layer of physical-emotional armor, and deadens our own energy level. It locks us into a certain inertia. Beyond our emotional patterns around food and eating, what is the correlation between being overweight and the power and energies in our bodies—creative, sexual, spiritual—that we are seeking *not* to feel?

If we "tune in," symptoms and muscle pains are actually a gift, telling us that somewhere we have gone astray, whether in our basic self-care (diet, exercise, etc.) or through ignoring the deeper currents that steer us to an authentic, sensual, and embodied existence. Are we expansive in life, or contained and restricted? Symptoms are often curious messages from the soul, strange messengers speaking a language of sensation—*soulspeak*—that we must begin to decipher and translate in order to understand.

Mindfulness and the Body

Few of us have learned to really pay attention. It takes a conscious choice to pay attention to what is happening in the body, especially in moments of energetic exchange or emotional charge. In the middle of a heated disagreement with a lover or a challenging situation at work, few of us are skilled at tracking our breath or noting our internal somatic messages. As with meditation or learning to quiet the mind, it takes repeated practice to hold such awareness; initially, we will probably fail miserably. Yet, as with learning a language or new skill, the more we practice the more fluent we become.

Because the body holds patterns that literally keep us ensnared in the ego's small story of who we are, the responses that emerge in difficult situations tend to be habitual ones. They remain locked in our musculature and breath. These old wounds of fear and shame (anger, grief, loss, etc.) are the dramas that we hang on to unconsciously, replaying and imprinting them over and over into the cellular memory of tightly held muscles and joints. Rather than restrict or discharge in habitual ways, if we can stay open and soft in our bodies during challenging moments, our experience will be quite different. By noting our held breath and muscular patterns, *by consciously shifting them in the moment of activation or engagement*, we begin to create new options for response.

Simply put, with awareness of body and breath, we gain choice. We respond rather than simply react. Instead of automatically constricting into a small, tight place of prickly hurt when one's beloved says something hard to bear, we are better able to breathe into the belly, letting it expand and soften. We will certainly still feel the emotion (with its hurt and vulnerability) but we will not be ruled by a habitual somatic response. Perhaps our response can be something like, "I can hold the truth of this and see what is here to be transformed. I choose to soften and let go, allowing this to flow over and through me. I grow into a larger, more expansive version of myself and see how this situation is a gift for my own evolving nature . . . despite the pain I feel in the moment."

Conversely, by noting the lightness and expansion we feel in moments of openness, pleasure, and joy, we begin to build a somatic resource to draw on. A cellular memory like the "relaxation response"—the opposite of the "stress response"—is a state we can consciously activate and return to. In this unrestrained, embodied place, we more fully sense and celebrate our wholeness. We sense our hidden but true identity: lover, poet, warrior, steward, or wild soul. With a bit of grace, perhaps we realize our interconnectedness to the Larger Story unfolding around us, along with the curious and imaginative gifts of our human experience.

Central to the way of the Sacred Masculine is the appropriate use of personal power. As men, can we feel our emotion or energy in the body—sexual arousal, anger, shame, etc.—without immediately having to act it out and lessen the charge? Or bury it? Consciously directing and channeling one's energy is not the same as shutting it off, clamping it down, or repressing it. When we allow the current to move through the bodymind, gradually integrating it with breath, the energy enlivens and animates but no longer controls or drives us. We build power and *choose* how to use it. We choose sublimation rather than discharge; flow rather than restriction.

One cannot have both growth and security. Whether in a mercurial emotional state or solid physical reality, we are not able to open to something greater and remain contained. In somatic terms, we cannot be simultaneously expanded and contracted. The parasympathetic nervous system mobilizes the body into a "fight or flight" response, whereas the sympathetic nervous system coordinates our reciprocal cycle of "rest and repose." One is a restriction and mobilization; the other is a relaxation and opening. They are opposites that do not work together at the same time. Generally in life when we say "no" to something, we contract, whereas "yes" is an expansion. Try it in your bodymind. Say no to something (say, something you don't want to do), then yes to something and note the difference in muscular tension, your belly, and breath.

With mindfulness of our somatic experience, we discover the ways we unconsciously limit our felt experience through our patterns, the ways we say "yes" and "no" in the bodymind. Such awareness grants us the freedom to respond in a new and authentic manner that embodies the soul. Expansive. Relational.

BREATH

In its common usage, *inspire* generally means "to influence, move, or guide by divine or supernatural inspiration" or "to exert an animating, enlivening, or exalting influence on." Its older, archaic meaning is "to infuse (as life) by breathing."[1] Indeed, *inspiration* is another word for respiration. Just like the breath, inspiration is expansive; it opens us. An invisible wind that blows through us, *inspiration* opens our being and unfurls a thousand banners of imagination that flutter against the changing sky. A primary portal for entering and descending into the bodymind, mindfulness of our breath brings us immediately into the present moment. The not-so-simple path of conscious embodiment—which includes noting our patterns of respiration—offers its own spiritual practice, repeatedly threading us back to the here and now.

As humans, our tendency is to restrict our breathing whenever we feel frightened, startled, stressed, anxious, angry, or any strong, uncomfortable emotion. A strange grace exists in this, for shallow breathing enables us to not participate in or fully *feel* an event. When we restrain the breath, emotions recede like timid deer into the thickets of the bodymind, where they remain hidden. We no longer see or sense them clearly. When feelings in the body are blunted, we no longer touch the sharp, jagged edges of our discomfort.

Eastern traditions have known for ages that shifting the breath alters our consciousness. The tides of respiration offer the option to open fully to our experience (and power) or to disconnect from it. Limiting the breath, reducing its volume, we decrease the oxygen and energy available to the brain and vital body processes. Restricted breath mirrors a stress response in which our nervous system is ready for "fight or flight." We function but our emotions dry up or become tightly constricted, and we do not have to drink fully from the river of feeling.

When we breathe into the shadows and restricted places of the body, we invite awakening. Sensation, memories, and feelings may trickle forward or rush forth in a surge of emotion. Yet this flood also irrigates and enlivens us to the full spectrum of the bodysoul's experience.

As men, we are not generally encouraged to feel fully. What is modeled to us is to constrict and squeeze off emotions and vulnerability. It requires no small measure of courage to turn one's gaze inwards, to breathe into the restricted places and face what lurks; we fear the iron-scaled dragon emerging from the dark reek of his shadowy den. And yet much of what we hold so tightly guarded with shallow breath and muscle tension is simply our personal mythology—the small stories of trauma, wounding, and limiting beliefs. To risk facing the dragon is to also lay claim to the treasure he guards. When we breathe deeply we will certainly uncover our pain and the ways we have unwittingly colluded to limit our experience, but we will also glimpse the golden possibility of our power, joy, and fulfillment as well. At our core we are luminous, wild, and creative beings who are meant to feel deeply. Our task as evolving men is to rediscover and awaken to that truth.

Learning to breathe fully and deeply—and to continue to do so in moments of emotional activation—allows us new options of response as opposed to our habitual patterns. Fair warning: you are likely to be surprised at how difficult it is to begin embodying the breath and excavating your somatic archeology. As emotions and stories are uncovered like old skeletons entombed in bodily earth, your defensive strategies and habitual responses will quickly step in to dissuade us from continuing further. The breath tightens and a host of familiar voices begin whispering or shouting, while squeezing with invisible fingers.

"Stop. Stay small, stay safe." "Don't rock the boat or dig this stuff up. Let it go and forget about it." "No one wants to hear about this stuff, anyway." "Choose something positive, instead." "Chin up." "Just keep busy."

We restrict the breath and the full emotional vulnerability of its natural flow, drawing safely back within our shell. Our bodymind holds us contained in a familiar, small space. By limiting our natural feeling and the breath—holding back our possibility—whom are we seeking to protect? Is this a pattern that still serves our highest evolution and transformation?

A fire needs oxygen to burn. Likewise, when we feel creative passion, our breathing changes to support our internal flames and energy. Breath offers a powerful means of fanning the flames, of building the energetic "charge" of the body and increasing the life force of the bodysoul. In Eastern approaches to health and spirituality such as yoga and meditation, breath has been used for millennia as an instrument of transformation. Conscious breathing cleanses body and mind, stokes the elemental fire, and quiets the constant noise of our internal chatter. Contemporary Western approaches to breathwork employ specific breath techniques to facilitate "rebirthing," clearing of past traumas, and entering expanded states of consciousness. In Hawai'i, the *kahuna* (traditional keepers of wisdom) understand that breath—along with chanting and dance—is a way to increase the mana (life force), which is closely interwoven with spiritual power.

Respiration provides inspiration not only in the drawing of air into the body but also in the stimulation of creative thought. Divine guidance, even. With each breath, we draw in the intelligence of the Cosmos present in every atom and molecule. Allowing our breath to be free and untethered frees the rivers of energy, creativity, sexuality, and spiritual connection to flow in new and unexpected channels. Deliberate breath helps rouse us from the slothfulness of inertia. When we awaken our creativity, we engage in reciprocity with Eros, embodying possibility and power. We become expansive. In a word, *inspired*.

I invite you to breathe fully into the body, to follow the tides of breath as an explorer who walks an unknown shoreline. Mindful. Curious. Let yourself be surprised at what emerges from the ocean depths of your being, washing up at your feet. With conscious breath, we open from the inside out. We unlock and free the soul, inviting transformation and escape from limiting patterns. I further challenge you to risk full-bodied breathing—*inspiration*—in the many realms and activities of your waking life: walking, engaging with your partner or loved ones, cooking dinner, washing the dishes, driving, work, waiting for the train, puttering in the garden, creative activity, making love.

In mindfulness of breath, one notices the subtle sensations and movement in the body. A somatic pulse exists, a ripple that seeks to amplify into larger movement. As this movement unwinds, it often becomes a rocking or a wave. Allow it to unfurl and increase as you stay with your full breathing, letting your body sway with the core movement. In doing so, you begin to unchain the soul's longing for authentic movement and allow its energy to move through the body in a wave. A soul wave. Like the esoteric *kundalini* energy that rises up the spine, soul waves in the body signal an awakening to a deeper level of embodiment and power. The wild soul is no stranger to this.

To breathe fully is to risk embodying one's power and brilliant possibility and to align with the soul's dream rather than with the ego's fears. We open rather than constrict, and this conscious breathing supports expansion of the soul's movement and longing. Unrestricted breath embraces both darkness and light, pushing neither away, to claim fully our passion and core energies. As with opening through our senses, tending to the breath aids in reclaiming the capacity to feel. Breath builds mana—life force—that, ultimately, is the primal path of power. Wholeness. Vitality.

The courage to become the man the Universe *hopes* you will be begins with a deep inhalation. Unleash yourself.

Breathe.

Methods for Reconnecting

The body is the temple of Eros and the wild angel of the soul. Certainly we need to nourish this earthly treasure by eating fresh and healthful food, drinking plenty of water, engaging in exercise that we enjoy, connecting with nature, stretching and bodywork, breathing fresh air, and obtaining enough sleep. Beyond these basic fundamentals, however, becoming consciously *ensouled* means living fully and mindfully in the experience of our breath, sensations, movement, creative expression, and authentic actions.

Rather than enlightenment, seek full embodiment.

Men's search for connection, passion, wholeness, and a more balanced approach to masculinity is less about reclaiming the body than it is about befriending, listening to, and cultivating relationship with it. How might we learn to finally be at home in the sensual, miraculous, and tactile wonder of our own skin? How might we begin to embrace a conscious relationship with the body and soul?

Ever a guide, Eros draws us with a somatic sense of allurement, longing, and power. On the embodied journey of ensoulment, we are aided by time in nature, ecstatic movement, conscious breath, and acts of creativity. Soul waves of awakening can be initiated through anything that brings the body alive with a felt sense of energy. *Exploring our sensate perceptions unlocks the door to feeling.* Anything that opens us in wonder, beauty, or inspiration guides us further on the embodied journey.

We can also begin to reconnect and awaken our relationship to body-soul through practices such as the Soul Skills and embodiment exercises at the end of each chapter in this book. Learn to notice what happens in your body: expansion rather than contraction offers a subtle, somatic clue to our patterns. That's it really: begin to pay attention.

On any quest, a map or guide can be tremendously useful. Someone skilled and fluent in the languages of somatic sensation and mindfulness can make our passage easier, as we are unlikely to find our way through this beguiling landscape of bodymind completely on our own. Healers, bodyworkers, movement artists, breath workers, martial arts instructors, and somatic therapists can all assist us in gaining deeper, more reverent and vital awareness of the body. Various modalities of breathwork, movement, dance, sound, bodywork, somatic psychology, yoga, and martial arts can prove equally useful. These methods offer enough relevance and importance that they warrant a fuller discussion in appendix B, "The Soul Shaman's Bag."

PAYING ATTENTION

In our lives of busyness and doing, trapped in our heads and ignoring our senses, we succeed in distracting ourselves nearly constantly. Thinking is valuable, yes, but most of us do it far more than is actually necessary. Apart from problem solving and discerning judgment, our cognitive functions are largely habit and distraction; we're obsessing about things that happened yesterday or that might befall us tomorrow. Our narrow bandwidth of attention buzzes and crackles with static interference: worries about debt; fantasies about sex or the intriguing new person we've just met; daydreams about winning the lottery; problems with the kids; fretting about the stock market; the sales target we must reach; the constant drama of our coworkers.

We will not find a life of connection, of authentic meaning, among the windmills of the mind or on the Internet. Instead we must learn the language of the body—speak it as humanity once spoke the languages of forests, rivers, and stars. When we free the body and breath, the soul follows. We must commit ourselves to a personal path of practice, to bodysoul practices that open the body, awaken power, and invite feeling.

As I walk in the afternoon windstorm, laughing and shouting like a madman as I charge animatedly through grassy fields, my entire body roars with raw power. Every cell sings full volume with the unlimited possibility of *yes*, shaking off the fleshy shackles of my fears and limiting stories. Muscles shed familiar, shortened patterns of movement and beg to be stretched and moved in new ways, exploring possibility. How quickly inertia creeps up on us, lulling the body into a tightly wound stupor from which we must struggle to wake. How far we are from any real sense of the wild soul.

I have begun to uncover the places in my body where I say no to life and my soul's longing, where I contract and restrict into the snug limitations of an ordinary existence. Tendonitis in a shoulder limits my strength, making it a struggle to release feathered arrows of intention and power. My lower back wobbles with issues of support. A tightly closed anal sphincter still puckers and pulls in with patterns of shame and fear. What other secrets and limitations does this body hide? Where does my aggression lurk, coiled like a venomous serpent and ready to strike? In what dark cave or rigid muscle do I bury my shame or lock away my power, hoping it will never be found?

Brother, pay attention. Tune in. Beyond awareness, the amount of energy required to hold these patterns of tension—energy consumed daily in keeping small and subdued—is tremendous. Too tightly restrained, we are captives of our own devices. Soul asks something larger of us; that we wake up and unleash power by coming fully into the body and opening our senses wide. Soul dreams that we will be more than just a trickling stream, that we will become the mighty river. Open the heart. Risk feeling deeply.

Polythesia (multiple perceptions and feelings through the senses) and breath form a "field of knowing" that activates the brain and bodymind's untapped potential. Far from being our lowest, animal-like somatic qualities, sensation and sensory awareness activate the mystic brain, where we access higher realms of intuition and transpersonal possibilities of knowing and awareness. Indeed, it is largely through our senses—and heart—that we experience and touch on the wonder of our existence, where the cosmic Mystery enters our consciousness in return. We are not separate. *Everything is relationship*. Our soul essence longs to be expressed in the world, connected in a visceral and polysensory way to the greater body of wonder that surrounds and envelops us.

The body is trying to wake us up and seduce us for the soul's purpose. If we attune to the body as the primary place where we dwell, when we cast our senses wide and heed our somatic messages, we become willing accomplices to our own possibility and transformation. We embody Nature. A sensual, embodied agent of global change emerges from within.

The body conspires with the soul to bring us awake, to move us closer to our dreams and the mysterious, elusive gift we have incarnated to bring to this world. To follow our longing and allurement is to heed the sensation of it as a guide; to apprentice to our own patterns and evolve past them. Through awareness of our habitual responses, we are invited to embrace both shadow and light, domestication and wildness. Fully inhabiting the body and breath, in recognizing and reclaiming the cast-off parts of himself, a man will finally discover what authenticity, power, and wholeness feel like. The Erotic Warrior.

THE SACRED MASCULINE

A sense of the sacred has largely vanished from the modern world. To invoke and embody the Sacred Masculine is to rediscover the holy in everyday life. Whether on the crowded streets of New York City or roaming pine-clad foothills, we partially achieve this through unfurling our senses and unlocking our hearts in an ongoing exchange with the other-than-human world that surrounds us.

Mostly we have forgotten (or never learned) how to pay attention. Yet we live in a fully participatory and evolutionary universe where, as Thomas Berry writes, "we are touched by what we touch. We are shaped by what we shape."[2] Drawn outward by natural beauty—this can happen anywhere, anytime—along with threads of invisible somatic connection and expansive breath, we evolve into a greater version of ourselves. We begin to detect and feel the Soul of the World. Whenever we open and expand in authenticity—the freedom of a nonhabitual, creative response—we move ever closer to the soul's dream for our lifetime.

Three defining characteristics of the Sacred Masculine are the appropriate use of authentic power, a sense of interconnected relationship, and an open heart. Developing a conscious relationship with the bodymind—its patterns, intuition, feelings, power, and primordial wisdom—is essential; equally as vital as nurturing our connection with the other-than-human world around us. The Sacred Masculine strives for deeper levels of embodiment and knowing, power and grace. Rather than containing or discharging, he learns to let energy fill and enliven him as a part of nature. As a wild soul.

The Sacred Masculine celebrates the earthly divine of the body—the angel of the soul—considering it equally as holy as a church, synagogue, temple, or mosque. If we can find holiness in an ancient book of verse or a fragrant redwood forest, can we not find it in the warm flesh of the human vessel? If one believes that humanity is created in the image of God, then the body must certainly be consecrated as well, and there is no part of it that is not sacred or worthy. Everything is holy unless we choose to make it otherwise or no longer honor it.

Celebrating the body as an intelligent, conscious agent of the sensual soul—a living poem, a breathing prayer, the ecstatic dance—is the path and practice of an awakened, evolving man. As John Lee observes, "When we engage in our lives with full breath, body and soul, then every act carries in it an echo of the sacred."[3] Living fully in the body—senses and heart spread wide like wings for flight—constitutes an act of sacred reciprocity. It's an active dialogue and exchange in which we are saying "yes" and "thank you" for the gift of being alive.

The prayer of the soul is that we embrace the beauty, power, and passion of the body as the embodied, earthly angel of our imagination and creativity. The soul dreams that we become bold, passionate, tender, and expressive men who openheartedly engage in a conscious communion with the other-than-human world and the Mystery. *Ensouled*, may we unleash the powerful dream that seeks expression through us. If nothing else, may we open our senses wide, breathe fully as inspiration, and dance.

Wildly.

Naked.

◆ ◆ ◆

Embodying the Erotic Warrior

Embodying the soul through the sensual body is the primary journey of the Erotic Warrior. He knows this when he unchains and builds his own power— creative, spiritual, sexual energies—and through dilated senses and open heart allows himself to be seduced into a courtship with the world. He emerges from his former shell to a life of passion, meaning, and connection. Movement and breath can break the shackles of shame.

The ever-present rhythms of the body and breath call us back to the present moment, pulling us into the deep currents beneath the surface turbulence of our daily lives. The Erotic Warrior seeks to become mindful of his body and of what is happening under his skin and in the tides of his breath. Whether riding the rapids or floating gently, he observes his own patterns that he might better understand—and shift—the somatic and emotional ways in which he limits his full participation with life. He trusts that his body is the healer and the teacher. Ensconced in bones and breath, he notes the subtle sensations and micromovements that hum and tremble for willing expression as they invite him to speak his truth, lower the shield of his heart, and step to the edge. When he risks novelty, he evolves.

Step into the fire. Breathe.

SOUL SKILL #3: MEET THE BREATH

One of the key ways we move towards conscious embodiment—or *ensoulment*—is by riding the breath. Mindfulness of respiration carries us into the present moment, the here and now. It anchors us and focuses our attention.

The rhythm of inhalation and exhalation is a relatively easy sensation to follow. Whatever you're doing—reading a book, cooking dinner, traveling in the car, waiting for the train or bus—simply note the breath. You needn't alter it (though if you observe superficial, restricted breathing, you may choose to breathe a bit more fully). Shallow respiration is one of the somatic ways that we limit our emotions and power. As you begin to notice your breath patterns, you gain the opportunity to shift them, responding in nonhabitual ways rather than ingrained, habitual reactions.

With each breath, we draw in the intelligence of the Cosmos. We feed our cells and oxygenate; we build mana. We expand our awareness beyond the noisy circus of our thoughts. We can even use breath to cross the threshold between worlds, to experience the transrational, and to explore realms of expanded consciousness and unity. Breath invites us to sink fully into the solid blessing of our bones.

EMBODYING SOUL SKILL #3: EXPANSIVE BREATHING

To feel deeply—an essential aspect of both Eros and the Sacred Masculine—we must fully inhabit the body. *Everything is relationship.* Improving our relationship with bodymind and bodysoul begins with the breath. Each inhalation opens the door to our senses and further widens our ability to feel. It inspires.

For this embodiment exercise, descend into your body and breath. Sit upright with feet planted flat on the floor or earth, about shoulder-width apart. Soften your shoulders, relax your neck and jaw. Inhale and exhale through your nostrils, imagining that you can breathe down into your soles and up from the earth. Breathe into your abdomen. Let your inhalation fill the sides of your torso, expanding and then rising up into your chest and lungs.

Allow your belly to soften and expand like a warm, fleshy balloon and notice what happens as you do this. As you begin to breathe expansively, observe what happens in your bodymind. Perhaps you'll feel sensations such as tingling, an impulse to tighten your belly, a sense of warmth, or a trembling voltage of energy or feeling that may feel strangely like anxiousness. Shame keeps us tightly bound. Are you able to relax your belly? Do you feel discomfort about letting your body be soft and open? Notice how easily you revert to your normal, unconscious breath pattern (most likely a shallow and restricted one), particularly when you begin to feel a change from expansive respiration.

If you notice any desire to contract and restrict the opening of breath, consider how this applies to your life at large. Alternatively, if you sense an openness and expansion, reflect how that mirrors your present situation. Whether constricted or expansive, *your body reveals the physical manifestation of how you habitually engage life.*

Repeat the exercise as often as possible, attempting to hold a dual state of awareness—still engaged in whatever you are doing while also focusing on expansive breath. After the initial experience, you can perform it anywhere—sitting in your chair at the office, maneuvering the car in traffic, having a challenging discussion with your teenager, tending the flames of the barbeque grill, or sweating and grunting in sex. Breathe fully and deeply while continuing to do whatever you are currently doing.

The goal is to begin loosening the restrictions we unconsciously hold throughout the day, becoming more expansive and open, and slowly building a charge of power in the bodysoul. Such is the way of the wild soul. The more deeply we become embodied, the more we evolve as conscious, awakened men and collectively embody the Sacred Masculine.

BODYSOUL INSIGHTS

For a more in-depth excavation of self, either during or after the Expansive Breathing exercise, spend some time with the following insights and unfinished sentences. As noted in previous Soul Skills and embodiment exercises, many valid and revealing approaches exist for exploring these queries—musing aloud; writing and journaling; drawing, sketching, or painting; singing and improvisational music; etc. With each question observe what happens in your body and breath as you read it, contemplate, and answer to your soul.

- Where in my body do I feel most restricted?
- My anger is locked in my . . .
- Through its aches, pains, and symptoms, what is my body telling me?
- What I notice about my breath is . . .
- If I listened to my body, I would . . .
- I normally restrict my breathing when . . .
- If I fully inhabited my breath, then I would also have to . . .
- How does my breath fuel or restrict my creative energies? Sexual? Spiritual?

4 MYTH, SHADOW, AND LIGHT

The crescent sliver of a pearl moon hides from my sight as I emerge from the cottage into a snowy night. The temperature is well below freezing and I'm dressed warmly in layers and a down jacket, a favorite cashmere scarf wrapped snugly around my neck, and a wool hat pulled down around my ears. A handcrafted elk-hide rattle emerges from a rear pocket and the tiny stones inside it—roused from their usual stillness and dormancy—roll and chant softly together in a rhythmic chorus with each step I take. Traversing the crystalline garden to the high deer fence, my snow boots crunch loudly in the freshly fallen white blanket, punctuating the silence in rhythmic fashion. The air is strangely luminous and misty like a living prayer of cloud, a night when magic is afoot. As I open the tall gate to the field, a rippling shudder reverberates through my bones and a tingle races up my spine with a small thrill. Stepping through the gate into the softly swirling mists, I have the sense of crossing over some invisible boundary into a shrouded, secret world. Crossing into Avalon, perhaps.

It is the night of the winter solstice and I am going into the dark to wed the Goddess.

Through mysterious dreams and my work of writing, it has become clear that I must embody the Sacred Marriage within myself in a very conscious and celebratory way. In these days and nights of deepening into soulful romance and evolutionary partnership with my human beloved, I am reminded that my primary relationship remains with the Divine Beloved. Wholeness and connection blossom through one's union with the Sacred Other. It is only a spiritual relationship with Source that can transcend our expectations, hold the weight of our projections, and offer the wholeness we seek. Our lovers, mates, and spouses are all "escorts to the Beloved" and embodiments of that larger

Mystery. The sacred marriage in the heart is our primary vow: the temple within which all our other relationships are consecrated.

On this snowy night, I am a groom who greets his mysterious bride who exists everywhere and nowhere. Something deep and ancient, embodied in all the forms of Earth, she is also in my own heart as a receptive knowing and intuition. As I walk, I notice a curious sensation at the top of my cranium—something between pressure and pain—for a passing moment of imagination, I sense that antlers are growing out of my skull.

In Celtic mythology, the Horned One, portrayed as a man with a stag's head and antlers, embodies the Sacred Masculine. Known as Cernunnos, the Lord of the Forests, who also rules the Underworld, he is a god of death and rebirth. With his great rack of horns and often depicted with an erect phallus, he stands as a potent symbol of masculinity and virility. In addition to his other roles and powers, he serves as consort to the Goddess. Lover and counterpart to the Divine Feminine, each year he is born on the winter solstice and dies on the summer solstice in an endless cycle of death and rebirth.

Cernunnos might very loosely be associated with the Greek and Roman god Pan, lusty lord of the forest glades who is embodied as half man, half goat. They are not the same, however, and he embodies an energy distinctly different from that of wild Pan. It is commonly speculated that these male, horned gods of the pagans—with their overtly sexual and libidinous appetites—were usurped by the early Christian church and morphed into the figure of the horned devil.

Yet Cernunnos couldn't be further from the devil or Satan. He exists in a hallowed relationship with the Divine Feminine, the bearer of all life, and together they embody the sacred marriage of masculine creative spark and feminine receptivity. Just as the Green Man offers a compelling archetype for stewardship and relationship, the Horned God is a powerful image of the masculine heart of darkness, power, and the cycle of life.

On this snowy winter's night—the longest of the year, when darkness beckons full and deep in its mystery—I'm compelled to embrace the Divine Feminine in a ceremony in which I symbolically present myself as the Sacred Masculine. Cernunnos I am not. Yet throughout time and myth, the gods and goddesses have frequently chosen lovers who were merely human, and I offer myself humbly as a man on his spiritual journey. All references to deities and mythology aside, my moonlight ritual on this winter solstice simply offers a metaphor for wholeness within the self. It is a symbolic welcoming and union of the masculine and feminine aspects of my soul. I celebrate the spark of creativity and life; the male energy of authentic action entwined in a lover's dance with the receptive, intuitive, generative energies of the Mystery.

I have a hiker's headlamp tucked into my pocket for precaution and assistance should I need it, but I go into the magical dark unaided by man-made illumination. A shy bride, the moon remains hidden behind her trailing veil of clouds, yet the white snow reflects enough of her silver luminosity to light my way. On a night when darkness reigns in its full glory, it seems best to embrace the shadows rather than walk in a circle of light. As the American ecophilosopher, farmer, and novelist Wendell Berry writes in his short poem "To Know the Dark":

> To go into the dark with a light is to know the light.
> To know the dark, go dark. Go without sight,
> and find that the dark, too, blooms and sings,
> and is traveled by dark feet and dark wings.

Most celebrations of the winter solstice focus on the light returning, but on this snowy night I'm choosing to celebrate the darkness, itself. Rather than something to be pushed away, I'm keen to welcome and embrace it. An integral part of the cosmos and the psyche, the richness of the dark is both essential and misunderstood. Darkness is more than merely the absence of light; the dark holds its own unique energy, a powerful and palpable force in its own right. It guards something vital and mysterious. It is the hushed breath of secrets between lovers and the elemental force to tear them apart. Like either the Sacred Masculine or the Divine Feminine, the dark embodies one half of creation. Truly, light loses its significance without the opposite to offer contrast and balance.

My boots *scrunch scrunch* noisily in the snow and silence as I wander in the darkness. I have no preconceived direction of where to walk, but following an unseen thread, I find myself drawn to a familiar place on the land, over the hill about a half mile from the cottage. At the edge of a dense band of woods and an open, snowy field, there is a threshold between shadow and light; it is a place that I often walk at night. Here, at this horizontal junction beneath a numinous sky, I halt my moonlit roaming.

The naked trees reach up like elegant, lithe dancers, tracing the soft bodies of the low clouds with ten thousand bare fingers. My wool cap is rolled down snugly over my ears but I can hear the faint murmur of wind amid the seeking, swaying branches. Away in the darkness, something startled crashes through the woods, trampling the stillness of the night and causing a flurry of wings to launch noisily forth from high, shadowed branches. On stealthily padded cat's paws, the silence returns and waits, listening to the song of itself as it gathers me in.

I notice a subtle shift in my body, a deepening of breath and an expansion through my senses and heart. Drawn outwards, sensing, I feel the touch of the secret world upon me—a delicate exchange, a streaming of energy to and from the heart—and I am reminded that something ancient, deep, dark, silent, and powerful still exists in the world.

As I stand alone beneath the clouded moon, my breath forms frosty clouds in the frigid air. I withdraw the leather rattle from my back pocket, the community of stones in its tawny belly now rolling with delight and speaking animatedly to each other. *At last we are called forth into purpose and voice and magic! We are moving again! Sing, sing!*

I begin to shake the rattle with a steady rhythm, peppering the silence. In my private ritual, I celebrate the darkness of this long winter night and of myself, knowing that shadow holds treasures separate and distinct from those of light. Here I will ceremonially wed the Goddess, honoring the Divine Feminine as an essential part of my own being, welcoming it as the part of myself that offers wholeness and healing.

THE ESSENTIAL DARK

Even as so-called adults, on some level we are all afraid of the dark. Our pulses quicken, senses become alert to sounds and possible predators (human or otherwise), and our imaginations run wild as strange beasts in the undergrowth. The dark harbors our fears and projections like a graveyard where the cast-off and buried aspects of our own shadows gather and wait. In urban consciousness, night is the realm of thieves, marauders, prostitutes, and those masked or hooded ones who inhabit the frayed edge of society's norms and rules. The undesirables, outsiders, and lawless roam the shadowed alleys alongside those seeking an escape, a thrill, or a rendezvous with danger and desire. Darkness hides our civilized persona—our restrained, daylight identity—while offering a realm charged with the energies of sex, the illicit, and the taboo. Freedom in one hand, fear in the other, darkness tempts and draws us. Or repels.

To a great extent, we seek to illuminate darkness whenever we encounter it. From electric torches to motion-sensing porch lights, from streetlamps to avenues of brilliantly blazing neon signs, we keep the shadows at bay. Our cities and settlements give off so much light they blind us to the stars; when seen from space, the electric glow looks like a luminous cancer spreading across the globe. In our brightly lit sprawl, darkness shrinks as rapidly as the wilderness.

As much as we fear it, darkness is essential. At the end of a day, night is where we rest from our labors and dream, entering the shadowed realm of subconscious and soul. The dark cradles us as we sleep, a function essential to our well-being; we cannot function without it. In sleep, we rest and recharge, renew and restore for another day's journey. We also drop the ego's daylight mask and surrender, willingly or not, to the deeper currents moving and steering our lives.

Descending and disappearing into the Dreamtime woven of darkness and sleep, we are defenseless. The conscious, rational mind is abducted by the soul and dragged into deep waters that swirl and roil with puzzling images. We find ourselves in bizarre but telling circumstances, surrounded by a curious cast of characters while engaging in acts that surprise, secretly delight, or horrify us. All notions of control stripped away, we are offered a mysterious brew: a potent potion of images and memories that the Dreammaker hopes will significantly alter the way we perceive our daytime world of nonreality. Dreams are powerful, cryptic invitations to plunge into the depths of subconscious longing. As many nature-oriented cultures know, beyond the nightly initiation of the soul, the Dreamtime is a gateway to other dimensions and parallel realms of reality.

Whether we are sleeping or waking, the blackness of night yields a potent time to explore the realms of soul and Mystery, and it is often then that the Sacred Other reaches out to us. Shadows glide, glisten, and gesticulate with the unknown and offer fertile ground for the imagination. Enfolded by darkness, sight fails and we are forced to rely on less-developed senses. We risk opening to different ways of sensing, feeling, and being. The dark invites us to open outwards, to become more sensitive and receptive rather than blindly blunder along as we normally do. Whenever we loosen and expand, new possibilities emerge.

In daylight we feel secure but in darkness we are vulnerable, and to embrace the dark is to face one's fears. Amid unrecognizable and unknown shadows, our trembling skin brushes against the great unknown of death. Whether we perceive death as the absolute end or merely an energetic portal through which our souls pass, our dread of this ultimate mystery is embodied in darkness.

Even as we fear it or associate it with death, darkness is essential for creation, new life, and rebirth. A seed sprouts only when placed under a protective and nurturing layer of soil with the light blocked away. When the masculine spark seeds the feminine womb of creation—in the Unified Field, the energetic spheres of psyche and deep imagination, or in physical reproduction—it is in darkness that life and energy generates. Gestation is an essential time of growth—a time of sacred waiting before birth when profound change and transformation is occurring but cannot yet be seen. In such darkness, energies evolve into molecules and matter; cells divide and gather to create new forms; seeds germinate and reach upwards towards their potential; bees build their sacred geometry of comb and turn the nectar and pollen of flowers into honey; and events draw mysteriously together to form pathways, destinies, and solar systems.

The fecundity of darkness is elemental. As energetic allurement, Eros and the void have spawned all Creation. In the vast cosmos, the visible matter of planets, stars, galaxies, and elemental debris comprises roughly four percent of what exists. Everything else is seemingly missing or what is termed "dark matter," and there exists the even more mysterious "dark energy." Though we sing the praises of light, for it allows us to see, all that we perceive in sight is only partly full of the missing matter of the universe. Darkness is everywhere and essential.

MEETING THE SHADOW

We live in a culture that is largely addicted to "light-chasing." Religion, New Age philosophies, Eastern transcendentalist spirituality, and even objective-conceptual thought are all primarily *ascendant* in nature, rising upwards—towards "higher" faculties of cognition and the light of Spirit. The unspoken operating philosophy is, "Light is good, dark is bad." We have inherited a collective distaste for the descent into the underworld realms of soul, along with the dark underbelly of human nature and mythic imagination. Furthermore, beyond our cultural inclinations, the male principle of energy tends be ascendant while the female is descendant, and thus men are often drawn *up and away*, rather than *down and in*.

The darkness within us is not a place of evil; it is simply a shadow. Shadows are primarily caused by something blocking or obscuring the light. In the case of humans, the "something" that blocks the luminosity of our being is a mental/emotional belief structure—or trauma—that we carry as our psychological map. Yet shadows are more than merely one-dimensional outlines on the ground; as with darkness, they possess depth, substance, and energy, as well. Just as night holds its own powers as equal counterpart to day, so too with our shadow and light.

In essence, we are only energy and consciousness, but as part of the human experience, we have fragmented ourselves into a spectrum—much as happens when light passes through a prism. Personal wounding, limiting stories, and cultural conditioning have all crowded in to limit our emotional bandwidth into a narrow range. This is particularly true with men, unwitting masters at patterns of emotional containment. A primary task for us as evolving beings is to honor and experience the breadth of our humanness, to expand from our restrictions, and to become full-spectrum beings.

All of us lock away parts of our selves. Jung coined the term *Shadow* (using a capital S) for the dark matter of the self. The aspects of ourselves that we deem unacceptable—uncivilized, flawed, perverted, weak, too powerful, or perhaps even dangerous—are swept collectively into the dank basement of the subconscious. Our self-prohibited creativity and carnal sexuality exist here, too. Hidden from our everyday mind, we imprison the uncomfortable facets of personality because we fear, judge, or have otherwise split from them. The Shadow holds all that we suppress, deny, or project onto others, and these repressed aspects of ourselves tend to show up as symptoms in bodymind.

Facing our inner, unknown self is rare in general society, particularly among men. Instead, we treat the symptoms that arise—anxiety, depression, anger, sleeplessness, pain, nightmares—and seldom look deeper into their true causes. Jung astutely noted that "people will do anything, no matter how absurd, in order to avoid facing their own soul."

Part of the challenge of the Shadow is its slippery and evasive nature. Like a slick, black newt excavated from the muddy pond, it wants to quickly squirm back into protective darkness. Sunlight—or honest introspection—can burn like painful death. When we finally uncover the wound or painful part of our psyche, the very discomfort we sought initially to bury floods through us, thus the tendency is to *keep* it buried.

An individual's Shadow forms early in life, when one's developing identity perceives that certain behaviors or attributes are undesirable. Perhaps being overly energetic, ebullient, questioning, or gregarious incurred the disapproval (or wrath) of an unhappy adult. Children and adolescents quickly adapt to their environment, deciphering how to best get their needs met and navigate the turbulent passages of social acceptance. We also incorporate the attitudes, beliefs, and behaviors of those primary relationships around us: parents in our early stages, peers in later ones. Deliberately or unconsciously, we mold ourselves into who we believe we need to be in order to win continued safety, support, recognition, love, or acceptance.

Like a lacquered black box at the foot of the bed where we dream, the Shadow holds those characteristics and aspects of ourselves that we have determined do not adequately serve our social roles (or at an earlier developmental stage, our survival), and it is frequently where we incarcerate the wild soul. Into this chest are also stashed the experiences, traumas, and wounds that were powerful enough to nearly overwhelm. For better or worse, we cannot simply get rid of these unwelcome, discarded parts;

they exist as part of us, holding their own energy and depth. For most, the only seemingly acceptable option is to close them into the dark, subconscious vault of the bodymind.

For both children and adults, a great deal of energy goes into protecting and simultaneously avoiding this black box. Over time, we become ego-based individuals with skilled, functional personas and we largely forget or ignore what's actually inside the dark chest. Some convince themselves that it contains something terrible enough that it should not be opened at any cost and thus keep their bodymind restricted and contained. Others peer under the heavy lid, feel the pain rise up in a wave of sensation and silent sound, and quickly shut it again. We walk or tiptoe around it, so accustomed to this presence that it is *almost* not there. Alas, there's no lasting escape from a shadow.

We drag the precious box with us when we move from stage to stage in life, bringing it to each relationship like a curious "hope chest" that brides once carried to their marriages. Our lover or mate also keeps one at the foot of the shared bed—strangely complementary if seemingly different from the one we have brought. Thus together begins a dance of trying to avoid one's own shadow chest while invariably tripping and opening the other's, letting loose the flurry of dark wings waiting inside. As a sort of modern day Pandora's box, the Shadow will most certainly be opened up in relationship. In a lover's eyes, a man sees his own light mirrored back to him as glittering stars; eventually he beholds his terrible darkness, too. *Because our psychological wounds formed initially in primary relationships, it is always in relationship that they will again be touched and called to sing forth.* Painful as it may be at times, the crucible of relationship offers a true opportunity for unveiling the Shadow—along with subsequent transformation.

Apart from intimate relationship, the contents of the shadow box escape in one's daily life, emerging through slips of the tongue or flashes of powerful emotion. Symptoms, too. They present themselves as curious identities with which we relate—victim, martyr, rebel—as well as in our projections and transference on others. For men, some of the common thugs that lurk in the dark alleys of our collective subconscious include anger and aggression, shame, fear, and grief, as well as memories of abuse, violence, and combat. The gifts and wounding we invariably received from our fathers are particularly profound, but many of these remain chained and hidden away until we unlock them with an open, compassionate heart.

Running around within the Shadow are also our childhood survival strategies that still rule like petty tyrants, keeping us small and seemingly safe. These fragmented sub-personalities supported us in childhood and adolescence as we sought to adapt to the challenges of family and social life. Often, the way we habitually respond to situations—the clever wit, the calm mediator, the "know-it-all," the joking clown—are masks worn by these subpersonalities of childhood. Unfortunately, we've worn them so long that we have forgotten they are masks that are meant to be taken off, and their true usefulness has largely played out. Our strategies also contribute to and shape our bodily patterns—muscular development (or lack of it), posture, gait, gestures, etc.—inseparable from our emotional structures.

These embodied strategies—guarding core vulnerabilities beneath them—effectively block our authentic unfolding and development. Whether in "acting out" through certain behaviors or in other habitual responses, a man's patterns are still "protecting" him from something perceived as dangerous: something buried deeper in the Shadow. Curious at it may seem, these strategies play out in helping us *avoid* an essential, often challenging, developmental task. They are ways of keeping us securely contained in small, confining, and familiar versions of ourselves. Sometimes it is our limitations that we have buried—trepidation of failure or success; a belief of not being good enough; a fear of rejection; a lack of permission; the potential of being overwhelmed by grief. Yet equally we hide or split off from any rising sense of our life force, whether as personal power, creativity, powerful emotion, sexuality, or spiritual expression. A wild soul is potentially ruinous to a neatly organized, domesticated life.

For men, the Shadow is the place where we have buried or blocked our connection with the Divine Feminine, both in the world and in ourselves. We have locked away the tender, receptive, yielding, intuitive, and relational aspects of self—the ones that ultimately must be unearthed, tended and nurtured if we seek a balanced, whole, and healing masculinity.

To go into the fruitful darkness is to face an initiation—a soul-centered one—and it is the hallmark of authentic adulthood. Consciously entering one's Shadow and unlocking the beguiling box of the bodymind demands vulnerability. Truly, venturing into the haunted and tangled woods of the psyche is not the normal choice. For most men, one of the messages that we have internalized is that vulnerability is not compatible with being *strong*. We have swallowed the cultural pill that equates vulnerability— being open, undefended, tender, feeling, receptive, intuitive—with weakness. Thus, in the imbalanced, pathological masculinity that pervades our cultural expectations, a man who *feels* his feelings (the possible exception being anger) is weak, not a "real man." In this approach, however, one becomes a rigid prison warden of the self; waking at night from shadowy dreams in a jumble of emotion, wondering whether the iron bars are in place to keep something out or something *in*.

UNDERWORLD JOURNEYS

Myths are stories from another time and place, always set apart from the period in which we are living. Even in this modern age, the power of such stories is that they help us frame the larger questions of our existence: Why am I here? How do I discover my destiny? How do I stand in relation to the world and these beings—mountain, buffalo, human tribe, juniper tree, Father Sky—around me?

In his visionary book *Nature and the Human Soul*, Bill Plotkin says of myths: "Whereas history enumerates the facts of how we, as a people, came to live where we do, and how our social, religious, and economic traditions developed, our myths whisper of the psychospiritual possibilities of our individual lives, of the realizable mysteries of being a human, of our often veiled relationship to the transpersonal (to both soul and spirit), and of our sacred and reciprocal relationships with the other beings of nature."[1]

Myths, then, inspire us with metaphors, symbols, and archetypes: they arouse us to what is possible as a human. They offer stories of death and rebirth, portraying the challenges and possibilities—the obligations, too—of the soul's journey. Myths reveal symbols and stories of the human collective and our soulful initiation, just as our dreams mirror and initiate the individual psyche. As much as history—perhaps more so—myth tells our *true* story.

Joseph Campbell observed that these cross-cultural, timeless tales hold four primary functions: mystic, cosmological, social-historical, and psychological. To venture into the shadows of one's subconscious is a mythic journey into the psychological Underworld. Whether through our nightly abduction by dreams or through a conscious choice to seek what we have buried beneath our skin, this self-exploration is a marked departure from the daylight world of the everyday persona and ego. The mythic stories of descent into the Underworld to face darkness and death—there to win some prize or boon before returning to the upper world—are uncountable. Each tale offers a metaphor for peering into one's own well of shadows and then toppling in headfirst. Swimming down through the cold dark water, however, one finds the gold coins that wait glimmering at the bottom.

In the quest for transformation and wholeness, our challenge is to remove the protective armor and walk into the shadows, undefended and alone. There, stripped for an initiation, one wrestles with the dark angel who appears. In this struggle—and sure defeat—a man develops an essential inner strength and emerges from the darkness bearing his gift to the world. Facing our Shadow is an ongoing process of soulful initiation or "soul making"—the tempering of our elemental character, abilities, and personal power that forges us with fire into something much stronger than we were before.

The poet Rainier Maria Rilke wrote repeatedly of the essential power and necessity of darkness for tempering a man's soul.

> What we choose to fight is so tiny!
> What fights with us is so great!
> If only we would let ourselves be dominated
> as things do by some immense storm,
> we would become strong, too, and not need names.
>
> When we win, it's with small things,
> and the triumph makes us small.
> What is extraordinary and eternal

does not **want** to be bent by us.
I mean the Angel who appeared
to the wrestlers of the Old Testament:
when the wrestler's sinews
grew long like metal strings,
he felt them under his fingers
like chords of deep music.

Whoever was beaten by this Angel
(who often simply declined the fight)
went away proud and strengthened
and great from that harsh hand,
that kneaded him as if to change his shape.
Winning does not tempt that man.
This is how he grows: by being defeated, decisively,
by constantly greater beings.[2]

SURRENDER AND DEFEAT

For us as men, the concept of surrender and defeat is generally a challenging one. To be defeated—whether by an adversary, a competitor, or one's own demons—is seen as failure. We resist losing because everything in our culture, along with our outmoded models of masculinity, is about winning and gaining. No one wants to be the loser. Yet if we continually resist vulnerability to avoid losses—in intimate relationship, in work or creative ventures, in parenting or community—we have essentially lost the most important opportunity of all: being broken to something larger and discovering our wholeness.

It could be well argued that part of the Shadow's larger role is to dismember our everyday consciousness of ego. Yet such a transformation almost always requires a conscious and willing surrender. If we resist by clinging to the small identity and cozy shell that we have carefully constructed, then the soul and Mystery conspire in other ways—trauma, sickness, near-death experience, shattering loss—to pry us open. A soul crisis arises. The soul crisis is a temporary and highly powerful state that may take any number of forms: a medical event; the end of a significant relationship; death of a loved one; existential angst over the loss of one's youth; or any sort of traumatic and seemingly overwhelming situation.

In my work over the years—private sessions, men's groups, support circles, wilderness quests, workshops—I've heard and witnessed myriad accounts of soul breaking us open to our Shadow and deep longing. Some stories are more dramatic than others—a man who has a near-death experience and then begins to reinvision his life; another man now finding himself financially bankrupt after the shattering loss of the successful business he had built over thirty years; the tragic suicide of a man's gay teenage son; the unexpected demise of a twenty-year marriage when a man's wife suddenly walks out the door.

Whether such a fissure erupts in the body or in the soul (or both), the soul crisis is a powerful moment of choice—one of life-changing proportions and impact. We either choose to let go and embrace the uncertainty of the situation—generally this feels like breaking fully open and losing the sense of who we are—or contract and remain in our overall patterns of containment. Such a critical juncture is usually accompanied by a tidal wave of emotion—grief, rage, despair—that life is neither *solid* nor what we thought it would be, or anguish over the choice we must now make. For men, the overwhelming emotions of the crisis may prove as challenging as the actual event, itself. Yet in every case, the soul's purpose in the crisis is to make room for something much larger, even if we cannot yet perceive what that may be.

No man embodies his soul without risk. When he faces his demons and wrestles with angels, his strength grows even when he feels pinned to the floor. In the ongoing tempering of "soul making" and authentic living, *the very point is to be broken open to something larger.* For our creative and imaginative essence to fully emerge, we must drop the protective armor and allow ourselves to move body and soul while simultaneously allowing ourselves to *be moved* by powers and circumstances beyond our limited comprehension.

When we confront the Shadow and embrace the perceived woundedness of self—taking the leap that we're afraid of; risking foolishness and subsequent mockery by our peers; facing our shame or confronting our murderous rage—we are wrestling with powerful forces, ones that most people choose to avoid. Whether through our deliberate choices or in an unlooked-for crisis, in these vulnerable moments our ego tastes the bitterness of defeat. So be it. We cannot emerge to our authentic self or soul until we break open and discard the restrictive shell.

Standing at the precipice, we must either descend into the dark abyss or turn back to the small life that we know too well, the quiet desperation of the "frantic waiting to die."[3] In the midst of our daily lives, often when it is least convenient but most timely, the Underworld journey beckons, drawing us to face our own Shadow and be tempered by the fires of soul-making.

THE GIFT OF THE WOUND

As with the darkness of night, the Shadow guards the gnarled and seemingly deformed parts of us, those characteristics perceived as wounds or flaws. Sometimes these deformities are physical attributes of the body: a burned arm, a shortened leg, a large birthmark, an acne-scarred face, a pronounced scar, a missing digit. Most often, however, these unappealing parts are in the imagination, showing only in the way we *perceive* ourselves to be ugly, different, flawed.

Consider that it might be our very deformities, woundings, and bizarre twists of limb that make us fundamentally unique and play an essential role in who we are and what we are meant to become. For those brave and vulnerable enough to face their darkness, a mysterious treasure awaits. In that painful place that we would choose to ignore, the one held so tightly in restricted breath and bones, rests an opportunity for integration and wholeness. The ebony cobra in its woven basket lies coiled around the glittering ruby beyond price.

Most psychotherapy and self-exploration aims to illuminate one's distress with the idea that as a man discovers these emotional injuries, he becomes more aware of the choices he subconsciously makes. Pulling off the old, worn bandages and exposing a wound to air can bring healing. Beyond uncovering the scar, however, is the vital step of discovering the *gift* of it. The deep wounding has another side that we have not guessed at, something like an undiscovered twin. As surely as our core vulnerability hinders us, this shadowed aspect—call it *trauma, psychological wound,* or *limiting belief*—has also *aided* us in life. In a curious way, it has served us in becoming who we are.

No matter how painful and limiting it may be, a psychological pattern rarely shifts until we understand how it has benefited us. As discussed earlier in these pages, we must also sense how the pattern manifests in the body if we hope to explore new options and transform. Like a familiar tune playing repeatedly or a movie in an endless loop, we replay the small story of our lives over and over. It's like a stage play we've seen so many times that we know all the lines, but we keep thinking there's going to be a different ending this time.

What would happen if we recast the characters in our internal play into different roles? What if we retold our habitual story with the formerly perceived villains—mother, father, employer, perpetrator, foreigners, or enemies—now portrayed as unsuspecting and disguised heroes? Imagine that each of these familiar characters (or situations, or conditions) however troubling, terrible, woefully wretched, angry, and abusive, actually appeared in order to offer us a mysterious gift: a treasure so cleverly disguised that it might take a lifetime and a radical shift in perspective to discover.

As the poet Rumi wrote, "The wound is the place where light enters you."

Understanding that the Shadow holds something essential and vital, what would it take to embrace the unappealing part(s) of yourself with compassion and forgiveness? How might your core wound actually nourish the man you long to become? Rather than being merely a tangled, dark place of constriction and protective containment, when we glimpse how our wound aids us we understand how it can further support our soulful expansion.

When we acknowledge and honor the gift and blessing of a wound, we make it sacred. To make something sacred is to *sacrifice* it. This is not simply a cutting away and being done with; rather, when we truly sacrifice something, we offer it in service or offering to something larger. Taking this curious twist a step further, consider that *the mysterious gift of the wound is a vital part of your soul's offering to the world.*

The meaning in this life surely rests in finding one's unique talent or calling—a dream buried deep within the heart—and holding that forth to the other-than-human world. Eros and Nature both lure us into soulful states of expansion, inspiration, imagination, and possibility. Yet as soulful explorers like Jung and Campbell have noted, it is only by descending into the cave we fear to enter that we find the treasure we seek.

A NIGHT VIGIL

One of the first significant times I chose to consciously enter the dark, I was in the semiarid, rugged mountains of eastern Oregon on a weeklong, solo backpacking trip designed as an escape from the confines of my urban life that I might chart some of the wild landscape of my soul. Four of my days in the backcountry were intended to be a fast: consciously abstaining from food (though I drank water) to facilitate crossing over into more spiritual realms of experience while encircled by the forms and forces of Nature. At my chosen campsite above a small, alpine lake, the man-made noise and busyness of my daily life dropped pleasantly away. Enfolded by the timeless sounds and energy of pristine forest, sleeping on the earth each night while not eating for several days, I deepened steadily into my nourishing solitude and time of reflection.

After a previous vision quest in the Superstition Mountains of Arizona—an early part of my apprenticeship as a guide for wilderness rites of passage—a wise mentor had enquired of me, "Who is the one who carries your anger?" Now I sat among the fragrant, knotty pines above a turquoise jewel of lake, seeking out the angry stranger of myself. I suspected that he carried the keys to my imprisoned grief as well. An Underworld journey had beckoned me and I was here to answer the summons.

Throughout my four days of fasting, I wandered the dusty, dry mountainside and sat in rumbling silence, observing all that unfolded around me. I held conversations with myself along with the ever-present, elemental wind, and I spoke also to many of the denizens I encountered: chipmunk, Stellar jay, beetle, Ponderosa, osprey, pine marten, and even some lichen-crusted rock. Separated from all modern distractions, I sank into the depths of my being, which, I discovered, were anything but silent and still.

Using various approaches from journaling to dialoging with Nature, from dreamwork to movement arts, I wrestled with my blocked anger as I sought to understand it. Where did it come from and what held it so tightly bound? I howled and shouted. I truly wanted to welcome this angry and vital power, to learn from it and embrace it, for I knew that meeting this part of my Shadow was essential to my healing, wholeness, and transformation. After a few days I felt raw and pummeled like a boxer after too many rounds against the ropes; anger yielded and I toppled headfirst into the dark well. Flooded by a deep, aching grief whose name I did not recognize, I knew its face to be my own . . . and every man's. In solitude among the whispering conifers, I wept from the very depths of my being and my soul poured out in hot, salty tears on the dry earth.

Hunger had abated after the third day of my fast and my body buzzed with a quiet, high vibration. Coursing with energy, I felt light, open, and powerful. I rang with the tone of a silver bell, my mind and senses gleaming clear and sharp as shards of crystal in moonlight. On Midsummer's Eve, the final evening of my fast, I stepped inside a ring of stones that I had ceremonially constructed over the previous days: the place where I would sit through the night, holding vigil until sunrise. It was a time-honored symbolic gesture; I wanted to embrace the dawn of transformation after remaining awake through a long dark night of facing the shadows. Thus far my Underworld journey of facing my Shadow had transpired in daylight; now I would greet the darkness itself in a literal, elemental way.

I will eat my Shadow and let it transform me.

In the ritual circle, I had gathered a few things: my small folding camp chair; my sleeping bag for warmth; dented, stainless water bottle; battered journal, and pen; headlamp; my elk-skin rattle; and a small candle lantern. As the dusky light of the sky faded with elegant, wide brushstrokes, darkness slowly gathered its soft robes of velvet around me. Feeling very alone on the mountainside, I lit the solitary white candle within its shield of glass and welcomed its comforting glow.

Neither stars nor glimpse of moon graced the early hours of the night, and it soon grew black as a foreboding cave. Unfamiliar sounds of the night realm pressed round me like noisy ghosts, the unseen creatures passing on their secret trails. My senses alert as an ever-sweeping radar, I listened to the darkness alive and breathing around me: crunching leaves and twigs under paw and hoof; the snuffling of breath and various snorts;

and once, a great tumult amid the underbrush, of something very large moving fast, just uphill from my stone circle. Triggered by the noises of the night, my fears bubbled up under my skin, the tiny hairs standing upright and erect. I could feel the constriction of my body, my breath shallow. If a cougar is hunting me, I thought, he'll take me silently from behind and I'll never know until it's too late. I blew out the candle lantern and vanished into the darkness, my eyes and senses wide open amid the shadows.

Through the long hours of inky blackness, I heard many of those furred and feathered ones who roam the night as they passed my vigil spot. I wondered and guessed at their identities: skunk, porcupine, mouse, shrew, raccoon, wildcat, deer, elk, and others. Surely others passed silently, ones I never heard or guessed at. I saw none of them but certainly they beheld me with their wide, dark eyes of wet glass. Perhaps they even paused as they shuffled by—sniffing the air with flared nostrils—puzzled by the scent of the quiet biped wrapped in a nylon tube of sleeping bag to keep warm, sitting upright and looking like a strange, large blue worm with a human head.

I leaned back in my Thermarest lounger and gazed up at darkly silhouetted trees, the coal slate of sky now sprinkled with a million sparkling diamonds. As the night deepened into the full splendor of its mystery, I listened to the softly sighing wind in the pines, speaking timeless secrets I could not comprehend. Not seeking to illuminate or even to understand it, I opened to the dark with my entire body and beating heart, all my senses flung wide like an invisible net into the deep fathoms of a charcoal sea.

Standing up occasionally to move around, I danced to keep warm and awake. Even in summer, the air was cold at night. For a while, I worked with a troubling dream from the previous night: speaking it aloud and letting a stream of associations flow forward with each retelling. I sang songs to those in the dark who would listen, further cracking open the silence with a baritone voice. As the hours dripped interminably by, thick and slow as honey, I sipped from some invisible but warm essence of life flowing in my core and summoned my courage for a "calling of the demons." I stood in the middle of the stone circle, rattle clutched firmly in hand, and shook it fiercely in the pitch-black darkness, calling each of my fears to step forward from the shadows to be seen and named and to speak with me.

I knew most of the shadowy figures that appeared, and, as I dialogued with them, I felt oddly grateful for what each had come to offer. Sometime into my ceremony of calling the darkness and my demons, I realized that I was no longer afraid. The cold fist of fear in my gut had softened and the dry constriction in my throat had eased open. As I stood beneath the tall, watchful evergreens and twinkling stars, I realized that my fiercest demon was actually fear, itself.

Even when Death finally arrived—a deep shadow stepping forward into the circle of pines surrounding me—I felt curiously unafraid. Even more surprisingly, his message was one of life, not death.

This existence is precious. Don't die an unlived life.

The shadowed aspects of myself—so long buried or projected outwards—retreated and I found myself wrapped in the strangely nurturing arms of darkness. With an open and compassionate heart, I welcomed the wounded, wretched, and abandoned parts of myself, calling them all home like orphaned and hungry children to the table. Perhaps I remained broken in many ways but I was deeply appreciative to be alive and oddly, imperfectly *whole*. Light and shadow entwined, each contained within the other.

In the final and frigid hours before dawn, a tremendous lightness of being filled my body, as if heavy and damp clothes had been finally stripped away. Afraid of falling asleep on my vigil, I sang further songs to keep myself awake, improvising words and melodies. The silver crescent of moon finally rose into view, slipping through the shadowed trees while the jeweled stars faded to a few bright points adrift in inky blue. The queen of the night trailed regally across the sky, casting her silvery incandescence everywhere like stardust so that darkness and soft light fused. Across the lake, the shape of the mountain slowly emerged as a great bear, revealing itself in a way I had not seen before.

Chilled and cold, with a start I realized that the pale light was more than moonlight; the sky was actually lightening. High above me, the *hoot hoot* of owls in two different pines on either side of my stone circle startled and delighted me. It was the first time I had heard the voice of these silent, winged guides since arriving at my campsite on the mountain, and my heart leapt with childlike delight. It would be another hour before dawn fully arrived, but the music of the night shifted into a new movement—a slow crescendo of pastel notes and hues as the impenetrable black of the sky surrendered to a pale gray.

I was emerging from the Underworld. Darkness retreated and the day world gradually reappeared in familiar, comforting shapes. Unseen little birds began to peep and sing all across the mountainside, celebrating the approach of light; I could not help but smile as I, too, greeted the dawn with a grateful song in my chest. I had consciously faced the long dark of the night, welcoming all my fears and shadows and recognizing that each carried a precious gift to offer on my journey towards wholeness and personal evolution.

PORTALS TO TRANSFORMATION

Conscious self-actualization has made great strides in American culture, but facing and owning the Shadow remains rare. Men tend to either resist searching and exploring the Shadow or pretend that it doesn't exist. Women are far more likely to seek out psychotherapy and engage in workshops, retreats, or groups that focus on healing and self-transformation. Yet we are *all* unconsciously acting out the Shadow in our lives from boardrooms to ballparks, from bars to bedrooms.

Apart from a soul crisis, there are multiple ways to consciously enter the Shadow and touch on the deep wound, each beginning with a deep breath and a quiet summoning of courage. Yes, there is pain in our personal darkness, but grace exists in equal measure, suffusing the night with crystalline starlight. To risk any of these shadow ventures is to come out of hiding, to show up for authentic work, relationship, embodiment, and healing. It is to face a soulful initiation of death and rebirth.

To uncover the hidden gift of a painful place or wound, a man might begin by simply asking the question of himself—what is the gift of this?—holding that query as he moves through his days, noting what arises in thought, emotion, insight, and sensation.

Without fail, intimate relationship will transport us directly to the wound as surely as an archer's feathered arrow flies to the waiting target. Love breaks us open. Though it demands a raw exposure, an honest conversation with one's intimate partner—framed with respect, trust, nonjudgment, and a compassionate heart—can open a window of enlightenment. Despite our best efforts to keep them hidden, no one knows our Shadows more intimately than our beloveds. Indeed, often they know them better than we do ourselves.

Extended time in nature offers a time-honored route to clarity, whether a solo day hike someplace semiwild and relatively untamed, or something more extended such as a wilderness-based "vision fast" or trek. Escape the urban world. Taste the wild. As with the earlier Soul Skills and embodiment exercises, while out on the land, observe and listen to what draws you. Speak aloud. Set the self-conscious part(s) of yourself aside and dialogue with the forms and forces that present themselves: trees, wind, rock, water, clouds, animals. Rather than expect a response in actual human words (though you may receive something along those lines), allow yourself to be open to images, feelings and random associations that arise, however strange or unrelated they might seem. Seek to expand your senses and nonordinary channels of knowing—intuition, feeling, imagination, sensation—in contrast to your habitual ones (primarily, thinking). Reach out with your heart's field.

As I have already noted repeatedly in these pages, awareness of our bodily patterns—breath, muscular, emotional—guides us swiftly and directly to our core material, both constrictive and expansive. Mindfully exploring the somatic places of restriction in our body using awareness, visualization, and movement—or dance—will often yield surprising answers. Similarly, tuning into our somatic experience whenever our wounds or Shadow is triggered will also open a door to discovery and transformation.

LIVING THE QUESTIONS

Whatever route you choose—or is mysteriously chosen for you—the Underworld descent and return may take awhile. You must understand that the process of entering the Shadow and unearthing its treasure is not an easy or rapid one. Growth is seldom painless, and you can expect some—or a great deal of—discomfort and difficulty.

Time moves differently in the Underworld and the soul has its own mysterious seasons. The cobra does not instantly or always willingly surrender its ruby. The gift of the wound may not be immediately clear. Indeed, it may prove quite mysterious and puzzling, appearing as a dream, a repeating image, an animal or an element of Nature, or a somatic clue in the body, all of which are easily missed by those not paying attention.

There is an extended process—years, sometimes—of living the questions. In discovering the gift of the sacred wound, we continue to engage in an ongoing surrender to *not knowing* the answers or outcomes. Bundled in dark, silken folds of Mystery, our soul talents are seldom unwrapped or understood easily. They are not quickly translated into daily experience, and they often require a new language, set of skills, or general way of being in the world. Even when discovered, the new resource does not instantly bestow magical powers on an individual or miraculously transform his life. It is not a magic wand. It is, however, a talisman for the continued journey of tracking Eros and following the soul's longing and, like an ally or guide, it travels with us as we seek and create our authentic offering to the world in work, relationship, and community.

In our modern, insulated, and increasingly distracted existence, we have a slim threshold for discomfort, whether from outer conditions or inner ones. Dwelling in carefully temperature-controlled zones of stimulated disconnection is a life of relative comfort and convenience. Popping a pill, whether Valium or Viagra, offers a convenient way to stay within comfortable emotional realms.

Similarly, we have a low tolerance for being in a place of not knowing. Most of us do not handle uncertainty well. We want to know what lies ahead and what's on the agenda, as if life actually offered a neat and predictable outline. We seek the readily available answer, easy remedy, quick fix, or promise of security—the one that rarely, if ever, resonates with the soul's expansion and our spiral path of transformation. We fear letting go of the rock we are clinging to in the river and allowing the current to carry us into the sea of possibility.

I recall Mitch, a young man at a workshop I attended during my apprenticeship as a wilderness "rites of passage" guide. From the opening day, something between us "clicked" and we connected easily in the group; he radiated a gentle warmth of spirit that I found refreshing and appealing. One of two roommates I was bunking with at the retreat center, at meals and in the late evenings when the circle had disbanded, he frequently queried me about my coaching and guide work. Repeatedly he asked probing questions about soul and its integration (or not) into daily life. From his words, I gathered that his life in Seattle was in a state of bubbling turmoil—work, school, and romantic relationship all fermenting and transforming. He was awake enough to realize that this period of upheaval was a sign of his soul's stirring and longing. He was carrying big questions around on his broad chest: Who am I? Why am I here? What is my true passion? An aspiring soul pilgrim, this man was on a trek to discover his authentic self.

A couple of months prior to our meeting, Mitch had undertaken a wilderness "vision quest" that bestowed a powerful experience on many levels. Yet he seemed disappointed in the outcome. Curious, I enquired what he had been looking for or hoping to gain.

"I thought it would help me figure things out. You know, like, *everything*," he chuckled. "I gained clarity on a couple of things but mostly I felt like I had been plunged deeper into my sense of chaos and turmoil. Like I had more questions than I went with. I felt . . . *still feel* . . . unraveled."

Sitting across from him, I nodded in empathy.

"It's contrary to what our culture tells us," I said, "which is that we should be able to figure it out. Identify the goal and then plan the steps to execute its accomplishment. Men, in particular, think this way—linear and rational. But psyche and soul don't operate on a straight line. *Nothing* in nature is linear, actually. Far more often, it's a spiral-like process. And here's the rub . . . *you can't figure it out.* Not from the usual perspective, anyway. It has to be *revealed.*"

His tall, lean frame sat on the edge of his bunk, chin perched in his hand, while his dark eyes glanced out the window at the velvet sky. He chuckled again.

"Working on yourself is so much, well, *work!*"

"The toil of an awakened lifetime," I added, realizing as I said it that perhaps my words sounded less than uplifting. But there's no easy road.

Certainly he had heard this analogy from a guide on the quest, but I reminded him about the caterpillar—that what emerges from the self-created cocoon bears no resemblance to what it previously was.

"There's a mysterious process at work. It can't be rushed. Frustrating as it may feel, you're exactly where you need to be. You're not a problem that needs to be fixed. Your authentic self is seeking to emerge, and it's a process that takes time."

Mitch's restless struggle is not atypical. Even when we're willing to face the Shadow and seek our soul's longing, the period of discomfort—of metamorphosis—offers its own challenge.

If we can allow ourselves the time to simply *live the questions*—to molt from our old skin that has grown too small—our light grows and our darkness lessens. We more clearly glimpse that we have something unique to offer in *all* our relationships, even if we're still unsure as to how this gift may fully translate into our daily work and authentic, soulful expression. As we dance with our shadows rather than fearing them, we also draw closer to childhood dreams and consider anew how we might embody them in the world.

A measure of one's psychological and soulful maturity is the ability to tolerate ambiguity in life. The darkness reveals its gift and we must walk patiently with it, turning it over and over in our hands like a rare green stone that glimmers in both sunlight and moonshadow. Only then do we detect the fine, calligraphic runes of soul poetry etched within its core that spell something like *blessing*.

DEATH AND REBIRTH

Nature and the universe endlessly repeat the cycle of death and rebirth. Great stars collapse into supernovas, transformed into new elements and fanning out on an invisible wind across the galaxies. The story of the cosmos—right down to our unique species—is one of metamorphosis through irrevocable transformations: a death of what came before and a birth of something new and evolved.

Here in our terrestrial experience, the seasons roll on like endless tides, calling life forward into expansion and growth or drawing it inwards for rest and renewal. However long and subtle (or short and extreme) they may be, the seasons affect each living thing. In the quiet barrenness of winter when so much seems dead, life is still moving and evolving in a hushed, invisible cycle as it prepares for its next transformation. Seeds and bulbs germinate in the dark earth, quietly gathering their resources to emerge when their innate intelligence collaborates with favorable conditions to bring forth their unique form and beauty.

Only after being buried through the long, cold winter do the bright crocus, trumpeting daffodils, and lusciously painted tulips rise from the soil (or soul) to share their beauty and celebrate sunlight with a colorful song. It is in the dark of the cocoon that a caterpillar liquefies—dissolving into a sticky matrix of goo as the hitherto dormant structures, the "imaginal buds," link up and form an entirely new being we know as a butterfly.

Why should humans expect to be different? In our electric world of illuminated darkness and busyness, we pursue an endless cycle of growth and productivity. Yet nothing in the natural world blooms or bears fruit constantly. Disconnected from nature, body and soul, we have forgotten that we, too, need time to lie fallow. The dark, quiet times offer a chance for turning inwards and introspection, for guarding the precious seed that waits buried in the soul, whispering softly its chants and dreams.

Still, we rush on disconnected. We speak of the "seasons of a man's soul," a poetic metaphor for our cycles of growth, harvest, death, and re-birth. Few of us, however, possess any *real* sense of these seasons, internal or external, due to our fundamental disconnection from earth and soul. We chase the light—electric or transcendental—constantly reaching upwards with cognitive mind and a seeking spirit, while fearing and resisting our inner shadows. Increasing numbers of us live in the sunny, warm regions where winter darkness is mild and hardly more than a distant memory. Nature's cycles of death and rebirth seem negligible and insignificant, amounting to little more than a casual change of wardrobe. Even for those who live in regions where cold months pass slowly in darkness, we remain insulated and spellbound in our industrial trance, pushing on in an endless daze of work, busyness and artificial light.

We continue to resist the descent into shadow. The ego—our everyday consciousness—fears its end in this material world that we perceive as reality. It spends a great deal of its valuable time busily building illusions of security and self-importance, basking in delusions of immortality, wearing masks, and avoiding shadows. The final termination of life as a breathing, embodied soul is inevitable, but there are less extreme forms of death that we meet along the way to the grave. As with the seasons, to truly grow we must continually die to the parts of self that we have outgrown, those aspects that no longer serve our unfolding, blossoming, and bearing of fruit.

All while following the glimmering threads of allurement and Eros.

At key junctures in our lives, we face the uncomfortable challenge of letting go of something that has formed a vital part of our identity: a career or relationship, a home, perhaps a dear friend, or a belief system. To lose this thing (place, identity, etc.) often feels like a death; in a sense, it is a minor passing away of the self we have constructed. Because they strip away illusions of safety and control, the ego resists these destructions of identity nearly as much as it does its final appointment with the Great Unknown.

If we concede that there are many sorts of death, we will also discover that nearly all of them also involve a rebirth. We can experience a death of old habits and patterns; the end of a role or relationship that no longer fits us; or the termination of a chapter in life. Any such demise brings transition, a crumbling of old structures, and an awakening or renewal as new forms and possibilities emerge. If we resist the smaller mortalities that beckon—when we cling to familiar comfort of the environment, routine, or small self that we know—we stagnate. Root-bound, we have only limited potential for growth. We remain stuck in stale patterns of inertia and containment. Avoiding the difficult choice or sacrifice for the sake of seeming security—refusing to risk the larger and unknown—we effectively say no to embodying our soul and its dream. We linger in a cage of our own making, for it is always *we* who keep our lives and stories small, not the situation.

As a man begins to delve into his Shadow, discovering the limiting beliefs bundled in body and breath, he must be willing to risk dying to his old identity and way of being in the world. We cannot have growth and security at the same time. If we are safely closed and contained, we will not evolve to the next level of our soulful development. We will not find Eros while shut safely inside four familiar walls. Locked in the gated golf-course community of the mind, we will *never* know the breathtakingly wild landscapes of soul that inspire the deep imagination and sing the heart awake with the beauty, wonder and awe that surrounds us.

Despite the overpowering emotion of it, a soul crisis is always the opportunity and invitation to push forward into something larger and unknown. In the cycle of death and rebirth, any ending is also a new beginning. The universe formed through a series of cataclysmic, irreversible, and nearly impossible events: as embodiments of the Cosmos, so too do we evolve. Like the gift of the "sacred wound," these moments of irrevocable transformation are often cleverly disguised moments of grace (though it is often only much later that we can clearly view them as such).

It is in personal darkness that one endures the "long dark night of the soul," facing the collapse of identity and projections, a death and rebirth to one's way of being in the world. *Authentic* adulthood—which is truly rare in our society—is the realm of soulfully initiated individuals, who heed their souls and have faced their own Shadows.

Death can be a curious ally, reminding us that life is precious and short. On our life journey, we are continually asked to live with the seasons of death and rebirth, to venture into the Underworld and return. Knowing that we must eventually lose everything in this material world, the larger questions of death and rebirth arise.

What is my relationship with death? What in me must die so that my soul may live? What limiting belief must be sacrificed so that I may fully embody the man my soul intends that I become . . . the one that the earth and Cosmos hope I will be? What in me needs to fade away so that I can embody the Sacred Masculine? The Wild Soul? Brother, few of these questions are likely to be easy, even if the answer is immediately clear to your heart and soul.

If there is one talisman that you must always carry, it is *courage*.

THE HOLY GRAIL

Countless legends and myths surround the Holy Grail, each evolving out of others and incorporating new elements over the ages. Early versions include the Fisher King, whereas later versions involve Arthur and his knights, and many of these stories contradict or overlap. In the earlier tales, the Fisher King is often critically wounded in his groin, a result (in some accounts) of being pierced by a lance in his encounter with the Dark Knight. Mirroring his impotence, his realm slowly becomes a wasteland, for the fertility of the land and that of the king are inextricably linked. Though events differ in various versions, the knights of the realm are commanded to seek out and return with the mystical Holy Grail, that it might bring healing to both the wounded sovereign and the realm. Some editions of the myth feature Gawain, while others star Perceval, and in yet others Galahad stars as the hero.

In the version recounted to me—told by a man who was a longtime friend and student of Joseph Campbell—when the knights are sent out to seek the Grail, they are commanded to go alone, not as a group. Each is instructed to enter the forest at *the place that is darkest for him*; anything else would be less than honorable and not serving of a knight, especially on so important a quest. Though only one man will ultimately be deemed pure enough to reach the Grail, each knight enters the wild, dark woods alone at the most forbidding part. Alone.

Over the ages, the Holy Grail has been perceived and portrayed as many things— from a spirit to a cauldron to a cup, from a vine to the descending bloodline of Jesus (the Sangréal). The most common and enduring symbol is that of a chalice or goblet, frequently claimed to be the one used by Jesus at the last supper with his disciples, or the vessel that caught some of the Christ's blood when the he was pierced with a spear during his crucifixion.

Beyond any typical associations with the Sangréal or the goblet somehow connected with Jesus, as a cup or chalice the Grail symbolically represents the Divine Feminine, the sacred womb of Creation. Its symbolic male counterpart is the blade, which when wielded by the Sacred Masculine becomes the sword of truth. Together, the chalice and blade represent the archetypal balance of male and female energies. The Grail legends offer a metaphor for seeking the lost feminine, the sacred bearer of life, who was cast aside and fiercely—brutally, even—vilified by the early Christian church. The healing of the king and the land will be achieved only by finding the Divine Feminine, as embodied in the sacred and elusive chalice.

The search for the Holy Grail embodies the quest for wholeness and healing. As with all myths, it is our greater, archetypal story that is retold. The Grail legends metaphorically reveal the union of the masculine and the feminine, the sword united with the cup. Blade and chalice together as one. In another facet of meaning, the holy cup also represents union: the vessel from which both the Sacred Masculine and the Divine Feminine drink to symbolize their marriage and connection. As with the womb, from the filled chalice the vine of creativity springs forth. New life begins—life that can be engendered only from a creative place of wholeness and union within each of us, whether male or female.

The Grail is a symbolic representation of the soul.

In our own lives, each of us as men must accept the same challenge as do the Grail knights. It is only by venturing alone into darkness that we will possibly discover and return with the elusive and healing chalice. As we begin to embody the Sacred Masculine—undertaking a quest to the most vulnerable parts of ourselves and embracing the hallowed union of opposites—we bring healing and wholeness to more than ourselves; we begin to heal and restore the realm and the world.

In many of the Grail legends, the proverbial question posed is, *Whom does the Grail serve?* Some have offered that, like a Zen koan, the question is not meant to be answered in a literal way. Instead, it serves as a question to be contemplated, an initiation of sorts that opens the mind. There is much to be said for simply living the questions rather than seeking to answer them, holding the place of *not* knowing. Yet in considering this famous question, I offer that the Grail serves the sacred marriage within each of us—the place of healing and balance. Furthermore, the Grail holds the image of the soul, "the truth at the center of the image you were born with."[4]

Far beyond a personal quest, the knights in search of the Grail are in service to something larger than themselves. In modern times, the fertility of the world-realm has largely been laid to waste by the continued dominance of the pathological, one-dimensional human masculine. By cultivating a more balanced and interconnected maleness—which always requires facing our Shadow—we bring about the return of the Sacred Masculine. We become conscious, creative stewards who understand and value our interdependent place in the web of Creation. Such awakened men are willing and necessary participants in the Great Turning at hand.

THE SACRED MASCULINE

The darkness holds its own elemental power, treasures, and mystery. If we seek to embody the Sacred Masculine and the Erotic Warrior, a descent into the shadows is necessary. It is a journey of initiation: one in which we evolve from patterns of inertia, containment, and old wounds into the expansiveness of the soul's authentic design.

The Sacred Masculine understands that the more he develops a conscious relationship with self—both darkness and light—the more aware and fulfilling all his other relationships become. He also realizes that the psyche's shadow wears many masks and disguises but can always be found in the body, tightly held in restricted tissues and shallow breath.

Suffering abounds in life but there is also the mystery of grace. A man makes his wound sacred by honoring the way in which it has aided him. When a man understands and claims the mysterious gift of his Shadow, it loosens its hold on him. A scar may remain but there is no longer something to heal. Facing the Shadow, we embrace our wholeness.

The darkness, the wound, and the sacred Mystery are inseparable.

Emerging from this Underworld journey—dismembered and ultimately *re-membered*—a man bears his unique gift and seeks to understand how it plays a note in the Song of the World. It is a process of living the questions and slow, soulful alchemy: slowly transmuting wounds and gifts into the true gold of human experience—the creative imagination in service to the other-than-human world. Through his Underworld journey, a man becomes an artist of creative and cultural transformation.

As part of his integration and owning back the Shadow, a man who embodies the Sacred Masculine uncovers what blocks him from welcoming the Divine Feminine—both in himself and in the world. He seeks to embody a union between the opposite and seemingly disparate parts of his self: masculine and feminine, inner and outer, spiritual and material. He is ever striving to cultivate his receptive, intuitive, sensory, imaginative, compassionate, and nurturing qualities, along with his personal power and mana.

Like the moon, the soul's treasure is a luminous pearl that can be found only in darkness. Go into the void. Descend into the frightening abyss of yourself. With courage, breath, and awareness, venture into the shadows and find what lurks there waiting. Let it devour and dismember you, that you might then discover and *re-member* yourself as whole.

We do not serve the world by hiding our talents and dreams—or refusing the quest to discover them. We do not find meaning in life, nor do we cultivate the life force of Eros, by remaining safe, domesticated, and gathered timidly with the herd. If we hunger for a life of authentic meaning—for relationships that inspire and transform, for a sense of true connection, for healing and wholeness—we must step forward and risk defeat through surrender. We must be willing to be broken open and to feel. Deeply.

◆   ◆   ◆

Embodying the Erotic Warrior

Eros beckons from the shadows as surely as from light. The Erotic Warrior accepts the challenge to enter the dark mysteries of love and Eros—to surrender to the deeper currents that carry him to a place of not knowing. He understands the paradox that in being broken open, a man becomes far larger than he ever imagined possible. Facing his demons and dancing with Death, he comprehends that these are strange, unlooked for allies on the journey of life. Like a phoenix rising from the ashes, it is only through fire and death that one is truly transformed. Mirroring the larger story of Creation, the Erotic Warrior's own life is a process of irrevocable and irreversible transformations, with every one of those deaths and rebirths actually grace in disguise.

The quest of the Erotic Warrior is to recover the Holy Grail of the Sacred Masculine and the Divine Feminine within himself. Drinking from that golden cup, he embodies the healing and creative union in all facets of his life, his dreams, and his ensouled offering to the other-than-human world.

SOUL SKILL #4: FACE YOUR SHADOW

Darkness and light are both essential to the full-spectrum of energy. Masculine and feminine, yin and yang, outward and inward: the space where we hold the tension of opposites is the awakened heart.

Rather than hide, run away, or continue to avoid or deny it, step into the darkness of yourself. Meet your Shadow. Taste it. Swallow it and let it transform you as it seeps through your veins. Accept that even with all your perceived "flaws" you are perfectly whole—and human. Your soul is not broken. Each of the challenging or disowned aspects of self carries a unique benefit, and healing and transformation occur as you discover that gift.

You are unlikely to awaken your soul in broad daylight or walk the long journey to embodying it while only under the warming sun. The seed of your soul sleeps in fecund darkness, waiting to be unearthed and allowed to expand. In the gift of the wound—*deep in our Shadow*—you may finally discover your offering to the world.

EMBODYING SOUL SKILL #4: MEET THE DARKNESS

One of the ways you can begin exploring your inner darkness is to spend time in outer, physical darkness—the realm where we frequently project our own Shadow. To step into the dark and embrace the unknown of it—the uncertainty—invites you to meet your demons, to wrestle with them, and be broken open to something larger. You are voluntarily going deeper into darkness with an open, undefended heart.

This exercise is best in a place where you can find true darkness: outdoors on a moonless night; away from city lights; in a cave. Though you may take a light for assistance in case of emergency, the point is to go into and explore the dark. Alone. As with every exercise, turn off your mobile phone. Ideally, you will give yourself at least an hour but preferably more. Dress warmly.

When you have reached your exploration site, turn off your light and allow your eyes to adjust (this can take up to twenty minutes to fully occur; in a truly dark place you will likely see almost nothing, even then). Open all your other senses to wide. Walk slowly or simply find a place to sit. Note the sensations in your body—contraction, cold, rapid heartbeat, etc.—along with your thoughts and fears. There is much to be learned from what you project is *out there*.

Offer yourself. Open your heart. *Feel* what's around you. Allow yourself to be changed, altered, and broken open by what you find—by what devours you—there. How the dark changes you is part of its gift.

Bodysoul Insights

After your time in the darkness, explore the following insights and unfinished sentences. Remember that myriad ways exist to explore these queries, as noted in previous embodiment exercises and insights. Also as noted earlier, with each question observe what happens in your body and breath as you read, consider, and respond.

- What do I keep locked in my Shadow?
- I would probably die if others knew this about me . . .
- I'm uncomfortable in the darkness because . . .
- I feel most shameful about . . .
- My least desirable trait or feature is . . .
- I am most afraid of, or likely to resist . . .
- What is the gift of my core wound?
- How does my wound aid me? How has it served?
- What is my relationship with death?
- What in me needs to die in order for me to embody the Sacred Masculine?

5 PLEASURE, POWER, SEX, AND EROS

In the soft purple haze of summer twilight, miniscule bats twirl and zoom erratically in the air. Through the large bedroom window, I watch their evening dance as I lie naked on the bed, quiet and placid at last. The waves of erotic energy rising up from the sacrum—a force that lifts my spine from the mattress, washing through my body like the rolling ocean—have finally subsided. My entire being feels fully enlivened and quietly glowing like sunset, while my energetic field is a crackling ball of nearly luminous energy extending several feet in every direction. I am light as air, a shroud woven of silver blue silk. After a full-body orgasm, I'm floating in an altered state of consciousness, drifting out with expanding galaxies in a dreamy state.

My beloved has slipped away to the bathroom for a steaming, post-coital, aromatherapy bath, leaving me space and silence to integrate the energetic expansion that ripples through every fiber of my being. I could easily transcend my body right now—instead I remain, savoring the subtle sensation still cascading up my spinal column while I watch the twirling bats outside in the fading, violet sky.

Our sex has been a full-spectrum event this evening, building from exquisitely tender to highly animated and aggressively rough, a thrusting dance of power and surrender. The wild soul fully unleashed. Yet I've remained deeply embodied in sensation and breath, fully present with my mate, saturated in the moment and the body with its shifting energies unleashed by the fire of erotic union. Steeped in sensation, when we engage in movement, breath, sound—a willingness to be open rather than restricted in any way—the erotic spiral becomes highly charged; the current of sexual/creative/spiritual energy flows as freely as a river.

Most men have no idea that orgasm exceeds ejaculation, that it holds potential for an experience far beyond the sharp and pleasurable rush of seminal fluid outwards. Or that we can enjoy a full-body orgasm *without* ejaculating. In an energetic, full-body orgasm a man is flooded with waves of sensation and power that can last several minutes, completely rearranging his inner landscape. Cultivated through breath and embodiment, it is a profoundly expansive experience, one that facilitates dilating from emotional somatic patterns in the most pleasurable way.

Observing the zooming bats, I'm supremely aware of the openness and expansion in my being. I am energized but hushed, every sense highly attuned to the slightest vibration. I feel as if I have just emerged from a deep and blissful meditation, not entirely certain which reality or dimension I inhabit. Every restrictive pattern or thought has exploded in a starburst, and my heart is wide enough to hold the world in loving, golden arms.

As my body continues to subtly realign and recalibrate, I muse on how the spiraling bats rely on a sense other than sight to navigate total blackness. They dream the daylight world, the one we call *real*, while the night realm of the invisible is corporal to them. There is nothing to fear in darkness. Bat tells me, "You fear what is not real. I seldom fear; only that which I can actually sense." They are warm-blooded creatures of shadow. Not unlike ourselves, I muse, except that we are attempting to navigate with limited senses while fumbling around even in the light of day.

Watching them dip, swoop, and zoom through the darkening sky, I imagine their sheer joy in flight and movement. I project a certain pleasure onto their existence—simply being alive and embodied in the moment as most creatures are; totally engrossed in the delights of flying, feeding, and fucking.

While my beloved silently soaks in the tub, the night outside descends like a velvet curtain. The air is so quiet that through the open, leaded glass window I detect a steady, soft *crunch crunching* in the garden, like someone grinding seeds to meal between heavy stones. The badgers have arrived. In the stillness, I can hear them eating the sunflower seeds and bird food scattered liberally beneath the tall wooden bird feeder. The long spell of dry weather has parched the earth and made their digging for earthworms, insects, and grubs a challenge, so now they arrive for a nightly supper here at *Chez Americain*.

Another mammalian creature of darkness, I smile. A powerful one, at that. When I peer out the house windows, the badgers' white-striped faces gleam in the pale moonlight. Nearly three feet long with impressive claws, one of them is especially brave. I can stand outdoors on the stone terrace, less than ten feet away from them, and shine a small light as he feeds and he doesn't run. He has few predators other than humans and our speeding, deadly cars.

Naked and quiet, my senses and heart wide open, I watch the nightly dance of the bats and listen to the hungry badgers. What if we all embraced our senses and our power—including our sexual energy—as freely as does every other living being on earth? Imagine us all navigating our darkness so adeptly. What if we apprenticed to our sensual being, becoming "pleasure scouts" as we nurtured our own personal power and life force?

In our quest for authentic passion and soulful meaning, pleasure and power prove curious stumbling blocks for most men. Yet this is also the arena where we stand to be significantly transformed if we deepen into embodiment and awareness. Pleasure and passion—the embodied dance of power and surrender, of action and receptivity—weave the song of Eros. It is the lover's tango of the masculine and feminine within us. As with all matters regarding the soul's erotic spiral, the gifts of healing, wholeness, and evolution are bestowed when we engage in these creative conversations. True authenticity emerges.

My bodymind as expansive as a fiery star, the small and subtle waves still ripple up my spinal cord to sequence out through my extremities. I reflect for a moment on my own sexual journey in life, considering the way it reflects and mirrors my unfolding process from places of tightly held containment and shame to free and integrating self-expression. Musing too that it is Eros that guides us along an evolutionary spiral and arc, ever inviting us to embrace more authentic versions of self.

PLEASURE

A graceful and nubile dancer, *pleasure* is one of the mesmerizing gifts of being alive. Far more complex and vital than merely the effects of neurotransmitters such as dopamine, or the sensory response to stimulus in the "pleasure centers" of the limbic brain, it transcends scientific, reductionist definitions. Not only is it lovely—essential!—to experience but also it draws our awareness back to the body and anchors us in the present moment, however fleeting.

Like any sacred or mystical experience, pleasure cannot be adequately discussed, considered, thought about, or explained; it must be *felt*. Just as we know beauty through our senses, and just as elemental beauty calls forth the soul within us, the same is true of pleasure. We are strange flowers closed up against the chill of night until pleasure invites us to unfurl, offering a glimpse of our true radiance. The more deeply we drink from the polysensory communion enfolding us—sinking into body and breath—the more fully we experience states of connection, joy, love, passion, and bliss. These phenomenal occurrences are all "warm" emotions in the body, dilating rather than constricting. Expansive and receptive, pleasure holds a key to a more open, connected, and relational way of being in the world.

The agents of seduction and mystery are everywhere, seeking to wake us from our trance and court us with inspiration and beauty—little birds in the garden; sunny, scented flowers; howling windstorms; hoot owls; luscious, ripe mangoes; amber honey dripping from its fragrant comb; pastel-hued sunsets; a lover's flushed, warm skin. Truly, pleasure is part of the Cosmic conspiracy to bring us fully alive and singing. It arrives through any and all our senses, a graceful Muse that reveals our true nature and nourishes the soul. As we move, breathe, sing, dance, play, make love, eat, celebrate, and create, the embodied soul IS pleasure.

Sibling to beauty and grace, pleasure attends the soul when it invites authentic expression in our being.

As an embodied soul, we most acutely perceive Eros through pleasure. I have offered that one of our primary tasks and challenges is to cultivate our life force and power—the erotic spiral. Through sensation and our bodily experience of pleasure, we can explore the deepest currents of our being. Pleasure is inextricably linked to power, and they are essentially joined in the same somatic current. When we deepen into our embodied experience—either leaning towards the pleasurable or constricting against it—mirrored back to us is our relationship with power.

Though this chapter is largely about sex, our relationship with pleasure—and power—is more complicated and comprehensive than merely our sexual nature. We experience gratification along a wide array of avenues—from touch to taste, music to movement, breath to stillness, solitude to communion. The ways to receive and give pleasure are limited only by our imagination. As with mindfulness and embodiment, pleasure draws us deeper into relationship with self and *other*: food, nature, lover, Spirit, even the environments we inhabit or move through. It invites us to pay attention and savor.

On a familial and societal level, the culture we are raised in leaves its imprint on the way we initially view pleasure (or anything, for that matter). Culturally, Americans are conflicted over many forms of pleasure; this is perhaps a lingering influence of our Puritan roots (probably an overly facile explanation). In other cultures—French and Italian springing immediately to mind—a great emphasis is placed on pleasure, particularly around food, wine, cooking, and gathering at the table. Similarly, other cultures celebrate sexuality in a far more accepting manner than do most Americans.

A wild soul always celebrates the lusciousness of sexuality.

Real pleasure nourishes on a deep level, feeding the soul through the expansive senses—a painted sunrise in the chilled air; a home-cooked meal shared with friends at a lovely table; the warmth of a gentle, tactile connection; the interwoven harmonies of a classical piece of music played on real instruments; a succulent, ripe peach dribbling golden juice down your chin; or the scent of washed earth after a hard rain.

Modern culture has cheapened pleasure. We've confused it with *entertainment*—or never learned the difference. Entertainment is more like junk food; it satiates briefly, often in a heavy, cloying way, but adds no real nutrient. It does not cultivate our life force or authentic essence. Overall, the American cultural relationship with pleasure is more about *stimulation* than about savoring or true nourishment.

Drinking a cup of Starbucks coffee on the run or driving in the car is an entirely different experience than sitting at an outdoor café and savoring an espresso in a porcelain cup and saucer, lingering and drinking in the surroundings. The first is merely a stimulant; the latter is something more worthy than merely the jolt of caffeine.

Beyond superficial entertainment—television, video games, magazines, gossip, etc.—our modern society has become addicted to many false forms of pleasure: money; drugs; a consumerist lifestyle; chic glamour. Drugs, in particular, offer a fleeting rush of shallow pleasure. The current popularity of MDMA—a drug that gives its user a blissful experience of warmth, happiness, and empathy, along with an increased sensitivity to sensation and music—has earned it the street name Ecstasy (or E, or X-TC). It achieves its pleasurable effects by causing neurotransmitters such as dopamine to flood the brain; repeated use, however, causes damage to the serotonin system and the myelin sheaths of nerves in the brain, and memory loss. Clearly, this is a false pleasure, not something that nourishes or ushers us into an authentic and sustainable expression of self.

Consider briefly your relationship to eating. Because it constitutes a daily part of being alive, consumption of food tends to be nearly as automatic as breathing and other body functions. Is eating something that you undertake as a task, a habit, or as a means to an end? Is food simply a supply of fuel? Or perhaps comfort? For most of us, food is a source of pleasure and often one we share with others in a social or communal way. Sometimes the food we're eating doesn't warrant savoring, as is the case with the majority of packaged, prepared meals. Yet even when we have something truly worthwhile to eat, we still we tend to gobble it down, only fleetingly aware of its scents, tastes, textures, visual appeal, freshness (or lack of it), or subtle energetic qualities. Eating even the simplest meal—a piece of tree-ripe fruit, a bowl of rice, or a wedge of artisan cheese—can be a daily ritual of pleasure and awareness.

Reflect on your daily life for a moment. Do you live in a setting that gives you pleasure? Have thought and attention been given to the energy, appearance, and arrangement of things in your home? Personal space? Workspace? We reflect our environment; if our surroundings are dull, cluttered, lacking in beauty or vitality, so too are we. How does the space around you, both indoors and outdoors, bring pleasure to your being? Places that we consider sanctuaries tend to offer some sort of happiness to our senses, through either beauty, aesthetic appeal, stillness, or other energetic quality such as openness.

Contemplating other facets of the pleasure spectrum, what is your relationship with touch and physical contact? Your ability to let loose and play? Are you comfortable and at ease in your body? Creativity can be a great source of pleasure: do you indulge your artistic and creative inclinations?

The majority of us are trapped in a love-hate relationship with our physical bodies. We have a distorted view of what the body *should* look like and struggle to attain some external notion of beauty or appeal. Few are the souls among us who authentically embrace their potential as embodied, sensual beings—those who can love their bodies for what they are. The bodysoul is a resource of tremendous power, one that remains largely untapped due to our fear and mistrust of it. To be fully alive in one's skin is to be a creative, sensual, and powerful being—which strangely terrifies most of us.

Your birthright as a creative being in the emerging cosmos is to be glowingly alive, powerful, beautiful, creative, sexual, and radiant. It is only you who hold this back, dimming yourself down to be not so luminous, alluring, or worthy of notice. To feel pleasure deeply in the body is also to glimpse the tremendous power and potential that waits carefully locked away. The soul dreams that, rather than deny the body and the exquisite gift of our senses, we will dive in to richly embodied, sensual power and passion.

As I write about pleasure, part of a poem titled "Wild Geese" by Mary Oliver rings through my head:

> You do not have to be good.
> You do not have to walk on your knees
> for a hundred miles in the desert, repenting.
> You have only to let the soft animal of your body
> love what it loves.

As with the longing of Eros, what brings you alive? Don't deny the body; open to the expansiveness at your sensual core instead. In considering the role of pleasure in your life, what do you glean about your ability to give and receive? To be open rather than constricted?

Pleasure brings us more fully into conscious relationship with both self and *other*. Whether we are marveling at beauty or steeping in expansive sensations, an energetic and reciprocal exchange is occurring. We are never separate from our fully participatory universe. Even when offering pleasure to others—caressing a friend, lover, or child; stroking an animal; offering nourishment on some level through foods, music, words—we ourselves experience pleasure through our own senses; thus we are simultaneously receptive. *The more we consciously embrace our ability to give and receive pleasure, the more we balance the masculine and feminine within.* Indeed, pleasure makes the wedding bed for the sacred union within each of us. In our quest for Eros and meaningful connection—a life of creative and authentic power—pleasure plays a vital role as our somatic compass and guide. For the awakened man, pleasure forms a part of his daily practice of soulful nourishment and expansion.

THE PLEASURE BARRIER

It is challenging to admit or even recognize that we have barriers around sensory enjoyment. Yet often we allow ourselves to give pleasure to others—sexually or otherwise—but not receive it ourselves. Conversely, some among us are fairly adept at receiving pleasure but in a self-absorbed way that offers little to others in return. Our relationship with pleasure is nearly as convoluted and conflicted as our relationship with power.

Whether it involves food and nourishment, touch, sex, or any other sensory delight, what are the judgments we hold about pleasure? Often an inner Puritan or ascetic speaks loudly with a critical voice, provoking a sense of guilt or shame (both of which are constricting emotions). A reluctance or inability to receive pleasure is a sure restriction of the life force and bodymind. There is often an overlap here with a "nourishment barrier": a block in the psyche that is usually the result of an uncompleted developmental task in early stages of life, one that inhibits the way we allow ourselves to take in that which sustains us. "Pleasure barrier" or "nourishment barrier," either one is a restriction of the elemental, authentic flow of core essence and energy.

In marked contrast to those who resist taking in pleasure, at the far end of the spectrum is the disembodied hedonist, chasing all sorts of gratification and sensory stimulus—food, sex, travel, extravagance. Scientists have documented that on a brain chemistry level, an addictive quality exists to such pursuits. Similar to rats in a laboratory that have their brains' pleasure centers wired for reward, a steadily decreasing dopamine neurotransmitter response is noted, the more they seek and gain the reward. With each gain, they receive less and less chemical pleasure, which in turn causes them to want even more, similar to a drug addiction. On a psychological level, the pleasure junkie actually seeks a sense of passion and power that he lacks within, chasing superficial forms of pleasure and Eros in an attempt to fill the inner, emotional void but with waning satisfaction.

If we pursue Eros and pleasure blindly—merely as a response to a stimulus—while never realizing that the real call is the soul, passion remains only a thin and fleeting ghost. *Embodied* pleasure is not about experiences that fleetingly light up our senses or about being ruled by our impulsive desires. Rather it entails a mindful, sensual celebration of that which is daily in our lives—everywhere—that nourishes the soul and expands our potential as powerful, erotic beings: sensory delight, beauty, breath, movement, authentic voice, creativity, lovemaking, inspiration. Because it arrives and arises through the senses, pleasure brings us into the body and anchors us in the present moment, deepening our conscious enmeshment with the web of life.

Particularly in regard to sex, most men would shake their head saying, "I've got *no* problems receiving pleasure in sex. The more, the better!" Certainly we hunger for erotic connection that bestows a stimulating sense of aliveness and release. Yet we all have a certain pleasure threshold at which we literally shut off and disengage—and subsequently discharge—the stimulating and expansive experience. In sex, as the pleasure and energy start to build, it doesn't take long before we want to "cum," to rush ahead to the big bang of orgasm. While ejaculating is certainly pleasurable, it is also a powerful discharge of energy. We are literally spurting our essence out, feeling contentedly spent afterwards. For many men who are tightly contained, exercise and ejaculation may be the primary ways they can open briefly to the power within. What would happen if we could raise the threshold—not simply for longer stamina in sex but to begin increasing our capacity for sustained, nourishing pleasure?

POWER

The earth is abundant energy held in potential and form. Our bodies, likewise. We activate this latent power through many avenues: breath, movement, sound, exercise, grounding or "earthing," sensory and embodied awareness, immersion in nature, creativity . . . and sex. When our mana is abundant and coursing freely, we feel a current of vitality in the body. Often it presents as a sense of lightness, tingling energy, warmth, a contented feeling of health and radiance, or simply abundant physical energy. Our life force—the erotic spiral— is an experience of motion, energetic vibration, creativity, and expansion. By facilitating expansion, pleasure aids to activate this flow of energy in our body, with sex offering perhaps the most pleasurable energetic expression of all. If we truly surrender to pleasure, in that expansion we also open to our authentic, somatic power.

Power in the body is visceral, a wild animal hiding beneath our skin, trembling. From a quiet tingling hum to mighty waves streaming through our cells and nervous system, it is energy. As a force, it animates like the tides of breath or a wind moving across the landscape. Our struggle as men is to become comfortable with power in the body and find appropriate, soul-enhancing ways to express our energy—fully inhabiting our wild soul. Part of that challenge rests in discovering our habits and limitations. When we feel the current of our body's energies, do we immediately shut down or discharge them? Or do we allow the power to flow and thus energize us?

The appropriate use of personal power is a key characteristic of the Sacred Masculine. In understanding the ways that we balance, wield, expel, or reject power, we must face the challenge of cultivating and channeling our personal energies. Particularly when we are stripped and naked, our capability to fully receive pleasure reveals much about our ability to build and sustain power, allowing it to course through us without reflexive, automatic discharge.

Just as pleasure is more complex than a dopamine response, sexual energy is more than just hormones. While useful for a partial understanding, biochemistry offers but one piece of the puzzle. Humans are far more complex and imaginative than merely biology and brain chemistry. Sexual arousal is a gleaming, central facet of our life force. When we feel sexually aroused, all our energies are activated.

Consider a normal day for most of us: our senses are dulled and overstimulated by our manmade environment; the hours slip by in a soul numbing and largely sedentary manner. We eat processed and packaged food for its convenience rather than taste or nourishment. Apart from exercise (which doesn't necessarily bring pleasure), often the only time that we noticeably feel our core current is in sexual arousal. This is the closest many of us get to *power*. Severely disconnected from the body, we may notice or interpret this only as feeling "horny," with a concentration of energy around our genitals.

When power (or pleasure) becomes a river in the body, the learned reflex for most is to constrict against, repress, or discharge. Examples will vary between individuals based upon personal character and childhood survival strategies, ranging from compulsive exercise (or sexual activity) to discharge the energy, to overeating and Technostasis—dully plugged into Internet or video games—to numb oneself. Too strong a current threatens to overwhelm us. What to do with so much force and potential? Who are we to be powerful, potent, sexual, alluring, creative, and alive? Unleashed, the true power of our erotic authenticity might sweep us away—forcing surrender to a force larger than our ego and its controlling, self-conscious desires. It could—and often does—wreck our tidily constructed life. Lacking viable options, rather than ride the rising swell as it becomes a wave, many of us choose (unconsciously) to restrict and pull in or discharge through work, exercise, sex, etc.

We've already noted that our troubled relationship with power often arises from our deep-rooted mistrust of the body and its desires. Experiencing the misuse of power—usually through violence—also influences our resistance to core energy. Whether we have been on the receiving end of brutal force, witnessed it, or unleashed it on another, we fear power in its inappropriate expression. A churning storm within, each of us holds the power to destroy as well as to create; you are the lover *and* the rapist, the murderer *and* the saint. In the grace of a conscious breath, we choose our path. Yet in limiting our energy for fear of what it *might* do, or how it may overtake and overwhelm us, we effectively limit all forms of generative creativity, as well.

Consciously or not, many men bear an internalized shame over the historical, collective misuse of power over centuries at the hands of the imbalanced masculine. Thus we unconsciously curtail our personal power so as to not perpetuate the cycle of violence and abuse others and the world. Buried alongside the shame, there also rests a profound grief over the lack of role models for balanced manhood and authentic power. Each of us faces a deep inner divide between the cultural expectations of what it means to be a man versus our personal, unique essence. How does our power—or our innate mistrust of it—arise from this solitary struggle?

Surrender and power are two sides of the same coin. Yet too many of us still associate *surrender* with weakness, as opposed to receptivity, which is essential for balance and wholeness. If we rigidly resist surrender—in the bedroom or the workplace—then we oppose the feminine in intimacy and relationship. The sensual, sexual dance between pleasure, power, and surrender offers fertile ground for integration, balance, healing, and transformation. The erotic spiral invites us to be seduced into the numinous mysteries of the sacred union. But first we must open and expand. Only then do the dance and courtship begin.

RAISING THE THRESHOLD

I'm going to be very blunt here: the way a man masturbates or engages in sex betrays his pleasure threshold. There is nothing wrong with sexual pleasure—solo, shared, or communal—yet for most men, masturbation is less about pleasure than it is an unconscious way to discharge sexual energy. And power. Like much of sexuality, masturbation and self-pleasure come wrapped in a dark shroud of guilt, a shameful secret stitched of cultural norms and taboos. Even the word "masturbation" comes from *masturbare*, to abuse.[1] After ejaculation, we generally feel relaxed, calm, and pleasantly spent. The current in the body has been dissipated and the tides of our energies return to their normally subdued levels. Sharply pleasurable as it is, the normal discharging of our semen is actually short-circuiting our greater capacity for pleasure.

Many men claim that they can't sleep unless they ejaculate each night, solo or with partner. Whether "jacking off" or "wanking" is simply a pleasurable habit, an addictive dopamine threshold pattern, or a way to subconsciously manage and discharge one's own sense of power—or all of these—it is worth considering the true function of such a need or tendency. Just as we must enquire of our somatic and emotional habits, what is our sexual pattern protecting us from?

When we begin to recognize our proclivities around pleasure and power, sexual activity can be a way to raise one's "pleasure threshold." Engaging in masturbation or sex as a pleasurable way to *build* energy rather than discharging it simply to "get off" opens us to new levels of power, passion, and embodiment. For nearly all of us, the rising intensity of pleasure and energy at some point becomes too much. Our sensory system is alight and we hit our pleasure threshold. Our choice (even if we don't recognize it as such) then is to discharge through ejaculation or, alternatively, to contain the energy and seminal fluid, allowing them to circulate in waves through the bodymind.

Retaining ejaculation is achieved through constriction of the perineal muscles between scrotum and anus at the moment of orgasm, thus blocking the release of semen. Specifically, it involves contracting the pubo-coccygeal (PC) muscle between the pubic bone and the tailbone (coccyx). Though it involves the same muscle, it is a much stronger contraction than the *mula bandha* ("root lock") often engaged in yogic practices to form an energetic seal and lock *prana* in the body. Using a sustained contraction and conscious breathing to direct the rush of energy up the spinal column rather than out the shaft of the manroot, the semen is blocked, thus reserving the body's "essence" or energetic charge, while the energy circulates inwardly in a full-bodied, inner orgasm. There is no ejaculation.

Being retained inwards, the quality of this experience is decidedly different from a genital-based, outward ejaculation. You don't "cum" in a spurting release. The experience tends to be more diffuse (though no less powerful), nourishing, and replenishing; energy streams through the central nervous system rather than depleting as it rushes out. As an added bonus, because the ejaculate has been contained, a man can usually experience multiple orgasms in this manner, making for a prolonged sexual encounter, which further raises the pleasure threshold and overall energetic frequency.

Erotic exploration offers a tantalizing and powerful avenue for self-discovery and transformation. As an experiment around creative energy, next time you feel sexually aroused and engage in either self-pleasure or sex, note your habits and patterns. After ejaculating, observe how inspired or energized you feel (or don't feel) to engage any sort of creative project. You could also repeat this experiment and *not* ejaculate, noting the sexual/creative/spiritual current, and consider the difference in energetic result.

Apart from ejaculation and orgasm, to engage in sexual activity—solo or joined—and be in a state of heightened erotic arousal without the need to "cum" is a powerful way to raise the pleasure threshold in our bodies. Experiment with self-pleasure or sex, focusing instead on breath, sensation, and energy in the body. In addition to the manroot, pay attention to the places you feel in your body—and those you don't. Are there areas where you feel dead, cold, numb, or blocked? Freed from the need to *do* anything but simply savor the mounting erotic energy, allow pleasure to draw you deeper into the bodymind. Rather than focus on the big bang, be fully present with yourself and your partner and the commingled waves of sensation. Let the entire bodysoul become a temple of sensory pleasure. When we welcome this fully embodied pleasure, we open to erotic, authentic power and thus raise our capacity for both in a mutually enhancing, upward spiral of energy.

Gabrielle Roth, movement teacher and author, says that in order to come fully into our power, one of the most essential tasks in our lives is to *learn how to make love*. Most people, she writes, "cannot make love in any sort of complete and satisfying way. Ours is a supposedly liberated, even libertine culture, but it is actually woefully underdeveloped sexually. . . . We are surrounded by attempts to achieve sexual satisfaction in almost every way possible except the deeply rewarding one. How many of us know how to have a total, full-body, cathartic, shaking-all-over sexual experience?"[2] Full sexual experience is a key route—fundamental, even—to healing ourselves.

Through embodied Eros—focusing on breath and sensation and being open to energy and to other—and raising our pleasure/power capacity beyond habitual, reflexive discharge, we invoke expansive states of awareness and being. We evolve. Eros guides us to evolve from the reptilian brain and the lower centers of the base *chakras*, to the intuitive, mystic brain, where our consciousness expands and transforms. The lower three, primary *chakras* of energy support the higher ones, with the heart as center and balance point. Truly, it is in the awakened heart that the path of the Sacred Masculine begins and ends.

When we build the energetic charge through breath, sensation, and containing our seed, more power develops and remains in the system— energy that is available for creative use. As we cultivate energy, we feel alive and powerful. Radiant. Bold. Authentic. Free. What will we channel this life force into? How will we direct this vitality and virility? And what will we dare to bring to the other-than-human world? As an awakened man, your challenge is to unleash and embrace this powerful self, moving closer to embodying the Erotic Warrior. And the wild soul.

THE SPECTRUM OF SEX

Early in these pages we noted that Eros is most frequently and commonly associated with our sex lives and our libidinous longing. The power of sex, desire, lust, and love has driven men and women to ecstasy and madness since time immemorial. A powerful expression of Eros, sex remains a beautiful invitation into the wonders and sensations of the body, and to a feeling of pleasurable connection, both physical and emotional. Even spiritual.

Brother, what is your shame at being a sensual, erotic being? What barriers and patterns of containment do you place around your sexuality?

Perhaps nowhere in our lives are we as powerfully conflicted as with sex. We yearn for it and fantasize; we actively seek it out, scheme, manipulate, bargain, and even lie for it. Yet along with the engorged rush of fleshly pleasure often come shame and guilt that bind us up in knots—at least until the desire grows strong enough to send us searching and stalking once again. Cultural biases differ slightly, some being more liberal about sex than others. Americans are both puritanical and prurient about sex; living in Great Britain I note the same pattern among the English (if Victorian rather than puritan). Wherever the thrusting phallus is unsheathed, our general mistrust and loathing of the body rushes forward in full force. Sex is juicy, flavorsome, messy, and carnal. In the naked physicality of coital intimacy, we are vulnerable and revealed; all our inadequacies so carefully locked away break loose, gathering around the bed like jeering onlookers. We find ourselves exposed in our concerns over the size of our manroot or our ability to "perform" or to please our lover, and wrestling with body issues and shame. "Erectile dysfunction," as we euphemistically call the inability to get or maintain a hard-on, usually has far less to do with physical malfunctioning than it does the issues bouncing around in our heads. While in the heat of the moment we may allow our energies to flow—even our darkest secrets to escape—as the passion cools, we quickly don our covering robes of shame and reserve.

As with all areas of personal authenticity, we have self-limiting patterns around our sexual nature. Sex reflects our sense of power or lack of it. It reveals the ways in which we are domesticated versus wild. Do we feel we must be quiet and hushed so neighbors or family cannot hear us engaged in pleasure? Are we able to be vocal and expressive, to ask for what we really want? Can we express our male tenderness and vulnerability? Sexual or otherwise, our patterns become obstacles that we unconsciously place in the way of getting what we actually want—they serve as methods to keep us small, safe, and contained. Yet as we evolve and transform in our consciousness, part of that journey involves our sexual evolution as erotic beings. What better way to examine our shields than stripped and naked?

As an expression of the erotic spiral, sexuality is an inherent part of our being. When it emerges from our core and connects us to the Other, it can be truly sacred. When we loosen our restrictive patterns, sex holds the power to free the soul, unleash our authentic energies, and offer a gateway to transformation. Whether straight or gay, sex extends across a wide spectrum—reaching from the heart-opening and transcendental to the habitual; from the merely physical discharge of energy in casual sex and anonymous encounters to the violent shadows of rape and sexual abuse.

Most of us are comfortably ensconced in the middle of the spectrum, where sex is a pleasurable, mostly physical connection. Male sexual activity is largely fixated on genitals, focused on the short rush of ejaculation rather than fully inhabiting the sensory pleasure palace of the entire body. As an avenue to deeper connection with self and other—and Source— sex remains mostly unexplored. In our younger days, particularly for heterosexual men, sex is largely a conquest and a bragging rite, a means of proving one's manliness (one-dimensional) to others and self. Though this is slowly changing, gay men tend to experience early sexual encounters in colors and shades of shame, fearing that they are actually *less* than manly.

In our erotic education over the years, hopefully our lovers teach us new avenues of sexual articulation, creativity, trust, and surrender. Just as with movement, breath, rhythm, emotional or creative expression, we develop a limited, habitual range of responses. Our options for authenticity and freedom become narrowed, confining us to a partial band of the sexual spectrum. We become less vocal, more predictable, less imaginative, and more contained. Our sexual partner also has her or his own tendencies, further complicating the dynamic. In a longer-term intimate relating, these sets of patterns can devolve into a dull, unimaginative routine of sex, neither partner opening to or getting what he or she really wants. Whether in our roles in bed or sharing secret fantasies, we limit our desires—navigating our partner's web of patterns and carefully censoring our expression for fear of judgment, ridicule, or even disgust. As sex stagnates, passion dwindles; the current of life force clogs and we begin to seek Eros and pleasure elsewhere.

There is more to address here than simply trying new sexual positions or incorporating toys or scenarios to spice up a sex life. Fantasies can take us into the imagination—sometimes a welcome realm—but then sex is largely in our head and we are less than fully present with our *actual* partner. (Admittedly, for some that may be the whole point.)

The widespread availability of commercial "porn" on the Internet has given us poor models of sex, offering a seemingly diverse cross-section of the sexual spectrum while actually whittling us down. Images of overly muscled men—waxed and gleaming well-hung studs who can fuck dispassionately for hours—are not representative of who most of us are as lovers. Such visual objectification sets up unrealistic expectations for both how we should look and how we should have sex, further fueling our insecurities. Typical "porn" only models genital-based "sport fucking": a monochrome, emotionless portrayal of sexuality that reveals a flat, one-dimensional definition of masculinity and sexual relating. Whether studio produced or the self-styled, *amateur* variety, "porn" holds a strangely addictive quality for many, the result being that the more an individual watches, the less able he is to be aroused with an actual partner without visualizing a scenario in his head. Sex becomes ever more habitual, less creative, and less satisfying.

Because sex can be so physically and emotionally intimate (particularly for the receptive partner), ideas about monogamy versus nonmonogamy are particularly difficult to examine and navigate without criticizing judgment—either our own, our partner's, or both. Explorations into open relationships, polyfidelity, or polyamorous expressions will likely bear the brunt of familial, social, and cultural moralizing, making it all the more difficult to find an authentic, meaningful path for sexual connection.

I'm thinking of a couple I know, a handsome man with startling blue eyes and a dynamic, voluptuous, long-time girlfriend. Matthew has had male sexual partners in the past, and Kelly is fully aware of her mate's equal attraction to men and to women. Side by side, his demeanor, speech, and movements are softer than hers; extroverted and ebullient, she offers a dynamic balance to his reserve. In a reversal of standard roles, in sex he prefers to be more passive while she enjoys being dominant. Yet for Matthew, an aspect of his erotic longing is not met within the framework of his sexual relationship with Kelly. Although they have discussed the possibility of bringing an outside, male partner into their bed—or Matthew's pursuit of that aspect on his own—Kelly isn't fully comfortable with sharing her man. The deep love between these two is obvious, even to an outsider. With open hearts and minds (and the aid of a skilled couples therapist), they continue to explore with each other, examining their deeper issues about trust, vulnerability, power, and surrender. Both of them are working to loosen restrictive notions of what their sexual relationship *should* look like, while searching for new ways to connect fully with each other in ways that continue to satisfy.

The true opportunity of sexual intimacy is to evolve to a fuller sense of the embodied, sensual, uninhibited self. Soul is the creative and erotic force in us that is free—seeking to be fully *ensouled* in the body rather than restrained by self-imposed limits and habits. In sex, as we open to the erotic spiral, when we set our shame and constricting patterns aside, we can navigate a broader section of the pleasure spectrum. As in every aspect of our lives, the more we transcend our patterns, the more we become transparent, authentic, and free. We expand and we liberate the soul to shine like a star. A hot and sexy one.

SEX AND SOUL APPEAL

Our ideas of sexiness have become increasingly superficial. Like chic glamour that we mistake for real beauty, society's notion of sex appeal is mostly an artificial construct based on appearance and mental projection. Hollywood media, the Internet, online dating sites, and "porn" have all served to reinforce our shallow concept of sexiness. Looking at a photo tells us little about the real qualities, character, or energy of a person— those facets where true sexual attractiveness sparkle.

Sex appeal is something more than an attractive face or a shapely bum, appealing breasts, or sculpted pectorals. The most physically attractive demigod or goddess in the world has nothing if there isn't an appealing energy swirling below the alluring exterior. Even the most striking beauty quickly fades into familiarity while, simultaneously, the inner qualities of a person emerge to be seen (ones which may be decidedly un-sexy).

Whether in a photo or meeting face-to-face, we project certain qualities onto a person: confidence, strength, wildness, passion, intelligence, depth. *What we generally perceive as sex appeal often reflects qualities that we wish for in ourselves—usually around power, vitality, and authenticity.* When those attributes that we have projected onto a sexual partner vanish (as they inevitably do in real life relating), whether or not the individual holds true sexual allure will then be revealed. Our popular notions of sex appeal are largely a game of smoke and mirrors. Among other things that it is *not*, sex appeal is not shrinking into patterns of self-consciousness. The moment we restrict our energy, our allurement diminishes. When the attractive and seemingly bold lover suddenly displays shame over the perceived "flaws" of her or his body, the captivating energy shifts and lessens. The enchantment weakens and wanes.

True sex appeal transcends the merely physical. The body ages and physical beauty fades, yet attraction grows. Mature, older individuals find partners attractive despite the fact that the youthful blush of beauty has diminished. The real appeal is energetic and invisible. Just as the soul resonates when it detects authenticity—as in elemental Nature or in other people—our senses, chakras, and energetic field all detect currents of energy that we respond to with resonance (or not). Sexual appeal is often the sense of power and energy we detect in a person, a palpable sense of the "life force." Like the vitality that we perceive in an athlete, it is an energy that exudes beyond the physical body. The ease and grace of someone at home in one's own skin is an air of subtle confidence, utterly distinct from puffed up bravado or a shield of sculpted muscles.

A friend of mine, a gorgeous female wilderness guide and therapist with an untamed spirit—a woman who inhabits her body like a wild-cat—once remarked, "People who embody their soul gifts are dripping sexy!" Exactly. What we sense in such people is a glimpse of their authentic power and creative energy, a sense of inhabiting and celebrating their essence and mana. The more a person is free and authentically at home with him- or herself—unguarded, nondefensive—the more the person generates a tangible force. More than sex appeal, it's soul appeal.

EMBODIED SEX

It is popular of late, especially with the rise of so-called tantric approaches to sex—largely focused on breath and sensation for heightened pleasure but having little or no deeper connection to tantra as a spiritual path—to turn our attention towards the more ascendant, spiritual aspects of love-making.

Just as the deep imagination of Earth and the Cosmos seeks expression through us, so too does the soul yearn for an embodied expression of uninhibited, sensual sexuality. Something more than middle-spectrum sex or "fucking," the soul longs for sex as a creative conversation in which each individual is fully present and connected in harmonic pleasure to the energies of the other. The soul's gift to us is wholeness; when we engage in fully embodied, nonlimited, and nonhabitual sexual exchange, we unlock an energetic healing on a myriad of levels of bodymind and spirit. Soulful, uninhibited sex is integrating and expanding.

Soulful sex savors the energy in the entire body, not simply the genitals. It employs conscious breathing and awareness of somatic sensation, honoring the full body as a temple of sensual pleasure. This sort of fully inhabited sexual exchange involves being mindful of one's partner and noting one's patterns. We observe the ways that we tend to split off and become less present in sex: the spectre of body shame, anxiety about performance, fear of criticism or rejection if we ask for what we really want, focusing solely on the other, etc. Yet when we are ensconced in the moment with each other, nothing *needs* to happen other than a full appreciation of the mutual pleasure. What are the desires, sensations and messages of the moment? As with deep listening through opened senses, in this expansive and receptive state an authentic response and desire naturally emerges—something more profound and revealing than our conditioned or limiting responses. What arises in soulful sex is free of our censorship, limits, and shame.

Often what surfaces in soulfully embodied sex are elements that we have repressed in the psyche and bodymind—a sense of power, a desire to be dominated, a need for roughness or a blindfold, a hunger for pain, a longing for deeper connection. These submerged desires often encompass a wider band of the sexual spectrum and can be profoundly transforming and expansive when explored in an embodied, open-minded spirit rather than one of shame or guilt. As surely as we have locked away our shadows, so too have we hidden away our radiant power and light. Sometimes what emerges is the need to be free of a particular role, either traditional or self-assumed (i.e., the dominant, strong male). Curiously, because partners are of the same gender, gay men often have a different and more liberated sense of versatility in sexual encounters—a freedom from habitual roles in bed, with either partner being dominant or submissive. Yet they, too, can devolve into stale, limited roles of merely "top" or "bottom" rather than choosing a more fluid flexibility.

When I was leading men's groups, one of the topics I frequently chose for discussion was "Sex, Intimacy, and Soul." A realization that crystallized for me in these forums is that as surely as we lack authentic rites of passage for manhood, so too do we lack true initiations around sex. As men, no one taught us to make love—certainly not in any openhearted or soul satisfying way. If we have learned at all, it's mostly been in an accidental manner along the journey, through our own sensitivity and the grace of our partners.

Many men have shared with me how difficult soulful, embodied sex is for them—even if they long for it. My thoughts return to an attractive middle-aged man in a long-term marriage, a participant in one of my early men's groups. As the opportunity for sharing moved round the circle, he confided openly.

"It's so hard for me to disconnect my head. I'm so damn mental, and I've never really been comfortable in my body. I'd much rather focus on pleasing. It's easier for me. Sure, I can receive, but it's still tough to get out of my head. I'm more often thinking about a fantasy than about the actual connection that's happening. I know it's my pattern but I can't seem to break out of it. We've been together so long . . . we're both stuck in our patterns, I think. I'm not sure that either one of us has ever really gotten what we want out of sex."

As evidenced by nods of empathy and subsequent sharing as the "talking stick" moved round the circle, his honest comments struck a chord with most of the group. Later, in a separate conversation, my invitation to this man was to explore a different approach to lovemaking, one that might help him descend from his head and begin inhabiting his body in a new way. Start with a lengthy, shared massage, I suggested, giving first for twenty minutes or so, then switching roles and receiving. I also encouraged him to find a time for this other than bedtime, when both are tired and ready for sleep, and to endeavor to make the event something other than the normal, too familiar routine—light some candles, burn some incense, massage with scented oils, play some soft music perhaps. The goal was to engage in an openhearted seduction in which he too would be seduced. I outlined some preliminary steps for connection with heart and breath and emphasized that during his turn of receiving massage his primary task would be to focus simply on the pleasure of being touched—breathing deeply with senses open wide. With no need to reciprocate or rush ahead to intercourse, simply focus on sensation and connection with his beloved. It mattered little whether he got an erection or if the massage led to full sex—he simply needed to allow the pleasurable sensation to build with breath and to savor it.

When we are fully present in sex—senses ignited by passion and secret desires set free—we unlock the door to true sexual intimacy, which is something far more intense than merely entering another or being penetrated. True sexual intimacy is an open heart exchange, each partner peering deep into the eyes of the other, beholding them as light and shadow while allowing ourselves to be seen fully in return. It is surrender to the flow—either pleasure or pain—of one's own power, the elemental forces of our partner, and the erotic aspects that seek to emerge. In true sexual intimacy, we are undefended and open to our desires, pushing nothing away, while trusting in the other. We allow ourselves to receive as well as give—to be the *ravished*, not only the ravisher.

No matter the gender of our partner, in the act of sexual penetration and receptivity, we embody the union of masculine and feminine. We symbolize the Blade and the Chalice as our united souls resonate in wholeness and celebration. Embodied, soulful sex is something beyond the merely physical—it is an emotional, energetic, creative, and even spiritual exchange. In the vulnerability of our defenses cast aside, protective shell wide open, we blaze unashamedly with pleasure and entwined rivers of raw power. Here, at the shared threshold of skin and soul, we burn with the fire of the sacred.

SEX AND SHADOW

As a vital expression of our physical power, essence, and "life force," sexuality harbors energies of both light *and* darkness. Like yin and yang, one does not exist without the other. We all contain both masculine and feminine elements; each of us is luminosity that dances with shadow, strength braided with vulnerability.

The Shadow often projects its darkness outwards, deflecting attention away from itself, and nowhere is this more revealed than in sexuality. We judge particular sexual acts as sleazy, perverted, or simply twisted. "I would never do *that*," we decry, with perhaps a bit too much vehemence. Consider the moralizing, fundamentalist preacher caught with a prostitute or a male hustler. Condemning others, we distance ourselves from our own inclinations, whether conscious or subterranean. "*They* are shameful and perverted, but I am not." We defensively label sexual behavior as risky, desperate, or decidedly nonspiritual, yet as with other areas of life, behind scorn lurks a secret envy.

What is sacred and what is profane? Such distinctions are largely the projections of society and our collective consciousness, tangled with our internalized judgments about right and wrong (i.e., homosexuality, monogamy versus nonmonogamy, exhibitionism, etc.).

Beckoning in the shadows, the taboo holds its own allure. What is it that we secretly desire? What are our darkest fantasies? What is the aspect of us that our ego—that segment of the conscious self that deems itself in control—will not allow to surface because the desire or fantasy is too raunchy, powerful, shocking, or shameful? Do we hunger to be the one who subjugates and penetrates, thrusting a punishing, pleasurable weapon of hard cock? Or do we secretly yearn to be utterly dominated?

Fucking is powerful. There is something primordially raw in penetrating (or being penetrated) at one's root chakra, the very energetic base of one's being. The everyday self is stripped bare in the ultimate vulnerability. Proponents of leather sex, sadomasochism (S & M), and bondage argue that it is possible to transform and transcend one's ego through such archetypal, role-playing sex. Without a doubt, the ego can temporarily dissolve its self-imposed restraints while kneeling cuffed or bound at the black leather boots of a mistress or master. Sexual roles, pleasure, and pain all invite surrender as we dance with the integral issue of core power and the ways we open to it or restrict against it.

Few of these shadowy experiences are fully embodied, however. When the erotic allure of power and surrender fails to reach beyond the bedroom, sex club, sex dungeon or "play room," the roles themselves become habits and self-limiting, offering few real options for integration. We must each question how our sexual roles perpetuate the ways we obstruct our authentic power. How do we own—and integrate—our Shadow beyond merely acting out sexual fantasies? Daylight or night, how do we invite transformation and integration in the other arenas of life?

Overall, gay men have more opportunity to explore their sexual shadows than do straight and bisexual men. Primarily this has to do with the less intimate and highly physical connection between men, the easy availability of sex—in clubs, saunas, parks, bathhouses, and bars—and a greater number of nonintimate or even anonymous partners. Regardless of sexual preference, in sex the Shadow freely sows shame and perpetuates its own fragmented darkness. It seeks out experiences or partners that degrade and reinforce that which has been banished to the subconscious as perversion or sleaze. "Shadow sex" can offer a portal to insight—even healing—but *only* when it brings us into a fuller sense of self, not a fragmented one.

Drugs are often paired with "shadow sex"—lowering inhibitions and raising the "high" that comes from unleashing the repressed psyche and its dark desires. Addictive qualities notwithstanding, acting out fantasies while tweaked on drugs only further compartmentalizes and fragments an individual. As with any sort of violence, rape and sexual abuse emerge from the shadows of our relationship with power. We have locked our anger and aggressions inside the body and breath, tightly bundled and waiting to explode, but the powerful energies of sex can rip the lid off the sealed box. "Shadow sex" has its own spectrum, ranging from consensual exploration with a partner (such as acting out a rape scenario) to a truly fragmented and pathological act of rape, itself.

Sex offers a doorway. It invites us to dance with shadows and face our fears, bringing both to the light of consciousness. Too often, however, rather than exploring the darkness, an individual can simply become addicted to or enslaved by it, enchanted by a profane incantation. In an exploration, questions must be asked and answered honestly. What in me is seeking to emerge? Does this sex bring me to a more authentic and expansive expression of myself? Does it nourish my creative energy or simply provide release? Am I opened to a richer sense of my erotic being or does it fragment me into something smaller and shameful? In what other areas of my life does this tendency exist?

SACRED SEX
Whether venturing through the dark underworld of eroticism or celebrating transcendental experiences of unified, spiritual bliss, the journey of the soul is one towards wholeness, consciousness, and integration. Fully embodied sex can open the gate, luring us into unexplored fields of beauty and wonder. Soul sex frees our longing but doesn't necessarily celebrate or exalt the spiritual essence of being. Nor is fully embodied sex necessarily *sacred*—all that is required is that we be fully present in our bodies, senses open to pleasure, exploring our longing.

Just as differing levels of embodiment exist, so too do levels of embodied sex. The most profound expression of sexual intimacy—one that opens directly to the spiritual Source—requires full embodiment *and* a heart-centered connection. In sacred sex, we cultivate not only the flow of energy in the body but also the shared, elemental energy being generated as the result of lovemaking. This is the ultimately authentic, vulnerable, and harmonic sharing of souls—embracing and making love to the holy mystery of our beloved. In the depths of our beloved's eyes and our conjoined heart fields, we see and feel the Divine. In this energetic ecstasy, we expand and merge into the highest realms of Eros and spiritual connection—unity, bliss, soul radiance. It is a fusion of souls in comingled breath; a resonance of shared vibration and frequency. A full-bodied orgasm in this state can catapult one to mystic realms of consciousness. Such an experience is generated only by love and truly openhearted connection, a harmonic connection with the song of the world.

Peak experiences—even mystical and sexual ones—can happen to anyone at any state of consciousness, yet an ongoing encounter of sacred sex at this level is generally available only to those who have evolved in their consciousness and opened their hearts. Sacred sex is an experience of expansion and emergence. In the arms of one's beloved—the sanctity of intimacy, truth, vulnerability, tenderness, and surrender—is most often where this rare and magical flower blooms. An ancient chant, it is undertaken and shared with presence, patience, breath, and joyful reverence. Truly, it is a celebration.

Fully embodied sex embraces the shadow; sacred sex transcends it. Exploding from the deep love and ecstatic bliss that partners feel for each other in sexual union, it obliterates notions of self and separateness, masculine and feminine—exalting both Self and Other as unlimited energy and mystery. Making love becomes a conscious, consecrated act, a radiant expansion of the heart while spiraling deeper into the beguiling mystery of the Beloved.

Soul is the secret song of the body and awakened heart. A full-body orgasm in sacred sex generates a harmonic shockwave of spiritual heart energy and sends it cascading through the Unified Field. In the embrace of Eros, when we channel our life force through the heart and outwards to the world as the energy of love, we are revealed as the luminous and powerful Sacred Masculine.

SEMEN

Whether he chooses to retain it or to expend it in a delirious rush of plea-sure, a man's semen is more than millions of sperm cells. It is his energetic essence. As the messenger of DNA, each sperm contains the biological blueprint as a living seed—the entire timeline of human evolution.

What if we regarded our semen as something sacred rather than merely "spunk," "cum," or "jizz"? Beyond being simply mopped up and tossed away on a rag or discarded condom, this most precious and miraculous stuff of life is too often charged with shame and fear. Heterosexual men contain it in rubber prophylactics to prevent their partners from becoming preg-nant. For most gay and bisexual men, the exchange of semen is tainted with anxiety around HIV. More often than not, we view our seminal fluid as something of a biological time bomb, something that must be discharged safely, rather than as any sort of precious resource.

In retaining ejaculate—cultivating an inner, full-body orgasm through breath and constriction of the PC muscle—one builds the level of cre-ative/sexual/spiritual energy in the body rather than depleting it. Eastern and esoteric insight holds that we are thus bathing and opening the nervous system and energetic channels. Rather than the typical outward orientation and expenditure of energy, when we choose to direct our focus inwards, we cultivate a more feminine, receptive energy. This is not to say that men should give up ejaculating simply to become more balanced or to embrace their inner feminine; ejaculation is part of the gift and energy of being male. Yet as we seek to evolve in innovative ways, we can become more mindful—respectful, even—of our semen.

What if our seed, in fact replenished every few hours (a miracle in itself), were generated only at certain intervals or time periods? Would we view it differently then, as a more valued commodity? And what if it contained a drop—or more—of our soul? How might sex be different if we viewed ejaculation as flooding our partners with energetic essence rather than simply "cum"?

In an unnamed poem, Stephen Harrod Buhner, an Earth Poet and master herbalist, shifts our perspective with his usual candor and style:

Semen is Latin
for a dormant, fertilized
plant ovum—
a seed.
Men's ejaculate
is chemically more akin
to plant pollen.
See,
it is really
more accurate
to call it
mammal pollen.

To call it semen
Is to thrust
An insanity
Deep inside our culture:
That men plow women
And plant their seed
When, in fact,
What they are doing
Is pollinating
Flowers.

Now.
Doesn't that change everything between us?

Rather than view it as simply something messy, inconvenient, replaceable, or potentially hazardous, celebrate your ejaculate as energetic essence. If semen is indeed a form of our energetic essence, then sharing it becomes a sacred act, one that is truly intimate. On a spiritual level, consider becoming mindful and selective of whom you choose to share it with—if gay or bisexual, whom you receive it from. Relish your orgasm and ejaculation from a different perspective, one of being a powerful energetic exchange with the Unified Field.

As biological messengers and expressions of the creative Cosmos, we each carry the seeds—or pollen—of the Tree of Life. Rather than an accident or unwanted mishap, what if we regarded it as a holy responsibility and a gift to be able to create a child with our essence? Holding our semen as a sacred charge, as an energetic gift and the spark of life, moves us towards a more spiritual expression as sexual beings and embodying the Sacred Masculine.

THE TEMPLE OF EROS

We have defined Eros as our energetic longing—a felt sense of the life force and passion that arises from the soul—an elemental force that far exceeds merely sexual energies. In a real sense, Eros is the impulse towards wholeness—the authentic essence within us seeking to emerge. It is an energy as fundamental and timeless as Creation itself, an ongoing story of death and rebirth, expansion and emergence.

Our soul asks something more of us than the small cage of ego we have created. Through its whispers and longings, it guides us to break free into something larger—the freedom of authenticity and what we were meant to bring to the world. Throughout the pages of this book, my encouragement to you is to *Go deeper*—deeper into feeling and awareness; plunge into openhearted vulnerability; dive headlong into the authentic possibility of yourself, including the way you inhabit your body.

The body is the temple of Eros. It is within this marvelous structure of flesh, bones, and breath that we celebrate our lives—and evolve—as full-spectrum, awakened men. When it invites us to open and emerge, *pleasure*—the true sort that nourishes the soul—serves our personal evolution. Receptive and open, we raise the sensory threshold, inviting our bodysoul to savor greater states of pleasure, openness, and power. We glimpse the potential for life as a wild, authentic soul who fully inhabits the bones and breath.

Full, uninhibited sexual experience—including full-body orgasm—heals and unifies us, for it is both expansive *and* receptive. Yet embodied sexuality mandates emotional freedom. If our hearts are closed, if we are emotionally guarded and restricted, we will not be able to experience a truly full-body, waves-of-energy and shaking-all-over orgasm. Nor transformation or ultimate well-being.

Soulfully initiated men are rare; equally so those who are soulfully initiated lovers. Though we lack a deep understanding of pleasure and valid rites of passage around sex, when each of us as men begin to reweave our collective agreements about sexuality we loosen the bonds of shame. As we relinquish the boasting and bragging of one-dimensional, genital-based sexuality and focus on sex as a portal to transformation, we evolve.

THE SACRED MASCULINE

Eros is evolutionary. An awakened man acknowledges that his creative, sexual, and spiritual currents are the same elemental force. He honors that this erotic spiral is a manifestation of his soul, something to be celebrated without shame or fear as he dares to explore the realms of "fully embodied," Shadow, and sacred sex. Straight, bisexual or gay, a man embodies the Sacred Masculine by considering his relationship with pleasure, power, and sexual expression from an openhearted stance. He understands that sex offers an opportunity for evolution and endeavors to become ever more present—and authentic—with his erotic energy.

In sexual expression, the Sacred Masculine withdraws his judgments about right and wrong, good and bad. He comprehends that we are all shadow and light, and that sex offers a wide spectrum of expression. He frames sexual exploration in terms of integration—whether it nourishes and cultivates wholeness in bodymind and psyche, or whether it fragments and keeps one chained in repeating patterns and roles that diminish and restrict.

With an open heart, make love to your Shadow.

As we venture beyond the borders of culturally defined masculinity, each of us on a quest to fully inhabit his life—and discover his passion— we follow the summons of Eros and allurement. Our birthright is to be creative, sexual, awakened beings who are bringing something of value to the world. Men who feel deeply, who wield their authentic power with a compassionate heart. As bearer of the spark of life, the Sacred Masculine seeds the womb of Creation. When we sow the Field of Possibility with intention, it brings forth prescient vision in form. Senses open, feet connected to earth, all the seemingly disparate parts of ourselves unify when we understand our destiny is to be the Sacred Lover, taking the world into our arms.

◆ ◆ ◆

Embodying the Erotic Warrior

Embodying the soul through the sensual body is the primary journey of the Erotic Warrior. He knows that when he unchains and builds his own power—creative, spiritual, sexual energies—and through dilated senses and open heart allows himself to be seduced into a courtship with the world, he emerges from his former shell into a life of passion and meaning.

Eros celebrates expansive, sexual evolution. The Erotic Warrior understands that embodied sex—fully present in body and breath—can help one evolve to the expansive realms of consciousness. In sacred sex and lovemaking, his very soul becomes a prayer to the Divine, interwoven in harmony with the song of the world.

In celebrating his erotic nature—honoring and cultivating pleasure, power and surrender—as well as the relational and spiritual nature of the exchange, he incarnates the Sacred Masculine. He becomes an uninhibited, sensual expression of the life force—authentic, vital, and free. Far more than an enlightened, embodied warrior, he is the archetype of the Sacred Lover.

SOUL SKILL #5: APPRENTICE TO PLEASURE

Befriending our body, learning to be at home in it, is a key method for nourishing the soul, building power, opening the senses and heart, and joining in conscious relationship. *Everything is relationship.* In giving pleasure, we also receive it.

Begin an apprenticeship to soulful pleasure. Pay attention to the many ways that pleasure finds you through your senses—visual, kinesthetic, olfactory, auditory, and gustatory. Like a pleasure scout, focus on savoring each experience while also noticing the expansion in your bodysoul.

EMBODYING SOUL SKILL #5: SHED YOUR SKIN

The body is the starting point for our soul's awakening and yet few of us are at home in our own skin. For myriad reasons, it may be an uncomfortable place to inhabit—injury, chronic pain or muscle tightness, or carrying too much weight. Many of us harbor a deep-rooted shame over the way our body looks, judging it harshly by an external notion of beauty or social acceptance. For the majority of people, the only time they are naked is when bathing, having sex, or perhaps sleeping.

One of the ways that we mask our discomfort and hide from others or ourselves is with our clothes. In all of nature, we are the only species that chooses to cover itself. Certainly there is an essential need to stay warm (lest we freeze and die) and to adapt to our environment; but mostly we wear our garments for reasons of style and shame. Nakedness helps us to remember—or learn—how often clothes are unnecessary. Clothing limits sensation and encumbers movement. It impedes the evaporation of sweat or the drying of rain from our skin. It is such a familiar habit of containment that most of us don't even give it a second thought.

Nakedness is powerful. It stirs emotions. Though it is our natural state, it isn't accepted socially and you're apt to get arrested if caught naked outdoors. If you've ever been to a clothing-optional beach or hot springs, however, the social interaction is decidedly nonsexual. Mostly it is free and relaxing, as if nudity were the most natural thing in the world (it is). Stripping us of our external labels and fashions, nudity is a great equalizer.

For this exercise, take off your clothes. The goal is to spend an extended period of time alone, simply being naked while observing what happens for you. In particular, note your patterns around body and breath, especially any impulse to constrict. Is it challenging for you to savor being unclad and uncovered? Are you judging your body? If you're experiencing shame, where is it concentrated? What is it like to simply walk around naked, perhaps working on a project or reading a book. Can you enjoy the breeze from a fan or open window on your exposed skin? What subtle nuances of sensation do you notice? Consider your core energy—do you feel creative? Restless? Sexual?

Admittedly, this exercise is somewhat limited by climate and living situation. If it is winter and your house is cold, you aren't likely to enjoy being nude (there's a very practical reason we have clothes, after all). If you dwell in a shared residence—children, extended family, housemates, etc.—and nudity is not acceptable in the household, perhaps you can be naked in the privacy of your room at a time when no one else is home.

For you as a sensual soul, part of the journey is to learn to be unashamed of your body—equally about sex—and to learn to cultivate pleasure simply from being in your natural state.

BODYSOUL INSIGHTS

To the best of your ability, record your sexual history. Recall each of your lovers and make a list. Write them down. Yes, all of them. What does this list reveal? What does it say about you—body and heart included. Which are the ones that taught you something important?

As a different exercise, write an open love letter to your collective lovers, thanking them for what they've given you on the erotic journey. Try writing this letter from your masculine aspect, then again from your feminine aspect.

Considering other aspects of pleasure, power, and sex, answer the following:

* What is my relationship with food? Body? Touch? Creativity? Play?
* Do I live in an environment/surroundings that brings me pleasure? If not, what aspects displease me, and what could be done to create a more pleasurable space?
* What is my shame at being a sensual, erotic being?
* What barriers and patterns of containment do I place around my sexuality?
* What is it that I secretly desire in bed? Sexually, what of me seeks to emerge . . . or is withheld?
* Write a soulful sex poem.
* What is most celebratory about sex? What is most shameful?
* How does sex relate to intimacy in my life?
* Does sex bring me to a more authentic and expansive expression of myself?

6 WILD SOUL, WISE HEART

The metal doors of the long, metal caterpillar slide open and I step off the underground train, earbuds firmly plugged in and weaving a sonic cocoon around myself. Walking through the station, the heels of my black boots strike the concrete in a rhythmic pace as I move deftly through the crowd towards the platform's exit. In a half second of decision, I steer left to ascend the long flight of stairs alongside the escalators rather than standing still on the mechanized transport. I'm in motion, choosing to remain so, and as I climb I focus on the sense of my leg and gluteal muscles pumping.

At the top of the steps, my heartbeat quickened from the considerable climb, I withdraw the small leather wallet from my front pocket and palm down, place my transit card on the electronic reader of the turnstile. Display lights flash green, there is a click of the waist-high barrier gate, and I pass through. Emerging on a familiar street corner in London's vibrant West End amid a swirling sea of people, I begin walking down the avenue, navigating spaces in the crowds where I can pass and move ahead, keeping to my brisk pace. I'm in the city for some errands, having journeyed in by train and now traveling via Underground and on foot in my usual style.

The sky is gunmetal gray and chiseled of heavy stone, ready to crush the old huddled buildings, crowded streets and public squares. The tangled streets of London are awake and restless, churning with dreams of ambition, unnamed longing, and quiet songs of despair. The roar of buses vibrates body and senses, but my shield of music shelters me from the brunt of the city's noise, while the mélange of languages and accents on the street around are also softened. Striding through the colored, living maze of pedestrians, the smell of exhaust and diesel fumes assaults, yet simultaneously I catch the enticing aromas of warmly spiced food from restaurants and takeaway shops.

Just a few hours ago, I was barefoot in my garden in the countryside, picking purple jewels of plums from a heavily laden tree and placing them into my wicker gardening basket. Now, I'm booted and cruising through the urban heart of the city's centre, a courier bag slung across my broad back.

As I walk, my focus resides primarily in my breath and bodily sensation. Here amid the crowds, I'm engaged in a moving meditation and despite the press and hum of the urban swarm surrounding me, I feel expansive. As long as I stay focused on my breath, my senses and heart can remain mostly ajar.

I'm an outsider here, a foreigner in almost every way, even in the world's most diverse city. Passing me, you wouldn't likely peg me as English, not with my olive skin, dark hair, and close-trimmed beard. More likely you would guess me to be Spanish, Portuguese, or Italian, perhaps now residing in London. A citizen of the world. Sounds nice, but really I'm an outlaw and today I am undercover, moving confidently along this busy avenue that I have come to know well.

There's a bubbling, streaming energy in my core, ready to break into a run at any moment or strike an impromptu dance on the sidewalk. Wouldn't the oh-so-reserved British be startled to see someone begin to boogie in public. The thought makes me chuckle and smile. It's palpable, this somatic electricity. If I was at home, I would put on some music and dance, letting movement sequence through my limbs, spine, and neck—allowing my soul to express its waves of authentic motion. I'd sing, too.

My eyes follow the downcast, drawn faces of the businessmen in dark suits and pointed leather shoes, the loudly animated tourists, happy on their English holiday. Occasionally I turn to catch an interesting window display or to let my eyes briefly follow someone I find attractive. I'm savoring it all today as I stride down the street. Feeling good. Comfortable in my own skin, I'm a quiet conspirator against the dull and ordinary, knowing that I'm better as an authentic original than ever I could be as anything else.

Underneath my stylish European clothes lurks something wild and not quite domesticated. This is not my normal or preferred environment but you wouldn't guess it from observing me. I move with a pliant grace, comfortable and at ease. My body feels strong and supple from a regular practice of dance and yoga, and long walks through fields and woods. The trim cut of my jacket tapers nicely from shoulders to waist, and I'm wearing a tailored, floral-patterned shirt from a rather posh London designer. Charcoal trousers hug legs, pelvis, and buttocks in just the right way, not too tight.

There's something about me that catches your gaze, something other than my wardrobe or features. Harder to define. I'm wearing a slightly wry, mischievous smile on my lips and there's a gleam in my dark onyx eyes. A man with a secret, possibly just a bit mad. Maybe my body is well-inked with sacred tattoos. Perhaps I'm wearing a cockring around my manroot. Maybe my secret is the healing energy I can summon in my hands that helps me "see" what's wrong when I lay them on someone. Or quite possibly I'm just hotwired into a sensual appreciation of life.

The entwined current of erotic, creative, spiritual energies animates my being—a subtle glow and energy closely aligned with true health. I hold your gaze just a little too long and go on my way, disappearing into the crowd.

You probably wouldn't guess what I'm carrying. Sure, there's a mobile phone, but rather than a laptop, files, or business papers, my satchel holds the following: my dented, stainless steel water container; a just-purchased bottle of Meursault *Premier Cru*; three well-wrapped wedges of artisan cheese from Neil's Yard Dairy; a container of fat, briny Kalamata olives; two organic, sweetly crisp, Pink Lady apples; a wood-handled Laguiole pocket knife; a photocopy of my passport and residence visa; my battered blue fountain pen from Paris; a small black sketchbook with cream-coloured pages; and a worn paperback copy of Rilke's *Letters To A Young Poet*. Each thing in its own way reflects an aspect of who I am—gourmand meets renegade, sybarite meets bohemian. A worldly Soul Artist on foot.

Today I pass through this urban world cleverly disguised in my fancy city clothes, sending my heart's energetic field into the crowd before me and reaching out to touch any bit of nature that I encounter in this concrete world. It keeps me grounded and open, my nervous system regulated, and my heart in a coherent rhythm.

Traversing the streets of this old city, I'm a modern day Green Man. Poet. Lover. Shaman. Fool. I am an Erotic Warrior—an Evolutionary, propelled by a sense of personal calling and the reason I'm alive. Deeply inhabiting body and soul, I'm living at the edge, quite a bit further into the realm of authenticity than society wants to go.

Seemingly I'm a long way from the Kent fencepost where revelation struck. Not really. We are never separate from the Mystery. Even here on a crowded avenue, the sacred and profane colliding in each breath and heartbeat, I am steeped in the *suprasomatic sentience* of our planet. Every single interaction offers a chance to embody my soulful authenticity. Share a bit of kindness, too, even if it's just the unexpected flash of a little smile.

In a couple of hours, arriving home from the station, I'll shed these boots and stylish threads. I'll stretch my legs, shake off the clinging energy of the city, and invite a bit of gentle movement into my being. Sometime later, at dusk or at dawn in the garden, I'll be barefoot on the earth and breathing deeply, my heart field cast wide, listening for the Song of the World—offering my own song of gratitude in return.

I wonder, can we live amid the frenetic crush and manmade hum of the modern realm and still fully embody our authentic wild souls? In thinking that we can have it all, we've lost so much.

Nature and Authentic Movement

In our insulated lives of artificial light and conditioned air, we have lost the elemental connection to the hours and moods of the day. Time is a linear commodity to be scheduled and managed, a numeric readout on a watch or a mobile phone. Day in and day out, as we work a routine schedule of hours in buildings that maintain a constant temperature, the seasons have faded to merely a display outside our windows—the chill or heat of which we experience primarily when passing to or from our cars. The overwhelming majority of us live in cities, an urban demographic and lifestyle very different from our grandparents or ancestors. Disconnected from walking and working outdoors, no longer are we engaged in relationship with earth and cycles of weather.

Nature is something that exists "out there" and far away, perhaps in a glossy magazine or a television show. In our manmade world, our senses are simultaneously overstimulated and dulled; most of us are numb. Enmeshed with each other in a near constant exchange of superficial information via mobile phones, email, WiFi, and online social networks, in our modern trance we think—or hope—we are making progress. Yet we are not really present to the deeper quality of life, Nature's rhythms, or the sensory world around us. As we become ever more sedentary and wedded to our technology, alienated from our primal nature, the body suffers its own hunger for meaning: a powerful appetite for sensual connection with the elemental world and a yearning for authentic movement.

The body *is* nature, inseparable from the sea of consciousness in which we swim and breathe. Despite the fact that the majority of us live in a disconnected fashion, the bodysoul remains braided into the cycles and rhythms of nature because it evolved through eons of at-one-ment with the natural world. The moment we step outdoors, a subtle expansion occurs—a nonverbal communication with the living, sensory world around us. Even in the city you can feel this.

Subtle as the changes may be, we shift with the seasons: our energy levels and rhythms; the shape of our bodies; the foods we desire to eat; the way we turn inwards or emerge outwards. The natural frequencies of the bodymind reflect nature and its cyclical variations.

Our senses are the threshold where we engage the world around us, where we stand in relation with the Sacred Other. A long walk in nature—even in a city park with its manicured grass and bright embroidery of flowers—stirs the senses and invites us into conscious, celebratory relationship with beauty. We open. When we climb a forested hill and hear the rustling whispers of the verdant canopy, when we feel the spongy earth yield under our feet and the fragrant breeze on our face, we are drawn into communion with the natural world and the timeless, Larger Story. Bodysoul expands when it senses its immersion within the Greater Mind or Field of Possibility—the *suprasomatic sentience*—and nowhere do we feel this more effortlessly than in the matrix of nature. Indeed, the natural world invites us deeper into expansive, sensory relationship because every living thing—the interconnected symphony of life and the elements—reflects and dignifies our soul. Nature and the soul long for each other because they are, in essence, the same: the embodied imagination of the Universe.

Nature facilitates an expansive state rather than a closed, disconnected, and contained one; it models interconnection, authentic movement, and flow. It reminds us of what we have lost.

As surely as soul longs to be expressed in the world through expansive, creative action, the body longs to move. The body *loves* to be in motion, equally for a cheetah sprinting across the dry plains or for giant ribbons of emerald kelp swaying amid the ocean currents. Movement is life. From the microscopic level of cellular exchange to respiration, from peristalsis to functional motor movement, life *is* motion. All that we perceive in the universe is actually energy—contracting or expanding, ever in movement. When we stop moving we die, both literally and metaphorically.

Certainly we move all the time: transiting from point A to point B, eating, walking, breathing, and everything else. *Authentic movement,* however, is something other than locomotive, functional, or patterned. It arises from the body's core and the deep well of soul. It is instinctual and organic in the way that a cat lithely stretches or a willow bends and shimmers in the wind like a graceful dancer. *Authentic movement invites us into the somatic experience of that which seeks to be expressed.* It is the gyrating of hips that have been held frozen for too long; the explosive strike freed at last from its prison in the shoulder; the slow turning and unwinding of the neck after trauma; the great shout that rises up from belly and storms through obediently restrained vocal cords.

Most animals know only authentic movement, for it is somatic and innate. Only we humans—saddled with our will that allows us to override our instinct and impulses—are severed from a natural, fluent connection to the body. In our lives of domestic captivity and tired machinations, we move in predictable patterns and rhythms; in the iron gridwork of our days, we are stuck in well-worn grooves and ruts that carry us always to the same destination.

If we pay attention and listen, the body tells how it wants to move and what yearns to be freed: muscular movement, sound, breath, or subtle energy. When we cooperate mindfully—listening, allowing, following, and exploring—the impulse evolves into full-fledged motor movement, sequencing in some sort of somatic (and often soulful) expression. Although we may channel this motion into movements such as dance or exercise, usually it begins as a subtle sensation arising in the core, a form of micromovement. Every wave begins with an impulse; in the body, authentic movement flows from an instinctual soul expression.

Nonhabitual. Nonpatterned. Nonlinear. Free and expressive. *Authentic movement embodies the soul's longing to expand.*

On a certain level, any movement is good. It offers physiological benefits and frees us from stagnation while enlivening the bodymind. But we need a different sort of muscle strength and flexibility as men—as humans!—and exercise is seldom embodiment. What we do when plugged into an iPod or watching television while on the treadmill at the gym is simply exercise. It energizes and strengthens the physical body but this sort of movement does not truly feed the soul or express its longing. Little of our quotidian exercise is truly pleasurable (do you *really* enjoy it?) and often it simply tightens us further, which is counterproductive to our ultimate goal of core, creative expansion and suppleness. Movement is the antidote to holding; it unlocks body and soul. Martial arts, yoga, dance, and movement arts can be highly beneficial in helping us to open and expand, yet in order to facilitate *authentic movement* they require a level of mindfulness—tracking sensation and embodied desire as it shifts through the subterranean wilds of the somatic landscape.

The way we move reveals us. Our rhythms and patterns speak volumes. I used to lead an exercise with bodywork students in which I instructed them to pair up and then go for a walk around the building and parking lot. One followed the other, observing and "taking on" his partner's gait and posture in his own body. How did this person move? What was it like to try on the person's rhythm and movements? At a certain point, they switched roles so that each had a chance to follow. Assuming their partners' posture and carriage was like putting on their clothes. How did they navigate the world? Sharing notes and observations after the exercise always revealed extraordinarily accurate insights.

The way we move is who we are.

To discover the soul's power, begin with the body. And breath. When we rouse from inertia and containment, when we move the bodymind in nonhabitual, nonpatterned ways, we begin to shift, transform, and heal. The deeper we descend into embodiment and authentic movement, the more we affirm a relationship with power, pleasure, and the soul's emergence. Studies on brain plasticity show that when we move and act in new, nonpatterned ways, we create fresh neural connections that support the novel behavior. As we repeat the innovative behavior, those new connections strengthen until, eventually, they become patterns and habits. Choosing to become more expansive—to move, breathe, and respond in unfamiliar ways—literally begins to rewire our thoughts and behaviors. We evolve.

Our bodies reveal Nature in all its intelligence and innate, untamed magnificence. We are primal, sensual, sexual beings—wild souls—bestowed with self-reflective consciousness and higher states of awareness. Yet nearly everyone is locked in fear and stuck in their familiar cage. Our ego never heals us, only the body does. And grace. When we begin to move naturally and authentically, as nature does, we become present in our skin.

We each contain the elements, alive and in motion, constantly creating anew. Even if you live in an urban metropolis, your body remains an undeniable part of nature. You may exercise it daily or hold it captive like a lion at the zoo, feeling only restlessness or hunger. Anger, perhaps. But the wild, graceful being—the authentic, embodied story of yourself—is still waiting to emerge.

WILD SOUL

In our thoroughly domesticated culture, we have lost the rhythms of our forgotten wildness. Even our perception of being *wild* is somewhat askew; rather than simply free and authentic, we tend to conceive of it as misshapen, violent, and destructive. As a part of nature, the soul is characterized by a natural wildness—a fluency of movement and expression—that has become largely foreign to us. In all of nature, it is only humans that have to *think* how to be, while every other being effortlessly embodies its cosmic blueprint. We are weaned from our creative impulses and trenchantly, steadily guided towards the prefabricated, rigid designs offered by society—ones that will suffocate and consume us.

In Nature, each thing is simply and unutterably itself. When we understand that soul is expansive and seeks to be in conscious relationship with environment and the other-than-human world—and that the allurement of Eros serves as our guide to wholeness—we begin to rediscover and reclaim some of our innate wildness whenever we loosen our restrictions and begin to free what is held or repressed. What wants to move? What are we holding back?

Often we sense—and feel—our soul's longing but remain unclear what action to take. Lost in translation, we hesitate in our actions. Friend, you must recognize that the deep yearning is actually a summons, a call to action, but not in the typical way our overly linear minds usually approach a task. Rather, it is more like a plant's natural impulse to grow towards and follow the sun's transit across the sky, an effortless unfolding of its inner intelligence. Our task is to reactivate the latent, wild parts of ourselves through the body.

In our tamed but frenetic lives, we must uncover the lost part of ourselves that remembers how to be free. Even if we have never discovered our authentic self before, it exists—primal, natural, and timeless. Our bodies and senses are wired for this. Indeed, the sensory center of our brain, the hippocampus, is most active when the stimuli and sensory data it receives come from a "real" environment, as opposed to artificial, technological sources or television.[1] Our wild, sensual soul and bodymind are activated to their true potential by the terrestrial world, not a virtual one.

Others have written with skill and eloquence on their interpretations of what it means to follow a path of soul and to become fully human. Discovering our various subpersonalities—the strategies, patterns, and woundings that drive our ego and complicate our soulful development— is essential, but there is far more to becoming "fully human" than merely having a wild mind. The soul is sensual, hungry, creative, and juicy. Most of all, it is somatic. Alongside discovering the psychological patterns that keep us restricted, chained, and small, we must learn to fully inhabit the sensual body—to rouse the bones and breath—if we are to awaken and rediscover our innermost, authentic selves.

Rather than sit on the therapist's couch and talk about your wounded, inner child, get down on all fours and slink shirtless through the dried grass, nostrils flared to the scent of dried earth and prickly weeds. We need to experience the "missing resource" for our development—nourishment, support, authenticity, boundaries, etc.—while noticing what happens under our skin. The body holds the soul's key.

Can we allow ourselves to dance naked beneath a full moon or sing with all our might in a thunderstorm? What would it require to unbolt the steel box of the vocal cords, to sing loudly or off-key, to unleash a shout—at a time other than while watching the ballgame (though perhaps that's a start). Learn to recognize your inner censor, critic, and judge, along with their insidious somatic patterns; when you breathe and bring movement into the pattern or support the collapse, it begins to loosen its authority over you. Speak your truth from the body.

What if you allowed yourself to move, to discover the energy, sound, and power held locked in the bodysoul? Not simply via exercise on a machine, athletic track, or playing field, but through exploring nonhabitual, nonpatterned movement. To undulate the spine like a desert snake, a copper sidewinder that arcs and slithers across the warm sand. What would it be like to allow your entire body to be consumed in powerful, ecstatic waves of *kundalini* energy at the moment of orgasm, your limbs flopping and flailing about as you bellow with pleasure?

A wild soul embodies the uninhibited truth of pleasure, pain, and power.

We're a long way from wild, most of us. Our bodies have lost their inherent vitality. Our life force is mostly unconscious. Repressed, even. How could it be otherwise when we consume primarily lifeless, packaged, and industrially farmed foods? Eating lifeless and inert foodstuffs, so *we* become. Repressed in body and soul, overfed but undernourished in every way.

In a world that daily becomes ever more technological, synthetic, and severed from the natural environment, soul hungers for something more rudimentary and earthy, genuine and connected to a tangible sense of place. It yearns for rounded edges and undulating curves, for nonlinear, natural stimuli and authentic movement. Most of all, it longs for connection.

In our efforts to be civilized and advanced—in truncating the wild soul—we have so alienated ourselves from any authentic sense of self and at-one-ment with the world that we cannot even understand that our basic problem is societal soul loss—evidenced by our hurtling deeper into societal chaos, personal angst, and environmental cacophony.

THE GIFT OF ATTENTION

As we begin to pay attention—to open the well-fastened shutters of mind, senses, and heart—we learn the world anew. Perhaps for the first time we notice the way a flower actually grows in a spiral manner or how the tendril of vine wraps round the wooden post, or the beautiful, chaotic intricacy of a woven bird's nest. In the same way, we begin to recognize the manner that we hold our breath, constrict our "guts," clench our buttocks or jaw—repeatedly pruning some deeper message or emotion that a wilder, freer soul could naturally express.

We may have no greater teacher than Nature. If we are paying attention, that is. The longer we spend outdoors, be it somewhere semiwild or even the tidy setting of a backyard garden, the more our perspective shifts. A subtle opening or peeling occurs, like sloughing off old layers of skin that shielded us or milky cataracts that obscured our vision. The more time we can spend in a natural environment, free of the mechanical noise of the city, the more our gradual delayering occurs. Each day we observe a little more, notice a few more details that we missed earlier in our habitual haze. We may even begin to detect the wild, nonhuman forms in the landscape, trees, and rocks, as if they were spirits expressed in living form. (They are, by the way.)

A wild soul has different powers of perception. Hearing the sound of wild geese flying, he stops and watches their flight, following them with upturned gaze and noting the subtle movement in his own body, a nuanced sensation of connection synchronized with each wing stroke.

When we cultivate a synesthesia of perception, which can occur only when we come fully into the body, our wild soul begins to awaken. We start to expand, cracking the calcified shell; we stir from the technological trance. We grow and evolve. The more we learn to appreciate—to notice, to stop, to listen, feel, and marvel—the further we facilitate this essential development.

The bodysoul knows. It guides us constantly, even when we are not paying attention (which most of us aren't). To what are we actually listening? And what are we feeling? What seeks to uncoil, expand, and unwind, moving us towards something larger and mysterious?

What if we conspired with our body to free what is held, rather than unconsciously collaborating to remain a prisoner? What if each day we did something not simply to move our energy and enliven the body but to feed our creativity? I say that you would move closer to reclaiming your birthright as a wild, authentic soul.

To what will we give the precious gift of our attention?

As men who embody the Sacred Masculine, we need to learn to "see" as an artist or explorer does, for in doing so we will recognize that the nonlinearity of the world is an essential aspect of its seamless interconnectedness.

NONLINEAR THINKING AND FEELING

Though the process began much earlier, perhaps with mathematics, our societal way of thinking has shifted significantly with the rise of what we call *science* over the past two hundred years. We find ourselves now in a world dominated by linear, analytical thinking; a mode of cognition that underscores—and perpetuates—our pathological disconnection from the rest of nature. Men have firmly embraced this form of thinking, for it embodies a purely cognitive/rational approach to life and notions of advancement; it feels safe from emotions, deep feeling, and intuition—the way of the feminine. Collectively, our seat of consciousness has become the brain, not the heart, and this has underscored our cultural, pathological disconnection from the body.

Yet it was not always so, and there are two primary modes of cognition that exist: the cerebral/verbal/intellectual/analytic one, and a heart-centered/holistic/intuitive one. For untold ages, the latter was our primary mode of gathering information about our environment and the world. On the timescale of humanity, it is only recently that have we given ourselves completely to the former.

Some will no doubt argue that as we "evolved" as a species, we developed our rational/linear capabilities and that this, in turn, has fostered our astounding mechanical and technological development (which we call "progress"). Yet it has also brought us to the point of near total disconnect from our environment with its cycles and rhythms, limits and essential restraints—an innate model of harmonious balance—to the point where we teeter on the edge of global crisis and disaster accompanied by a societal pathology that breeds ennui and a pervasive lack of existential meaning.

In our modern division of mindset, we could describe this verbal/intellectual/analytic mode of cognition as a typically masculine one; the holistic/intuitive/heart-centered mode is certainly more feminine.

More accurate would be to say that the analytic/rational/linear mode of thinking—which is inherently shallow—represents the *imbalanced* masculine, as opposed to a whole and integrated one.

Whereas everything else in nature allows its inner intelligence and organic blueprint to emerge and evolve in an organic, nonlinear fashion, humans singularly have become entrenched in a linear, disconnected mindset at odds with everything in the natural world. Straight lines do not exist in nature (or the cosmos), only spirals and arcs.

Even falling objects, which seem to obey a linear descent, do not. Our planet spins on its axis while orbiting the sun, cruising at 18.5 miles per second. The solar system itself is hurtling on a spiral (not truly elliptical) trajectory through the galaxy at 155 miles per second. The seemingly straight path of the falling object, if it falls for one second, has actually traced a spiral at least a hundred and fifty-five miles long. Exclusively, nature is made up of and uses spiraling geometries. Nowhere do we encounter a straight line.

On a certain bodily level, we realize that these two differing forms of cognition exist. Yet for most men (and our superficial level of embodiment), anything other than mental remains mostly theoretical, vague, untrustworthy, and lacking in hard evidence. Because we identify with our heads (brains) as our primary seat of identity, it's understandable that we choose the linear, analytical mode of cognition; it entirely supports our ego and undeveloped, provisional identity. Our primary mode was taught to us; it's almost solely what (and how) we know. The other form of knowing is intuitive, abstract, and natural, but undeveloped, nearly forgotten, and largely discredited. Why should we even bother to switch our dominant channel?

Because the natural world—of which our bodysouls are an intrinsic part—is not linear. Our path forward in reinventing and reimagining our collective future as a species will not be linear, either. Nature already models and mirrors for us much of what we need to shift and reinvent. As the burgeoning field of biomimicry reveals, when we emulate nature's design rather than impose our rational, analytical process, new solutions appear. Inventor and entrepreneur Jay Harman, in his recent book, *The Shark's Paintbrush: Biomimicry and How Nature is Inspiring Innovation*, illustrates countless examples in which inventors and businesses are learning from nature's models to create innovative, green solutions.

"From sharks, whales, and dolphins to lizards and leeches and butterflies to trees and seashells, there are thousands of species already teaching us about engineering, chemistry, materials, science, fluid dynamics, nanotechnology, medical devices, and on and on."[2]

Biomimicry employs the understanding that nothing in nature is linear, and neither can our thinking be, exclusively. The point is not to cease thinking analytically or in a rational, cerebral way; certainly that has its uses. It allows me to edit the pages of this book in a systematic, logical format, for example; keep an organized schedule; balance my checkbook; and make sense of various other puzzles. The emphasis is *balance* between the modes—lessening dependence on one and increasing the other—in an evolution towards wholeness.

As we have steadily been consumed by our rational/linear cognition, Western society has simultaneously lost its access to the feeling sense, along with the imaginal realms. "Imaginal" does not mean *imaginary*; rather it is the world of archetypes, where the human psyche meets the mythic—the Soul of the World. Describing the domain where the mythic and mundane interpenetrate each other, Henry Corbin first coined the term "imaginal" (he called it the *Mundus Imaginalis*), which was later employed by noted Archetypal psychologist and author, James Hillman. Entrance to this domain is gained by crossing the threshold of senses, open heart, and inspired imagination in moments when a door is left open and the Mystery slides in unexpected to dance in the rooms of our shifting, expanded awareness. Descending deeper into embodiment, one of the most important things men must do is learn a heart-centered way of knowing. This is more than simply *feeling*, though that is certainly involved. It is a stepping away from the mental towards a more somato-emotional, intuitive way of knowing.

Repeatedly I have stressed that when we are receptive as men, we embody the creative union of masculine and feminine within ourselves. The very nature of receptivity—allowing, yielding, welcoming, malleability—is itself nonlinear. As we become more practiced and fluent with receptivity, more flexible, we become less rigid and linear in thought, action, posture, and movement. In a reciprocal fashion, as we develop a more heart-centered, intuitive mode of cognition, we naturally become more flexible and receptive. Mirroring his mental outlook, a receptive man's body moves in an authentic, natural way.

Receptivity allows a man to engage in a different sort of conversation with the world: one in which his ear tunes to dialogue, to nuances of language and sound, to diversity and differences of opinion and expression in a truly open exchange—rather than argue simply to win a point. When we are receptive and open and listen, whether to another being or simply to our own intuition and creative impulses, and then take appropriate, nonhabitual action on what we have received, we embody the creative union of feminine and masculine. Wholeness.

In the martial art of Aikido, rather than meet an attack in a linear way with opposing force, the recipient turns towards the force, yielding to it, and in doing so redirects and diffuses it.

When we learn to feel and "see"—and taste, listen, touch, move—in a nonlinear way, we cooperate with and mirror nature. We move *with* rather than *against*. We evolve towards the expansive, intuitive heart of a balanced, sacred masculinity.

LEARNING TO TANGO

There are countless ways to be a wild soul, to begin learning through the heart—apprenticing to life in a visceral, palpably expansive, and intuitive manner. A dear friend of mine lives in Taos, New Mexico, where he runs an artisan bed and breakfast inn. A talented bodyworker, cook, and gardener, he is a man who works ceaselessly while running his successful business; he also possesses a remarkable eye for creating beauty in his environment, as his appreciative guests will attest wholeheartedly. A couple of years ago, in his late forties, he discovered tango dancing. Though his husband doesn't share the excitement, nearly overnight, tango became my friend's great passion.

His new love has inspired him to dance multiple days each week, and recently he remodeled his garage into an appealing studio filled with natural light. It boasts a gorgeous Koa (a native Hawai'ian hardwood) floor where he can dance and, ultimately, teach. "It's the most difficult thing I've ever studied," he told me early in his tango journey. "It requires learning with my body in an entirely different way."

Visiting him in Taos in the late summer, one afternoon I sat with him having coffee in a pleasant courtyard of shops in the historic district, a stone's throw from the plaza. Ominous gray thunderheads built up over the Sangre de Cristo mountains, threatening an afternoon shower, and the high desert air smelled distinctly of resinous sage. Every so often, the fast-moving trill of a hummingbird zoomed past overhead. My friend's lithe, dancer's body was draped easily into the outdoor chair, and I was struck by his enthusiasm and passion and questioned him further regarding his self-discovery through this dancing form of Eros.

"What I love about it is that it requires me to tune into what the other is feeling in their body. It's more than just learning steps and moves, more than even being simply a somatic type of learning—it's learning in an *emotional* way. Literally, it's a dance between the cognitive, thinking self and the feeling self. And I'm learning this at fifty!" He laughed warmheartedly, darkly bright eyes flashing and expressive hands leaping upwards into the air.

"You know what's most fascinating of all? As I'm learning all this, emotionally, I'm also learning about my relationship with my father. I realize that I've always been about emotions but my father wasn't. He was silent and analytical and distant, and we could never connect. Now, all these years later, dancing tango and becoming an instructor, I'm really learning about myself . . . and my father. It's this beautiful opening of the heart. And it's all because it's happening through the body and emotions. *Sensing* rather than thinking."

When I queried whether he would describe the form of tango as linear, he replied, "It's totally intuitive. The leader knows moves and steps, but what he chooses is entirely based on what he feels in the music."

Much of my friend's life is orderly, concerned with the daily details and demands of running his business, but here is a man living from his wild soul and heart, navigating the world largely through a feeling sense rather than a strictly analytical and rational mode. Indeed, one of the things that I admire most about him is his dancer's fluidity in moving from one state to the other, balancing a heart-centered, artistic, feeling sense—evidenced in the appealing environments, food, and creations that define his Soul

Artist approach to life—with a practical, focused, and highly skilled cognitive ability. I salute him for following and dancing his Eros, substantiating the Sacred Masculine in such a passionate and elegant way.

TRACKING THE WILD SOUL

Beyond exploring authentic movement and response, sensory orientation, and nonlinear, dominant thinking, what does it mean to have a wild soul in the modern world? Whether we live in an urban zone, a suburban sprawl, or a rural setting, how do we embody this nondomesticated essence of self? Surely having a wild soul implies something more than beating drums in the woods, undertaking a contemporary-style vision quest or a pilgrimage to Burning Man in the Nevada desert, and then returning to our "default" lives at the office.

Regardless of where we dwell, we can embody a worthy percentage of our innate, subdued wildness—our natural authenticity. Body and senses are the borderlands, and one's profession and residence matter little (at least initially). That said, a wild soul is not likely to be welcomed within the confines of a corporation where conformity is important and rewarded; nor is someone well entrenched in such a setting likely to risk embracing the startling authenticity that a wild soul always personifies. Similarly, a wild soul is almost entirely at odds with our childhood survival strategies—particularly the ones that kept us orderly, small, and safe, like the "inner good Boy Scout," as I call mine—the ones that still lurk in our Shadow and attempt, often successfully, to run the ego show.

Robert Bly, author, poet, scholar, and father of the mythopoetic men's movement in the nineties, offers us some insightful advice:

One Source of Bad Information

There's a boy in you about three
Years old who hasn't learned a thing for thirty
Thousand years. Sometimes it's a girl.

This child had to make up its mind
How to save you from death. He said things like:
"Stay home. Avoid elevators. Eat only elk."

You live with this child, but you don't know it.
You're in the office, yes, but live with this boy
At night. He's uninformed, but he does want

To save your life. And he has. Because of this boy
You survived a lot. He's got six big ideas.
Five don't work. Right now he's repeating them to you.

It's time to stop listening to those old strategies. If you want to reclaim your authenticity and freedom as a wild soul, that is. Much of what fills these pages serves as a field guide, not only to Eros and the Sacred Masculine but also to ways of returning to the wild, untamed essence. In your attempt to discover what such a person might look like, certain key words may offer illumination—creative, intuitive, feeling, heart-centered, nonanalytical—but here are twelve notable characteristics of such an individual:

- *A wild soul embodies radical authenticity.* He personifies the freedom and courage to be himself, to not follow the herd. It means speaking his truth rather than a habituated, acceptable, or clever answer. He strives to find work that has meaning—soul work, offering one's unique talents—something more than merely a paycheck.

- *A wild soul's passion ignites his dream.* The golden threads of allurement and the summons of Eros lead the wild soul onward. He dreams and creates, whether as a "hobby" or as his work in the world. He heeds his innate creativity and expresses it in a tangible way, his life a physical manifestation of the erotic spiral of creative, sexual and spiritual energies.

- *A wild soul is inspired by natural beauty.* He has a drive to be enfolded in nature's embrace, coupled with a desire to protect it, and understands that each thing has a right to be here and a role to play. More than likely, he will be found outdoors rather than in.

- *A wild soul inhabits the body differently.* The body is a source of pleasure, power, learning, and communion through opened senses. Not just a fleshy stick figure, the wild soul reveals a certain openness of the chest, a looseness of gait, a spark of life in the eyes. Breath is less restrained. Everything in his carriage is less *held*, less domesticated, more authentic and free.

◆ *A wild soul is always reacquainting himself with the world.* Sensing the interrelatedness and wholeness of things, he allows the world to present itself for discovery (rather than simply imposing a linear, analytical, scientific approach). He learns equally from the body—its feelings, impressions, sensations, and patterns—for it too is a part of nature. *Show me. Teach me. What is the message here? What seeks to be discovered?*

◆ *A wild soul dwells in the untamed borderlands.* An "edgewalker" who knows that vulnerability is also a teacher, he accepts that it is only at the edge that he grows and evolves. Evolution happens at the fringes, never in the status quo or the safely familiar.

◆ *A wild soul trusts the seasons.* He remembers that life is a cyclical rhythm of seasons, a series of passages. He knows that everything, good and bad, will change and pass away, perhaps to return in a slightly different form or perhaps not. In a restless world, he has patience (or strives to).

◆ *For a wild soul, life is an adventure.* With open heart and senses, he perceives life as a journey—sometimes a challenging or painful one—leading him to a unique destination beyond his imagination. In his own way, he is an explorer, seeker, and wanderer.

◆ *A wild soul navigates in both light and shadows.* He inhabits the day world and the night world, at ease in both with senses cast wide. He willingly risks his Underworld journeys and understands that wounds always carry gifts and that the sacred and the profane are simply two sides of the same coin.

◆ *A wild soul has capacity for self-reliance.* Nourished and fed by both nature and community, he is also willing and able to fend

WILD SOUL, WISE HEART | 183

for himself and to find his own way in the world using the tools
at hand (whatever he's carrying with him).

♦ *A wild soul recognizes, respects, and responds to wildness.* He feels a
somatic resonance in breath and bones—a camaraderie or soulful kinship, even—with the elemental and non-domesticated,
whether that be human or 'other', sound and movement, image,
mythic archetype, weather, or landscape. Wildness mirrors our
depths and true nature back to us.

♦ *A wild soul is a heart-oriented outlaw.* He relies on experiential
sensing, a direct perception of the world through the heart rather
than cognitive, analytic thinking. He is a renegade who eschews
the orderly, civilized, and totally domesticated—all the opposites
of wildness—and sheds his shoes (sometimes his clothes, too).

Though I have used the pronoun *he*, note that none of the above-listed
qualities have anything to do with gender or masculinity. As the union
of the masculine and feminine within us, soul itself is beyond gender.
I'm pleased to know many wild souls who are women—reflecting on it,
currently it seems that I know more women who meet this basic outline
of criteria than I do men. Clearly, brothers, we have some learning and
catching up to do.

Domestication begins early. In the classroom and at home, nearly every
one of us has been trained out of our innate eroticism and creativity, our
souls forced into tight, regimented boxes until we have successfully learned
and internalized the message: *Authenticity and wildness are not welcome.*
Conform and adopt the roles given to you. Let fear and shame keep you small.

Yet our blueprint is to be fully ensouled as a living thing that seeks
only to grow, in communion with the natural world of which we are an
intrinsic, inimitable, and erotic part. If we follow our Eros and allurement—descending into the bones and breath, casting our senses wide
while fearlessly revealing our heart and facing our shadows—we can
recover that wild, elemental, creative aspect of our being. We become the
untamed, radically authentic one the Universe *hopes* we will be (and conspires to help us become, through all manner of encounters, lessons, and

opportunities). A modern-day vision quest is not required, but some sort of soul pilgrimage and initiation will be, most definitely. On that personal soul quest, the body offers the starting point as well as a compass. As outlined in the chapters of this book, this can happen almost anywhere. *Almost*. And you must be willing to step out on your own and go further than polite, restrained, distracted, and domesticated society wants to go—following a faint trail that only you perceive and that leads into the thickets. Or the jungle.

WELCOMING THE OUTLAW

As we loosen the iron shackles of family expectation and societal pro-gramming, our soul becomes more wild and we will notice a curious shift in our own psyche (and bodymind). Decreasingly are we willing—or even able—to remain in roles that blunt or demean our creative spirit, whether at work or at home. Realizing that our underlying hunger is never truly assuaged or fed, we will be less entranced by the junk-food distractions of modern culture. Narrow lives within the rigid, linear framework of the cities and urban life will begin to chafe and gnaw, becoming ever less comfortable or appealing. In the geometric grid of our cities and neighborhoods, we feel constricted. The breath cannot be inhabited fully. Something wild grows within, and we will find ourselves allured more and more to Nature—not merely as an escape but as a way of life. It is the place where we feel most fully ourselves, ever more at home when we are immersed in the living, shifting, breathing, animate world. Such is the way humanity has evolved, a part of nature not *apart*, and even if we have never lived so in our current life, our cells and soul remember.

When we are free of the realm of concrete sidewalks, where rustling trees and open space surround us rather than apartment buildings and parking lots, or suburban lawns and side-by-side houses, we begin to notice (and appreciate) the shifts that occur in our body. Distanced from the electric hum, no longer bombarded by manmade noise and electro-magnetic fields, shifts happen not only in our awareness, but in the brain, as well. We begin to think and act differently. Emerging behaviors that may seem novel, different, or odd to friends and family—to ourselves, even—are often simply the authentic, wild soul emerging. We may have dwelt in a city our entire life, but the wilder our soul grows, the more we uncover and inhabit our unmanicured edges, the stronger our desire— need, really—to live in a place that reflects that nondomesticated essence.

On all levels—brain, heart, biochemical, and soul—we are shaped by our environment and deeply affected by it. Ever more intense burns our desire to be in a place that supports our expansion and growth, where we feel connected to something greater, where we feel an affinity for the forms and forces of a place (such as its landscape and seasons), and where our intimates are living beings rather than "things." Or work. In almost every way, civilization is at odds with nature. Stephen Harrod Buhner puts it bluntly and brilliantly, as usual:

> "'Nature is,' as Henry David Thoreau understood so well, 'a prairie for outlaws.' Those who go into Nature become, of necessity, *uncivilized*. Thoreau was well read. He knew that the word *civilized* comes from the Latin *civilis*, meaning 'under law, orderly.' Ah, his little joke. *Civilis* itself comes from an older Latin word, *civis*, meaning 'someone who lives in a city, a citizen.' Those who go into wilderness, into Nature that has not been tamed, are no longer under (arbitrary) human law, but under the all-encompassing, inevitable law of Nature. They go out from under human law. They are no longer citizens, they are not orderly, they are not civilized—they are outlaws. When you go into wilderness, something happens, something that civilization does not like. (That's why they cut it down, you know.)"[3]

Ultimately, what the wild soul seeks—and discovers—is a *living* experience that is nonlinear and nondomesticated, something quite other than a mental construct. For when our human senses are immersed in the other-than-human world, we are activated as antennae of perception. Steeped in that primal experience, bathed in streams of information and sensory images that flow in every moment, the soul awakens through the body's field and Earth's touch. We are *fully* alive, the way we were when we were young. Simply put, to use our senses most productively, to fully inhabit the self as a wild soul, we must go out from the cities.

An interesting thing happens when we taste wildness, in ourselves and in nature—we begin to hunger for it. As if it were some vital nutrient we have been too long deprived of, one we didn't know we were lacking until it was reintroduced, the more we eat and drink of it, the more we will be revitalized. We transform and awaken. We change.

Don't go back to sleep.

The deeper we venture into nature and wilderness, the more our own ordered regularity—and our willingness to be ordered—disappears. We become ever less concerned with fitting in and social niceties, trimming our hair and wearing shoes. Popular trends seem oddly puzzling, even laughable. Conservative thinking dissipates, and we are ever more fixated on discovering our own authenticity and the unique, sometimes gnarly, manifestation of that expression.

Our bodies begin to change too, regaining a renewed sense of health, vitality, and vigor. We feel less atrophied, inelastic, and unwell—the standard side-effects of domestication. Movement comes more naturally and *feels* natural. Somehow in this transformation, this rewilding, sweat seems essential, as if we are now clearing out the channels that have been clogged, hardened, and paved over in a "civilized" life.

More and more we learn that the living things we observe and sense around us (body included) are our real teachers, and that to learn from them we must embody a different kind of cognition: the mode of sensing rather than thinking (just like other wild things). Whether in the way we tend our garden or a hive of honeybees, or through the spiritual path of love with our beloved, we begin to grasp the difference between *studying* something and *apprenticing* to it.

We become more comfortable with darkness, both external and our own inner shadows. When we have wrestled openly with our own Shadow and the spirit of death, the blackness of night, whether in a fragrant pine forest or alleyways that reek of trash and urine, no longer evokes the same sense of fear. And the wilder our soul grows, the longer we are steeped in nature and wilderness, the more fully do we realize that something deep, dark, ancient—powerful and silent—*still* exists in the world. Watching us. Waiting. It is a knowing that comes not from the mind but from the expansive field of the awakened heart.

WISE HEART

In considering its importance to an evolved masculinity, perhaps it helps to understand more about the heart, less as a mechanical pump as we've mostly been taught but rather as an organ of perception—one that generates the largest electrical field in the body.

Recent scientific heart studies reveal that the heart is far more than simply a cardiovascular pump that circulates blood. Our primary life organ is formed of ten billion cells, each synchronized in electrical, wavelike patterns; 60 to 65 percent of those are neural cells, the same kind as in the brain, and they function in an identical way. In essence, the heart is a specialized brain with its own nervous system, whose role is to process specific types of information—largely from the senses.

In utero, the heart is beating before the brain is fully formed. As the regions of the brain develop, they grow from the bottom—the primal brain where our emotion centers are localized—and expand upwards. In a real way, the thinking brain grows out of the emotional centers. Thus, long before the cerebrum, or rational, thinking brain, exists, there are the emotional brain and the beating heart.

What we are learning in research centers is what ancient wisdom has long held to be true: rather than the brain, the heart is the master organ and governor of the body. In fact, the heart is actually a major organ of perception. All living beings (and matter, in general) generate an electrical charge and energetic field from the bioelectricity of the body and movement of atomic particles. Though it is a faculty that modern humans generally don't cultivate, we have the ability to detect energetic fields through the heart's field. Primarily, we sense them as emotions and nonverbal, intuitive flashes rather than articulated, verbal thoughts. In a two-way arrangement, impulses enter the heart via the electrical field—composed of sensory interactions with other types of electromagnetic fields—and are transmitted to the brain, which categorizes and then sends these data back to the heart and rest of the body.

Generated predominantly by the constantly swirling vortex of blood spiraling in channels through the cardiovascular system, the heart's electrical field is significantly the most powerful produced in the body: it is approximately five thousand times greater than the field generated by the brain. The heart's field not only permeates every cell in the body but also radiates outside us and can be measured up to ten feet away. Clearly, we are electromagnetic beings, not simply physical ones (as if it were even possible to separate these). In a very real sense, we are an electromagnetic expression of our physiological processes, cognitive functions, and emotional expression.

Heart communicates with the brain through four primary means: neurologically, through the transmission of nerve impulses; biochemically, via neurotransmitters and hormones; biophysically, in pressure waves (which also create electrical impulses); and energetically, through electromagnetic field interactions. Combining the various and complex elements of these four methods of communication—including countless nerve cells, noradrenalin, dopamine, ANF (atrial naturetic factor), and pressure waves that generate an electrical current—the heart plays a central role in blood pressure, emotional processing, hormones, homeostasis (or *homeodynamism*), and our electromagnetic field.

Our body rhythms are entrained by the heart's more prevalent rhythm. *Entrainment* is the phenomenon whereby two independent rhythms synchronize with each other; the strongest rhythm draws others into synchrony. In a room of pendulum clocks, the largest pendulum will *entrain* the others, with the result that they will all begin swinging in the same rhythm. In what appears to be a universal principle, entrainment is also a phenomenon that appears in music, chemistry, biology, psychology, astronomy, and other fields. When our heart emits *coherent* patterns—at one beat per second, these are essentially the same frequency as the wavelength found in nature—the brain and the rest of the body entrain with those rhythms and we function at optimum capacity. Most of the time, however, the heart actually produces so-called *incoherent* rhythms, which are tied to our mental-dominant and frequently distressed state of being.

Coherent is better.

At the moment of coherence, a wide-ranging array of beneficial physiological effects begin, and the cardiac rhythms phase into a seamless, sine-wave-like pattern. The autonomic nervous system divisions (sympathetic, parasympathetic, enteric) begin to synchronize with the heart's pattern, and the body moves directly into a more parasympathetic-dominant mode ("rest and repose" versus the "fight or flight" of the sympathetic mode). As we relax, the autonomic system readjusts, triggering a tide of helpful hormones and neurochemicals, while stress hormones such as cortisol are reduced. There is even a chemical effect in the eyes, causing them to become soft-focused with an emphasis on peripheral vision.

The brain and heart are meant to work coherently together, not in a hierarchical arrangement of brain over heart (which has become our typical mode of navigation in life, particularly for men). When this heart-brain communication flows—in coherence and positive heart entrainment—connectivity increases between the brain and the entire body. Apart from physical health benefits, it is an expansive state that can be felt as openness, lightness, ease, and *flow*, creating a powerful energetic field and catalyst for healing. A new mode of cognition is activated, a holistic/intuitive/sensory one, which heightens creativity and a sense of alignment in the bodymind.

Few of us live in a state of heart coherence, however, for we have long been habituated to the mental, analytical mode (which generates *incoherent* cardiac patterns). Our education and culture focus on developing the brain, not the heart, and we are addicted to a verbal, intellectual, analytical form of thinking and cognition. Early in our lives we are trained out of using our hearts to guide our actions, directed away from its intuitive knowledge and understanding. Unlearning this pattern does not come quickly or easily, and acquiring this skill later in life feels awkward; it requires time, practice, and patience.

Our heart has an astounding ability to detect and synchronize with other types of electromagnetic fields. To initiate heart coherence, we need only focus externally on our environment, reaching out through our senses and *feeling* something—a tree's roughly furrowed bark, for example—which shifts our site of consciousness to the heart rather than the head. We can also begin coherence by focusing on the heart itself. Almost immediately there will be a change in breath, an involuntary inspiration, a signal that early coherence has been triggered. This is followed by a subtle somatic expansion and opening. The simple veering of focus alters the heart cycle and simultaneously cascades a series of responses on all levels of physiological and cognitive functioning. Writing about the intelligence of the heart as an organ of perception, Stephen Harrod Buhner states that "simple attention to these [natural] stimuli is sufficient."[4] Linear, mental thinking breaks the state, however, and results in disruption between the heart and brain fields, the typical *incoherent* pattern.

As we increasingly focus on the heart and our senses, shifting consciousness from the brain, coherence increases. Something begins to stream into us through our expanded heart's field, a quiet tide of life force and information, which we largely perceive as affect and emotion. The Soul of the World speaks in a language older than words. To begin to decipher and learn that ancient form of communication, we need only understand that there is always a response in the heart to what is presented to the senses.

Breathe. Listen. *Feel.*

We are once again touching on the invisibles here: a world of energy, subtle perceptions, and emotion. This style of sensing or feeling is both underdeveloped and underappreciated in Western cultures. Yet we all do this on a certain level, as when we walk into an unfamiliar room full of people and quickly "sweep" it over with some invisible sense, detecting how it feels—whether it seems safe and inviting or bristling with unfriendly eyes.

The living intelligence and creativity of the Cosmos permeate everything from atoms to cedar trees to supernovas. We dwell in a fully participatory and reciprocally sensing universe; *we cannot perceive a thing without it also perceiving us.* Despite claims of science, there is no such thing as a truly objective experience. What we touch, observe, or interact with also touches us in return.

In this form of sensing, of reaching out to an *other*, there exists a moment when each being experiences something unique in the other. It's a feeling for which we have no word in our impoverished English language. The Athenians called such an awareness *aisthesis*: the experience of feeling the touch of life, of a particular kind of other-than-human awareness on us, in return. For the ancient Greeks, the organ of aisthesis was the heart, that part of us that is capable of feeling. It was understood that this exchange, this nonphysical touch between the human and nonhuman worlds, opens moments of perception and understanding, when insights flow into us that can arrive no other way.

Where we most powerfully feel this sort of exchange is in the living realm of Nature. When we reach out and touch the wildness of the world and Nature's soul, something new—and essential—arrives in us. As with the breath, we open in *inspiration*. The mindful observer notes that in this mutual "touching" or sensing, in addition to the affect or feeling, there is also a simultaneous change of physiology. A somatic response ensues: a dilation of the heart's field, a deepening of breath, a relaxation or "settling." *Everything is relationship.*

Although it is not offered as such in this final chapter, learning to sense with the heart is decidedly a soul skill, one that can transform our lives profoundly. At any time, we can extend our sensory focus to something alive or natural, and *feeling* it, trigger coherence (and its accompanying beneficial shift in physiology). At the end of a mental workday, step outside and connect with whatever living thing greets you—a stand of bamboo, a flowering shrub, a small green lizard, a purple clover blossom in the lawn—and let your mental dominance and heart incoherence shift.

The way of the Sacred Masculine is also the path to healing, transformation, wholeness, and conscious relationship. The challenge is to heed the direction of our expansive hearts, not solely our brains. For us as men, how would our lives be different if we acknowledged the heart as a primary sense organ and source of guidance? What follows is merely one example.

HEEDING THE HEART

One of my "soul brothers" is a park ranger, often fond of wearing a white Stetson while in the field. For years he lived and worked within the pastel-hued, dramatic landscape of the Grand Canyon, a rugged environment that fed his wild soul on many levels. Walking the dusty trails through shifting seasons of intense heat and freezing cold, he came to intimately know that arid land and its diverse array of desert denizens. My friend has a keen intellect, a talent for poetry, a passion for cooking, an athletic body, and a guiding sense of soul. He is strong and direct in some ways, soft and yielding in others, and I consider him to be a rare and admirable example of a well-balanced guy. He possesses an unusual sensitivity and empathy, yet for most of his life, in matters of the heart, he settled for an approach of "this will work for now." A curious sort of disconnect, it was as if his heart abided silently before it could come to life, somehow mirroring the desert that waits patiently for the blessing of rain in order to finally burst into ecstatic bloom.

A couple of years ago, what began as a "literary love affair" with a wild, beautiful woman—a psychotherapist, wilderness guide, and dancer whom he had known for some time—quickly accelerated. He found himself in a territory he had not explored previously, complete with a somatic imperative that he needed to dismantle his well-established life in the desert and move to the mid-California coast to be near her. "It was a knowing in my body, along with a trust that this would unfold as it needed to . . . in all the right ways." Though he had not heeded his heart in this fashion before, he understood that he needed to follow its call with direct action, which included leaving the Canyon and essentially starting anew. Their soulful wedding—an overnight camp-out in the coastal mountains, complete with a sweat lodge ceremony—unfolded less than a year later.

He and I sat on the deck of their charming Carmel Valley home, enjoying a cool evening on the cusp of the autumnal equinox. Sharing a twilight meal we had cooked together and a bottle of well-crafted wine, we watched a great pearl of moon rise from behind silhouetted fans of the silvery oak trees. Like homing pigeons, our wide-ranging conversations always circle back to the sheltering roost of soul. When I asked him questions about deciding to follow his heart's guidance, he reflected quietly for a moment and then said, "It was more than simply wanting or longing to be with her. It was a somatic sense of openness. Rightness. While it meant dismantling my life and taking a huge leap of faith, my path was also absolutely clear in a way it never had been before. Actually, it was a similar sort of knowing to what I would get when on the trail in the Canyon, all my senses open. A visceral sense that I was as much a part of that landscape as was every other desert creature."

As my friend continued speaking of his body's wisdom, he placed his hands on his chest and abdomen.

"This is what I know in my heart and I will follow. My heart and belly are not separate, and I know that's a sign. If I allow heart and belly to guide me, as it's doing, the path keeps illuminating itself. The next step will become apparent."

He realized that he didn't have to figure anything out other than taking the step his heart dictated—albeit a significant one, nothing less than ending his current chapter of life and transplanting himself to a new, unfamiliar landscape. "No matter how much soul work we do," he said, "our wounds persist. I knew they would be triggered in this new relationship and love—how could they not be? But I will come to this place with my heart and wounds and offer myself willingly."

Illuminated in the glow of the fire built in the portable hearth on the deck, he smiled, something like wonder and contentment in his blue eyes. "She is so different from me! And I get to spend the rest of my life learning how to be a human in this world, walking a path with heart . . . and there is no more rewarding journey than that."

As I observe him and his beloved together (she is also a dear friend of mine), creating a home and building conscious relationship on many levels, I witness the beauty of awakened, intimate relationship—not only with each other, but with Nature and their environment. In an ongoing work with their own hands, they are constructing a lovely garden to yield a significant portion of their food and have planted an orchard of fruit trees. Their vision makes many nods towards sustainability, including the installation of massive catchment tanks to capture water for the property, as well as tending several colonies of honeybees at the bottom of the garden. In each of these remarkable individuals, I see a balanced symbiosis of masculine and feminine, while the dynamism of their marriage reveals the holy union of the Sacred Masculine and the Divine Feminine. Inspiring to witness, they are bringing light to their Shadows and tenderly—boldly—walking the path of the wise heart, two beautiful and soulful outlaws exploring the wilderness of love.

MOVING THROUGH THE WORLD

This chapter began on the streets of London, navigating the busy modern world with a sense of the soul's energy, movement, and a heart-centered awareness as my compass. On the journey to becoming a fully authentic being—a Wild Soul—we must learn to free what is held (or for some, cease from continually discharging our vital energies): movement; emotions; power; pleasure; life force. A wild soul isn't destructive; he is radically authentic and free. Virile. Creative.

In a daily life too often framed in despair or existential angst, the deep yearning we feel is actually a summons—a frozen soul seeking freedom to spiral and unfurl creatively. Yet our inertia and distraction, our fear and restrictive patterns, firmly fix us in place. Eros guides us through the body's somatic messages and we must pay attention and learn to read those signals. For when we begin to inhabit the body and breath differently, so too do we begin to move through the world in a new way. With heart as primary sense organ, our entire perspective shifts, becoming more acute, as do our powers of perception.

It requires but a simple shift in perception—focusing on the heart itself, or reaching out with open senses and the heart's energetic field—to initiate a significant recalibration that can entirely rearrange the way we engage and inhabit the world.

When we discern and sense with the heart, we interact with Nature and the Soul of the World, and their energy flows into us. At first this may seem terribly subtle, perhaps even imaginary, but with practice the streaming becomes clear, immediate, and powerful—a mode of perception clearly felt in the bodysoul (indeed, *feeling* is always its primary channel). Experiencing the world in this way begins to shape us in precisely the way we are meant by Nature and the Cosmos to be shaped. Loosened from our well-practiced restraint, our innate wildness and authenticity emerges, along with a certain energy, vitality, and grace—our mana embodied.

In an upward, transforming spiral, the more our life force, power, and personal authenticity—including movement—increase, the more strongly we are drawn to channel them into further pursuit of Eros, allurement, and our soul's creative work. It is a positive feedback loop, self-generating a life of ensouled vision and action.

As we soften our mental and somatic armor and dilate the heart's field, a shift occurs. Breath deepens instantly, gaze relents, body relaxes. We move differently. An easy grace animates us, a counterpose to the linear, segmented, mental-dominant mindbody. Once again we become warm, welcoming, sensual flesh rather than a hardened, protective exoskeleton.

The world is erotic, a lover waiting to be discovered and made love to. Eat the wild. Eat your Shadow.

Authentic individuals don't just inhabit their bodies in a different fashion; they inhabit the world differently. Alive rather than numbed. Feral rather than fashionable. With a wild soul and a wise heart, they inspire others to loosen up and savor the dripping, honey-like, raw sensuality of life uncontained.

THE SACRED MASCULINE

The Great Work at hand—a reenvisioning and reimagining of humanity's sustainable future as a species—will be accomplished by the work of men and women who have collectively embraced the Sacred Masculine and the Divine Feminine within, celebrating the soul and the sacred. Every one of us is the Universe, embodied. Each one of us can be—indeed, must be—among those creative souls who are waking up to the challenge we face. As we heed Eros and evolve our notions of masculinity, moving into radical authenticity—welcoming our wild soul and wise heart—we become catalysts for change through creative vision, deep imagination, and purposeful action. We embody new options for living and loving.

In a mechanistic, reductionist universe, soul sharing is impossible. It can occur only in an animate, breathing world, steeped in wonder and expanding possibility. For this, we must learn to experience and savor the world anew, to inhabit and move through it in an evolved, polysensory way. As an Erotic Warrior or wild soul, a man remembers that the poise of the white egret standing at the water's edge, watching intently, waiting to strike as the wind stirs his feathers, is the same conviction and truth in his own breath and bones. We are not separate.

When you open your heart and sense through your field—engaging in a holistic/depth/intuitive mode of cognition rather than a linear/analytic/verbal one—you cannot help but be changed. The spectrum of your experience widens, drawing you to evolve into a full-spectrum being. Compassionate. Accepting of diversity and the unfathomable, mysterious complexities of interconnected relationship. Willingly, shamelessly drunk of the intoxicating beauty and pleasure of being ensouled in this material existence. And this can happen anywhere, even on a crowded city street, sitting on a park bench, walking the dog, or noticing the bright flowers smiling in a neighbor's window box.

The Sacred Masculine invites us to inhabit our senses and wild, compassionate heart, to descend into the sensual body and soul, and to build the authentic power of our life force as we offer our unique gift to the other-than-human world. There is a reason you are alive.

Everything is relationship.

◆ ◆ ◆

Embodying the Erotic Warrior

The Erotic Warrior seeks to recognize his habitual patterns of action, movement and expression, and as an exploration of his deeper, authentic nature, he experiments with nondominant, unfamiliar possibilities. He also routinely shifts his awareness from his head to his heart, reaching out with open senses to experience the Soul of the World in an intuitive, nonlinear, holistic mode of perception—knowing this facilitates his own evolution as a conscious man.

In the Great Work at hand, he knows that Earth is dreaming awake the Sacred Masculine and Erotic Warriors, beckoning men to emerge into an authentic, heart-centered masculinity, each with a gift to carry. He knows that his essential wildness is welcomed as the heart of his humanness, and that he perceives the world differently—animated, alive, intelligent.

Dancing, he lets his life be a wild love prayer to the Beloved.

SOUL SKILL #6: EXPRESS YOUR BODYSOUL

Movement is the antidote to holding. The body was designed to move, and it wants to move. It *loves* to move. One of the primary ways that we begin to soften the rigidity and holding in our tissues—and thinking—is through conscious movement. As we loosen our body armor through expressive movement, dance, breath, sound, and singing, the soul emerges in newly authentic ways.

Authentic movement arises from our core and follows its own volition. It is nonhabitual, nonpatterned, nonlinear, animated, and free, expressing the soul's longing to expand. Whether swaying like a noble tree in the breeze or dancing like a madman beyond all limits, when we bring movement to the bodysoul we begin to open. We crack our shell of containment and emerge into something larger. Wild. Erotic. Alluring. Powerful.

EMBODYING SOUL SKILL #6: DANCE WILD

If you don't have any good dancing music, the prerequisite to this exercise involves obtaining some appropriate tunes. For this sort of expressive movement, it's best to dance to something that doesn't have words that you understand, because words and lyrics tend to take us into our heads, imposing a set mood as we sing along. Better to stay with the feeling and movement that arises simply from the music itself. A wealth of world music awaits your discovery, and much of the modern, electronic music can also be quite good for this sort of movement, especially if it's wordless. Percussion always awakens and moves the soul's timeless, primal energy. (The first sound we heard and felt in the womb was the cadence of our mother's heartbeat.)

You'll also need a decent set of speakers that enable you turn up the music to a good volume; loud is better because it moves us in a different and more powerful way. Keeping the volume low to protect your neighbors is politely courteous, but be mindful of overly inhibiting yourself. Using a portable music player with earphones or "earbuds" is not as good as simply being able to dance freely, partly because you're holding onto the player (and earbuds fall out, etc.).

Whether it is in your living room, bedroom, or garage, you need enough space where you can move freely without bumping into corners of furniture or objects. Slide any furniture out of the way. Make some room. Put on some comfortable clothes that allow you free movement—clothes in which you don't mind sweating. Or get really vulnerable and simply strip down naked.

Men seem reluctant to dance, as if it is silly or uncool. We're often afraid to let down the guard of our carefully constructed persona and allow the body to move the way it wants to. Dancing is not something that our culture generally equates with *manliness*, and there seems to be lingering prejudice that professional male dancers must be gay. Yet dancing brings the body and soul alive as does nothing else, quickly unleashing our power and wild soul.

The first thing to lose (other than possibly your clothes) is your self-inhibition. This isn't about *dancing* or exercise as much as it is simply allowing your body to *move*. Following the music, give your body permission to express itself however you feel inspired, without any regard for fancy steps, "moves," or looking good. No one is watching; let yourself go. Explore.

Give yourself twenty minutes to a full hour when you can be alone, turn up the music, and shake things loose. Although you *can* explore this exercise with a partner, it isn't about dancing with someone (and you may find yourself feeling inhibited rather than fully free). Primarily it's a solo experience of allowing movement to unfurl and unwind in your own body as you follow the music and the beat. (At a later date, when you feel comfortable, bring someone else to the exercise and discover how it changes everything—a whole new realm of moving authentically in relationship with another. Juicy, indeed.)

Breathe. Let the music coax you from old, stale linear habits. *What wants to move?* Allow it. Follow it deeper into your dance. Loosen your face, jaw, and neck.

Dance to free your body from its tight patterns that quietly and incessantly limit your expression. Dance to uncage your soul. Grunting, gasping, shouting, or laughing, free your voice and let sound emerge. Shake your buttocks and wondrous body, whether it's sleek or rotund. Pound your chest. Dance your Shadow. Emote your longing with the entire body. Express your repressed anger and rage, tearing down the world. Slap your thighs and your glutes. Dance with the lover of yourself. Tear off your clothes and dance your crippling shame. Let your manroot flop about in every direction, thrusting. Swing your hips and release the uninhibited sexual energy locked there.

Explore different rhythms of movement, noting what patterns you are repeatedly drawn to and which ones you resist. Do you enjoy only the slow, safe, languid movement of rolling waves in your body, or are you wilder, exploding with chaotic energy? Move in ways you're not accustomed to: eruptive; staccato; lyrical. Breathe fully and deeply. Spin like a dervish until everything falls away except your open rapture. As the Wild Soul, rediscover pleasure and power in raw, uninhibited movement. Sweat your prayers.

Afterwards, let your body come to stillness. Notice how you feel. Observe whether your senses feel more open and expansive. How are you now moving through your familiar space? The world . . . ?

BODYSOUL INSIGHTS:

Once you've explored some ecstatic, nonpatterned movement and dance, consider the following statements and queries. Alternatively, select a few of them—maybe the ones that seem most threatening or off-putting—and literally *dance* them. Utter the statement aloud and then dance until the truth of it emerges from the depths of your being. Of course, you can simply write, journal, draw, or otherwise explore the insights, always noticing the response in your body and soul.

- Where in my body do I feel the most restricted?
- My anger is locked in my . . . (finish this sentence).
- What I most need to withhold from the world is . . .
- The danger of being a wild soul is . . .
- I cannot move freely because . . .
- If I could embody and move like a wild animal, it would be the . . . (name the animal).
- What about my life is linear? Nonlinear is . . .
- What I most long for is . . .
- What do my patterns of movement reveal about me?
- If I followed my heart as a primary sense organ, I would probably discover that . . .
- The devil in me knows that . . .

CONCLUSION
THE WHITE HART

One day near the end of my time living in Wimbledon, something rare and beautiful graced my life. It was in the county of Kent, southeast of London, where I was scouting for a countryside house to rent so that my partner and I could move away from the city. I was riding in the estate agent's car after viewing a cottage near the village of Penshurst. As we drove along a narrow, winding road through wooded hills on our return to Royal Tunbridge Wells, I glanced out the passenger window and down into a shaded dell. Below me in the dappled glade, a realm of sunlight and shadow, an all-white deer stood with her neck upturned, nibbling on the green tree leaves. My wandering mind snapped to attention, my eyes blinking in near disbelief. The pale hooves and pink ears revealed her as a true albino, a special manifestation in the animal world.

"There's a white deer down there!" I gushed excitedly to the agent as she steered the car around a bend and my momentary glimpse of the white one vanished.

My amazement seemed completely lost on the agent, a middle-aged woman with tired sadness etched deeply into her face, her eyes dull, flat pebbles. As she navigated the twisting road, her dry, pale hands held the old BMW steering wheel like the curled, cracked feet of a lifeless bird.

"There are deer all through these woods," she replied matter-of-factly in a southern English accent.

"But this one was all white," I explained, attempting to emphasize the uniqueness of what I had seen. She turned her head slightly and regarded me with a look somewhere between puzzlement and smug condescension. Clearly, enduring my American enthusiasm added another heavy stone to the basket of burden she carried.

For me, the serendipitous sighting of the white deer seemed a gift of grace. Really, what were the chances that I would happen to glance out the car's passenger window and down into that dell—an aperture of mere seconds—just in time to glimpse the rare creature? While my life has been well-populated by such fortuitous moments, they never fail to feel like magic. A sense of cosmic connection, at the very least. Glimpsing the snow white doe struck me as a good omen that the challenges I currently faced—including my thus far discouraging house hunt—would resolve in good fashion.

A few weeks later, shortly after relocating to a tastefully renovated English farmhouse not far from Leeds Castle, I encountered another white deer. A male. It was late in the afternoon on a chilly, gray Sunday in April, and we were visiting the grand estate of Knole, an absurdly large manor house surrounded by a thousand-acre deer park that has existed since medieval times. It was just as we were departing the great park that I spotted him, the silver-white stag grazing silently amid the ancient trees. He raised his head and wide set of horns and looked in my direction. My heart skipped a beat and something like a song of joy expanded within my chest. I reminded myself to breathe.

Wondrous manifestation, I whispered.

For days afterwards, I found myself thinking about my brief but in-spiring encounter with the majestic one.

As with the white buffalo sacred to the Native Americans, the white hart is something rare, decidedly apart from the other males. Only once in a great while does he appear, a mysterious confluence of recessive genes and destiny. His very presence arrests our attention, his rarity a treasure. Standing in the mists, he seems almost otherworldly and ghostlike. Sadly, he is often hunted by those of conquering minds who seek only a trophy for their wall, those who do not fully realize the significance of his exis-tence: shallow men who would kill merely for sport and a twisted sense of power and accomplishment.

The white hart has been a symbolic totem in Britain and the Old World for untold ages, steeped in mythology and symbolism as a rare, elusive, and kingly creature. In Celtic times he was seen as an Otherworld messenger and a harbinger of impending change; an embodiment of the

Lord of the Forest, and sometimes the noble companion to the horned god, Cernunnos. From Arthurian legends, in which he represented unattainable knowledge, to early Christian beliefs, in which he represented Christ and his presence on earth, the silver stag evokes something transcendental. The snowy hart is also an inspiration, a glimpse of something mysterious and magical, yet far more real than any unicorn or imagined creature of fancy.

This special being seems a fitting symbol for the Sacred Masculine. As a horned male, the stag embodies a virile and unquestionably masculine energy, something inherently wild and beautiful. His rippling power and easy grace are unmistakable. Alert to the presence of danger, he is fierce when needed and can defend himself or his mate when challenged, yet mostly he lives in quiet communion with the forests and fields. A seamless and vital part of his surroundings, he is also a uniquely beautiful element in the web of life.

It is not such a far leap from *hart* to *heart* and this, too, seems deeply relevant to the Sacred Masculine. At his essence, the Sacred Masculine is the bearer of the awakened and compassionate heart, infused with conscious gratitude for the wonders, beauty, diversity, abundance, challenge, and mystery that surround.

In our fractured and fragmented world, the Sacred Masculine has reappeared. In many shapes and forms, he courts the Divine Feminine to engender the world's healing and restore balance. Already he is among us, an archetypal energy working for change and awakening, standing up for ecological preservation and social activism, while recognizing our mutual interdependence as a species.

Like the white hart, it will be the bold, unique, and different individuals who begin to reshape and redefine our outmoded notions of healthy, admirable masculinity. Evolution occurs at the fringes, never with the status quo. Mirroring nature's evolution (for we are never separate), new, unpredictable, and creative qualities will emerge on our collective journey, further shaping and defining what it means to be a multidimensional, conscious man.

We are the ones at the edge, generating change in the world by ensouling the body, transforming our own lives, and bearing something of inestimable value. Embodying power and grace, the silver stag emerges from the tangled, darkened wood. The Green Man lives, stepping forth to teach us about stewardship, while the Erotic Warrior guides us towards a soulful embodiment of Eros.

A brotherhood of the white hart is born.

SPIRITUAL ECOLOGY AND THE SACRED MASCULINE

Nature teaches us through its patterns, both visible and invisible, that everything is interdependent. Each is part of the whole, no single element more essential than the others. This is humankind's great stumbling and learning: to begin owning our significant impact and disconnection, to recognize our place in the web rather than continue destruction or false mastery over it. The other-than-human world is a *communion* of beings, not simply a collection of *ecosystems*, and we can no longer carry on bull-dozing it aside, exploiting everything as resources, or perceiving other life forms as somehow separate, inferior, or *other*. What anthropocentric hubris. Without the miraculous kingdom of plants and trees we would have no oxygen to breathe. In reality, from fungi to invisible microbes, it is everything *nonhuman* that makes our life possible—including the ten trillion cells in our bodymind that are essentially *other* yet united in relationship, a sort of superorganism.

Ecology is defined as the relationship of an organism with its environment or surroundings. Ever rooted in conscious connection, the Sacred Masculine personifies a *spiritual* ecology. We are stewards here. Service to Gaia as a biospiritual being propels us into a new level of awakened relationship in which, increasingly, our choices and a commitment to deep ecology become paramount. We choose locally to support the community in which we live, moving away from an unsustainable way of life in whatever ways we can and seeking new options. Through our individual resonance with surroundings—triggered through open senses and heart—we deepen our love for Gaia, who is, above all, an embodiment of the Divine Feminine, a stunning example of Universal creativity.

The Sacred Masculine involves more than just stewardship, however. Husbandry and stewardship are a reawakening of the sacred—a conscious custodianship of body, mind, and spirit included, for these are never separate from the larger whole. Microcosm mirrors macrocosm. Soulful manhood embodies essential, holistic qualities within us, a union of opposites. Thinking does not give any sense of wholeness; feeling does. When we tune into our senses, heart's field, emotions, and intuition, we *feel* a wholeness and connection in bodymind. In an evolutionary loop of positive feedback, our sensory perceptions of wholeness then lead us deeper into feeling and polysensory awareness, further enhancing our sense of connection and well-being.

An exchange in an expansive, heartfelt, sensory way with the Soul of the World allows its essential goodness—its innate morality and wisdom—to flow into us in return. We begin to perceive the deeper messages and communications of the world and our biosentient planet, spoken of and celebrated by healers, shamans, poets, artists, lovers, and mystics through the ages. This is something more than aisthesis; it is the emerging dream of Earth itself.

In surrendering to the sensual unfurling of the soul, we embody the Sacred Masculine and begin relating differently to each other and the planet. When we deepen our communion with the other-than-human world, we come to realize the importance of service and interconnectedness. Planted in our local communities and networks, we become representatives of global change, triggering a collective shift in consciousness. We are visionaries of cultural renaissance. Green warriors. Sacred lovers. Soulful outlaws.

EROS AND EMBODIMENT

What grace to have a bodymind on this journey! Despite the aches and pains of it, the smells and raw animalness of carnality, what a gift to be inseparable from this sensual mass of matter. How intoxicating to feel its power and pleasure, and how humbling to feel its frailty.

Far more than some highly complex machine that rolls us through our mechanical days, the body is a remarkable canoe meant to ferry us into deep waters of Mystery. The more we unfold the sails of our sensate perceptions, the more we detect the subtle, energetic aspects of our being. We are steered further into intuitive and mystic realms of connection and consciousness. The senses are not simply basic and sensorimotor; they offer a direct link—a bypass of the cognitive and rational brain—to the psychic, subtle, causal, and even nondual states. *The sensual is transcendental.* The heart's energetic field, our senses, perceptions, intuition, and imagination are an integral part of an invisible network through which Gaia communicates. We are immersed in and inseparable from the *suprasomatic sentience* that animates everything.

Some will argue that there are higher spiritual realms or levels of conscious development beyond the seductive luminosity of this psychospiritual world. I don't disagree; I have experienced such causal states in waking, dreams, and deep sleep. However, this is a book about the soul and our uniquely human journey to embodiment and *ensoulment,* not the highest realms of disembodied consciousness. The awakening that humanity requires at this moment of the Great Work is one of primary, sensory connection with the other-than-human world and our environment. We require a terrestrial evolution in our collective agreements and intersubjective worldviews. Using a term coined by ecological theologian Thomas Berry, what we need is not transcendence but rather *inscendence.* Embodiment rather than enlightenment, I say. In this life, our job is not to transcend being human but to become *fully* human.

The prayer of the soul is that we embrace the beauty, passion, pleasure, and power of the body as the vessel of our imagination and creativity. To do so is to know authentic Eros. To live fully *ensouled* is to be free and highly evolved as a unique embodiment of the Cosmos, offering our gift to the world, untethered as a wild soul.

Embracing the Challenge

How is it that we resist the infinite intelligence that animates everything in our world, from our bodies on a cellular level to the whirling of distant galaxies? We long for road maps and definitions, for certainties when the only constant is change, rather than trust the ambiguous and mysterious process that guides life's infinite possibilities. We seek to figure things out with our linear, mental capacities (and usually, one's controlling ego) rather than surrender to the invisible forces that draw us to the distant and unknown sea, like water, always along a nonlinear course.

Over the years, I have come to realize that we all hold the keys to the locks that keep us prisoner. In my work with others and my own struggles to risk a larger, more authentic life, over and over the way makes itself clear: to fully inhabit my body through expansive, ensouled practices. Intuition, quiet reflections, mysterious and enigmatic dreams all serve their purpose, as does the continued work of recognizing Shadow and recurrent patterns. A sense of Nature, from which we are largely severed, proves indispensable in our deeper transformation and healing. Yet in my experience, reinhabiting the body is our first task, for it unlocks all the other doors.

The Soul Skills emerged as a way to offer tangible, practical steps to reconnect to one's bodysoul and personal authenticity in a seemingly soulless world. As I stated in the introduction to this book, the skills work anywhere, and each offers its own passkey to the bodysoul's portals of wisdom.

As awakening men, we face several challenges. We must understand that the deep longing we feel—for *something*—is essential. It is the summons of Eros and the soul, the entry point for the larger life that awaits us. Our soulful restlessness is not a symptom of something waiting to be fixed but something authentic seeking to emerge. The impulse towards wholeness is fundamental. Timeless. Despite the way it may seem, brother, you are not alone.

The summons requires courage. *Soul courage.* It demands the bravery and conviction to emerge from your protective shell and strike off in a direction—on your own, at first—that leaves the familiar village behind. We need guts and temerity to face an Underworld journey of shadows and dismemberment, to die to a small life and be reborn into something much larger. If and when you return, you will be changed significantly, no longer able to fit back into the diminutive role and shallow conversations that once suited your former self.

We must invent something other than the packaged, one-dimensional, one-size-fits-all design that society offers—a cheap, mass-produced model that limits us to mediocrity. You are meant for something better, far more powerful and alluring. In the personal evolution of soul and spirit, our invitation and challenge is to dilate to the deeply creative Source that seeks expression *through* us. We must choose to say yes to it by expanding beyond our ego's patterns of fear, inertia, and containment, emerging from a dark night of shadows into the promise of the dawn. We find ways to *lean into* the situations that challenge our familiar restraints, to push to our customary edge and beyond. In this, we grow. We evolve.

Embracing our inescapable vulnerability remains a large hurdle. Most men don't really know what being compassionate means. Or vulnerable. If we are going to steer through this world with our heart, we must be prepared for the likelihood that it will take a few bumps and knocks along the way. Accept that you are flawed, broken, and yet perfectly whole.

Perhaps alone in all Creation, the unique contest of being human is that we have the terrible power to say no to our creative, soulful evolution. As the Yorkshire-born poet, David Whyte, has written, it is only we who "refuse our own flowering."[1] We diminish our power and pleasure, restricting our own flow. In dozens of ways daily, we repeatedly turn away from our sensual, vital power. We retreat from our awesome potential.

In many ways, humanity has reached the edge of a precipice. We can shake our heads in dismay and despair, lamenting that the hour has never seemed darker. Just remember that it is always darkest before the dawn. In many ways, the hour is growing bright, as untold thousands around the globe begin to wake up to the Great Work at hand.

Brother, you are summoned on a soul quest into the darkest parts of yourself to unearth and reveal your true light and *giveaway* to community and planet. The world hopes for your unique and priceless offering. Gaia listens for your drum; she awaits your song. The dawn of the soul and humankind's creative evolution with Earth is at hand. What will you dare to bring from the depths of your awakened heart? The energies, archetypes, and metaphors of the Sacred Masculine are needed for the Great Turning at hand, and whether as Green Man, Erotic Warrior, wild soul—or simply *yourself*—your work is essential.

Don't go back to sleep.

A FINAL BLESSING

When we embody the Sacred Masculine as the Erotic Warrior or Wild Soul, we venture beyond the borders of our culturally defined masculinity into the wilderness of the awakened heart and creative soul. Collectively we are reimagining what it means, not simply to be a man, but to be fully *human*.

The biosentient entity we call *Earth* is dreaming awake its own evolution through us, and despite the bleak headlines, a spiral of consciousness is growing. Exponentially. In following Eros and those golden threads of allurement, deepening into *ensoulment*, truly we are serving the Soul of the World.

It is arduous, this journey. At least initially. If it were easy, everyone would do it. Nearly all will hear or feel the summons of Eros at some point (perhaps many times throughout their life) but turn away. You must have profound soul courage, along with the conviction to become your authentic self at any price. Anything less is too small for you and doesn't serve the world.

Brother, as you begin to discover your passion and awaken, as you come to fully reside within the contours of body and breath, emerging through your senses and wild, masculine heart, you will undergo a change. You will evolve and transform. Celebrate that.

Traversing the wide, lonely desert—the crowded urban streets, the dull maze of suburbia—in search of the lost city of soul, remember that you are not alone. When light is lost to the dark, trust that a bright diamond of morning star will reappear on the horizon to guide you.

The Brotherhood of the White Hart now gathers, a circle of wild souls who will bring the Sacred Masculine to life and change the way we inhabit the world. Fathers, sons, brothers, husbands, lovers, and elders, we will reinvision and transform what we leave to our children and future generations. It is an age of miracles and we have a couple to perform together in service to something much larger.

On the grassy hill crowned with a circle of trees, in that ring of luminous, wild and evolutionary souls—visionaries, teachers, inventors, healers, builders, leaders, stewards, artists, poets, shamans, story tellers, coaches, guides, gardeners, revolutionaries, and more—I'll look for you.

I'll know you from the gleam in your eye, the way you inhabit your bones and breath with assured ease, and the resonant tone in your voice. I'll recognize your visionary passion, profound imagination, and unrestrained laughter. Too, I'll detect the faint otherworldly scent, the dark glimmer of power, of one who has descended into the Underworld and returns bearing something essential.

Holding your gaze, I'll nod in approval at the spiral painted on your chest and smile at your calloused, dirty bare feet. A wild soul, you are. In the convening circle, I'll know you belong with us by way you dance like an embodied, ecstatic fool. Shamelessly.

Erotic Warrior, your time has arrived. And we've been waiting for you.

Standing here in the expanding circle, witnessed by all who have gathered—human and *other*—for the Great Work, I ask, *brother, what do you bring?*

There is a reason you are alive, and you are charged with discovering it.

Friend, until we meet in that circle on the hill, I offer you this Blessing for a Wild Soul:

- As you depart the old life that has grown too small, heed your curious, beguiling allurements. (Take your passport, wallet, and dreams . . . leave the rest.)

- May you loosen your shackles of shame and be willing to walk naked to the gods.

- Understand that the derision, mockery, and scorn of those who do not understand what you seek—or feel—masks their own fear.

- May you shed the expectations of others in favor of your own emergent truth.

- Maps are useful but learn to follow the compass of your soul.

- May you have the strength to be alone—and value your own company—until you discover your true soul tribe.

- When you enter the forest at the point where it is darkest for you and descend into your Underworld journey, may you return with the Grail of the soul.

- May you engage the world in a less linear, more intuitive way, recovering a sense of breath and authentic movement.

- Understand that the body is unlimited, untapped potential energy held in kinetic form.

- Realize that your entire being shifts—even your health—when you navigate with a coherent heart.

- May you recognize the underlying importance of claiming our value as conscious men and that which we are bringing forth.

- Remember to continually give yourself away in generosity, knowing that our actions define us in the world.

- Trust that you are never separate from the Mystery, and that grace unfolds in the most unexpected ways in unlooked-for moments.

- May you reawaken to the sacred and make room for it in your everyday life.

- From your heart, bring something precious, vital, and hitherto unseen to the Great Work at hand.

- May you find the place in the world and community where you truly belong as an authentic soul.

- With your heart and senses open wide, in quiet moments may you hear the timeless Song of the World. Be unafraid to sing in response.

Appendix A
Barefoot on the Earth

In our modern world, the majority of individuals are tired and "burned out." This is not simply from work and the pressures of making a living, but from mental and psychic drama (ingrained but nonproductive patterns, poor communication skills, conflicts of differing worldviews, dealing with immaturity, etc.). It also has a great deal to do with the fact that we do very little to actually *nourish* our bodysoul.

Nearly every one of us has been seduced into the modern madness—either the "hurry-busy" disease or the technological trance, or both. The early promise of computer technology, email, and the Internet was that these advances would give us more time to spend on other things—the ones that really matter. Instead, these conveniences have invaded nearly every aspect of our lives and gobbled us up, so that even if we are not working constantly and responding to endless emails, we are glued to our smartphones, browsing the web and sending text messages. Truly, it is an addiction.

We are working harder and longer than ever before, continually engaged and distracted, chasing entertainment rather than true nourishment. Technology supports our linear, mental nature; rarely does it nourish the soul.

How difficult it is to awaken when everything and everyone around us draws us further into the illusion of connectedness. Back in the States, as I walked through the airport in Salt Lake City on a visit, my gaze was drawn to an advertisement on the wall, where large words read, "Imagine what it's like to really connect." The sign was an ad for a technology company promising faster and seamless Internet connection (as I recall), but I found myself musing on the irony of the slogan. Most of us have come to believe that our blind wedding to technology brings connection, when

211

so often it delivers exactly the opposite. At airports, hotels, and restaurants, I see families sitting together but wordless to each other, all glued to their various electronic devices, communicating with others elsewhere, *somewhere*. Meanwhile, everything except the most blatant and intrusive goes unnoticed.

Imagine what it's like to really connect.

It begins with taking a breath and paying attention to what surrounds. Opening the senses. Expanding the heart's field. It means slowing down. Tuning our attention in to our own bodysoul, recognizing our patterns . . . and surfacing from technoworld.

Continually entrained to the fast, staccato rhythm of city life, immersed in the noise and chaos of it, how do we pause? How do we reconnect to something more natural, healing, wholesome, and soulful?

The Soul Skills point the way. As outlined in the Preface, they are designed to work anywhere, and each in its own way facilitates openness and expansion in the bodysoul. They nourish the soul, while also aiding to build a sense of power in the body and deepen us into conscious relationship (both with self and other). In a word, they help us to *reconnect*.

Dozens of soul skills potentially exist. In closing these pages, I offer you one more, specifically for living in the soulful vacuum of Technoworld.

◆ ◆ ◆

SOUL SKILL #7: DISCONNECT TO RECONNECT

Soul is timeless and elemental, fused seamlessly with bodymind and inseparable from spirit. As with every living thing in nature, its imperative is to grow, to connect, to embody its blueprint. Earthy, grounded, tactile, and terrestrial, soul is fed by the timeless, not the technological, and it moves with rhythms that we are quickly forgetting and losing.

To nourish the soul, slow down and disconnect from the wired world—even for just a small portion of the day. Turn off your phone (or leave it behind). If only for a short respite, pull out from the continuous stream of email and texts. Forego the Internet and television. Eschew the technological distractions and conveniences and come back to the pulsing, breathing bodysoul. *Unplug.*

Breathe. Be here now.

Now, go outdoors.

EMBODYING SOUL SKILL #7:
BAREFOOT ON THE EARTH

Nature is the soul. We *feel* it in the body. Simply step outside the four walls, ceiling, and floor that typically contain you and notice what happens when you are outdoors. Even in a city, our senses open in a different way and we will find ourselves drawn (if only in a visual sense) to whatever bit of nature we encounter: tree, flower, grass, river, open sky. Even if we are not completely comfortable in a so-called natural environment, our bodysoul remembers. Automatically, it expands.

The soles of our feet are beautifully designed as electrical conductors through which the earth's electromagnetic energy and health-generating negative ions stream into our bodies. Multiple studies have documented the healthful benefits of negative ions, including their potent anti-inflammatory effects. Yet with the advent of cushioned, nonconductive, rubber soles in our footwear, most of us are effectively insulated from this elemental, healing energy that serves to keep our bodysoul balanced.

Find a place where you can be outdoors and shed your shoes. A patch of grass or earth is preferred, though the earth's energy also travels through concrete (asphalt and tarmac, with their petroleum content, are different and far less effective conductors).

Allow yourself twenty to thirty minutes to simply stand or walk barefoot on the earth. You can also sit or lie down. In a short amount of time, you will begin to notice a faint tingling in your legs, a pleasant sensation, as your electrical field begins to "ground" and recalibrate with earth's natural frequency. Ideally, you will do this daily (and you will soon begin to notice some interesting beneficial results).

While you're "earthing," allow yourself to simply relax as much as possible. Unplug from the modern world. Stay off your phone. *Disconnect to reconnect.* Take this time to pause, to open your senses and your heart's field. Breathe deeply and fully. You may choose to revisit the embodiment exercise for Soul Skills 1 and 2 and incorporate them with this barefoot time. Explore this exercise as a standing or walking meditation, one in which you don't necessarily have to clear or attempt to silence your mind but, instead, come fully into your senses. Allow the beneficial effects of being barefoot on the earth to gently recalibrate your body, mind, and spirit.

If you emphasize heart coherence during this exercise—focusing externally on your environment, reaching out through your senses and *feeling* something, say, a tree, or focusing on the heart itself—you will further amplify the positive physiological benefits cascading through your being.

At the end of the given time, notice how you feel. Consider your mood. Also note whether any pain or discomfort that you normally feel in your body has diminished. If you find this exercise challenging in its requirement to slow down to "soul speed," what does that reveal about you and your life?

◆　◆　◆

The modern world that we live in does not promote health; the very matrix has become unhealthy. The natural environment, including the earth under our feet, is the true source of health. Healing is natural for our bodies, not supernatural, especially if we can reconnect and plug back into that source of healing.

The importance of soul nourishment in a busy, technological world notwithstanding, overly simple as it seems, if you engage in barefoot "earthing" each day, your overall sense of well-being will shift considerably for the better.

Go outdoors, my friend.

Note: For a fuller discussion on health benefits of "grounding" in a barefoot manner, I recommend two sources. The recently popular book, *Earthing: The Most Important Health Discovery Ever?* by Clinton Ober, Stephen Sinatra, MD, and Martin Zucker (2010, Basic Health Publications), offers a straightforward read, focused mainly on documenting the health benefits. For something less overtly medical or scientific that attunes more to the spirit, I highly recommend the lovely and deceptively simple *To Be Healed by the Earth*, by Warren Grossman (2007, Seven Stories Press).

APPENDIX B
THE SOUL SHAMAN'S BAG

Not so long ago, individuals and cultures understood the connection between body, soul, and nature in a more compelling and integrated way than we do now, largely because the soul was not perceived as a "thing" or separate. In particular, they understood the relevance of breath, of voice in song or chant, of rhythm and percussion, and dance or movement. This was something quite apart from "art" or performance; rather, it was an integral aspect of living in a fully sentient world and being connected to its soul. A few contemporary cultures—Native American, Maori, Hawai'ian, and other Pacific Islanders spring to mind—still value and celebrate these traditional methods of connecting body and soul, but mostly it is a way of being that we have lost in the modern world.

To truly embody the soul, one must become aware of its language and movement, the way its longing *feels* in the body. Tuning in to these sensations and subtle movements brings us quickly to the doorstep of the soul, as surely as working with dreams and stepping out into nature. An embodied soul uses the somatic instruments of sound, singing and music, rhythm, dance, and breath to fully awaken. Yet for any of these tools to achieve their most powerful effect requires setting aside fear, shame, and old patterns of limitation. Coming out of hiding in this way—whether on a therapist's couch or in a martial arts studio—is vulnerable.

The body is the angel of the soul, yet we exist as fully human—seduced by our longing, sexual and otherwise, wrestling with both angels of shadow and demons of light. As we seek to become ever more embodied and soulfully authentic, what will we continue to imprison? What will we risk sharing? Dare we expose the shameful, undesirable parts of ourselves—anger, lust, fear, unworthiness—or will they remain tightly locked in jaw, vocal cords, and body armor? Whatever we seek to bury or hold in the body will still escape elsewhere, arising in dark dreams, powerful projections, and revealing speech.

We can learn a great deal from books, videos, online resources, and "new media" (YouTube, etc.), but there is much to be gained from finding a skilled practitioner of these methods, a coach, or therapist and working directly with them. Almost certainly, such knowledgeable individuals will help us travel further along the soulful journey than we would go alone.

Like the Soul Skills, the following body-centered tools aid in opening the aperture of soul. In their own way, each assists the bodysoul in expanding from habitual patterns that tend to keep us limited and stuck in our small stories. Certainly what is presented here is not an exhaustive list. What follows is merely a jumpstart for further exploration, a few time-honored pathways to exploring realms of personal authenticity and soul. They are means for embodied living, powerful talismans in the *soul shaman's* bag.

BREATHWORK

Breathwork, in its variety of permutations from basic mindfulness to deliberate manipulation of one's pattern, offers a profound way to reinhabit our bodies. Simply learning to pay attention to the breath, to become aware of its patterns and holding, opens new doors of self-awareness and consciousness. Do we routinely hold or restrict our breath? Is our respiration shallow or full? There is a distinct relationship between our habitual breath, the way we dwell in our bodies, and our soul's sense of power. Learning to recognize—and shift—our habits of respiration is a primary tool for facilitating deeper levels of embodiment and *ensoulment*.

As noted in the chapter "Ensouling the Body," when we breathe into the shadows and restricted places of the body, we invite awakening. Sensation, memories, and feelings may trickle forward or rush forth in a surge of emotion. Yet this flood also irrigates and enlivens us to the full spectrum of the bodysoul's experience. Conscious respiration—particularly in moments of emotional activation—allows us new options of response as opposed to our habitual patterns. It is also a way to recalibrate which part of the autonomic nervous system (parasympathetic or sympathetic) is dominant and shift our consciousness into altered states.

Soul Skill #3, "Befriend the Breath," offers a simple introduction, yet many different modalities of breathwork exist for your exploration, some Eastern in their origin, some Western. A few of the better-known approaches include yogic practices such as *pranayama* (alternate nostril breathing), rebirthing breathwork, Reichian approaches, and holotropic, transformative, integrative, and shamanic breathwork. All assist in one's quest for more profound levels of embodiment and personal authenticity.

Unleash yourself. Breathe.

DANCING AND AUTHENTIC MOVEMENT

Perhaps the most powerful way to reconnect with the body on a primal soul level is through movement and dance. Breathwork, yoga, and other tools serve to open the body; literally and metaphorically, dancing *moves* the soul. (Like other artists, dancers intimately know the soul's energy.)

Dance teacher and movement expert Gabrielle Roth suggests that we need to discover the rhythms we resist, for they represent lost dimensions of our being. Whether it's a high-energy Nia class or simply dancing alone in your living room, movement shakes things loose and opens us. Moving offers freedom from stagnation, a sense of play, and a release of energy. At its most profound, dance and authentic movement offer an embodied way of shifting our core patterns of response and engagement.

Moving the body heals the soul.

Soul Skill #6, "Express the Bodysoul," encourages you to dance on your own rather than with a partner (at least for the initial experience); yet of all the avenues listed here, dance is the most communal and social. Indeed, there is something powerful and uniting—tribal—in dancing together. (The crowded floors of dance clubs, though they offer their own sort of transcendental experience—complete with light, smoke, and sweating, half-naked gods and goddesses—do not generally offer the best avenue for authentic movement.)

Roth and other modern innovators of ecstatic movement arts have given us a malleable framework that focuses on free expression rather than on any set of structured movements or steps. In most urban centers in the States (and a growing number in Europe), one can find a dance studio where at least one day a week some sort of communal, ecstatic dance (such as the 5-Rhythms, the popular format developed by Roth) is offered.

Get up and dance. Dance as though no one were watching. Dance your howling anger, dance your dark shame, dance your secret lust. Realize that these held emotions are simply strange and curious gifts in disguise, energy waiting to be tapped and transformed.

SOUND

Singing is powerful in its ability to open the closed portals of the psyche. When one sings, especially when that sound is supported with breath, the entire body becomes a resonating chamber. Just as with other tools in this appendix, sound unlocks the held and restricted areas of the body, mind, and soul.

Any singing is good. It doesn't matter if you're on key or not. The very nature of singing tends to make us feel happy—looked at the other way around, it's something that we tend to do *when* we're happy. Yet like dancing, some of us don't engage in it because we fear we're not proficient or good enough; perhaps we have been teased or chastised in the past for our vocal efforts. To hell with talent. It is an entirely different story when we're working to enliven and free the soul. To free the soul, what matters is simply that we are creating authentic sound and discovering a sense of freedom in that loosening of our patterns of self restraint and censorship.

To sing—particularly in front of others—is to risk being heard. In a real sense, it reveals something raw and potentially unpolished about ourselves. Such actions are always risky and vulnerable, catapulting us directly to the edge of our comfort zones.

Rather than familiar songs and actual singing, explore simple sounds and making tones. A long, drawn out *ohm* for example, in different keys and vocal registers, will wake and enliven the body. The practice of chanting extended vowel-sounds has been a meditative practice for millennia. Studies on meditation have found that simply focusing on a sound (such as "ohm") inside the mind—without generating the actual, physical sound—for a sustained period results in positive effects in the bodymind.

As a tool for embodiment and soul expansion, generally we are more interested in audible, self-generated sound from the vocal cords to loosen and free the bodysoul. Try "toning" for five continuous minutes and note the profound difference in your voice, bodymind and energy level.

Start singing. In the shower. In the car. To your children, mate, or lover. Sing to the plants in the garden and the moon. Sing to the Soul of World.

BODYWORK

A general umbrella term, *bodywork* covers therapeutic techniques that involve working with the body, either in a direct fashion such as manipulative therapies (massage, etc.), breathwork, or "energy" healing.

A large score of bodywork modalities exist, with most of the better-known ones relating to massage therapy (such as Swedish massage). A brief list of hands-on, manipulative bodywork forms could include massage (sports, deep tissue, integrative, Esalen, etc.), shiatsu, reflexology, Feldenkrais method, Rolfing, Structural Integration, Alexander technique, Trager, Somatic Experiencing, Watsu, WaterDance, applied kinesiology, bioenergetics; Ayurvedic *abhyanga* and *urdvartana*, Somatics, Bowen technique, Hakomi, Craniosacral, postural integration, Myofacial release, lymphatic drainage, and more. Other modalities that are less directly manipulative of tissue and fascia, such as "energy" work, include Reiki, Polarity, Healing Touch, Jin Shin Jyutsu, Jin Shin Do, Zero Balancing, marma point therapy, biofield energy healing, and chakra balancing. New forms of bodywork continue to emerge.

On a certain level, any sort of therapeutic work and healing touch offers benefit for body, mind, and spirit. Whether it helps us expand from restrictive patterns in musculature and fascia or open the energetic pathways known as meridians, or *strotas*, bodywork supports a higher level of positive integration in the bodysoul and personal awareness.

Many types of bodywork can trigger emotional release (some actually hold this as a goal). In general, bodywork is a highly effective adjunct and complement to psychotherapy, especially if the body therapist has additional skill or training in the field of psychology—or is simply deeply skilled and empathic, able to hold a healing space for whatever emerges in a session.

A client will reap the most benefit when a skilled practitioner encourages him to participate in the work and his own healing process rather than simply being "worked on." Guiding an individual's awareness to the places in the body where he is constricted, blocked, or held invites a deeper understanding and opens a window for change.

Depth and Somatic Psychology

The vast majority of psychotherapy is palliative—talking about our small, limiting "stories" helps us to feel better. With the help of a therapist, hopefully we gain some insight into those tales, cycles, and patterns in the process of telling them. Put bluntly, the goal of most traditional talk therapy is to assist individuals to better cope with life and our own neuroses. Yet while talking about our "issues" can feel tremendously cathartic (even though most men resist it), very little true transformation occurs unless we also address the body. As a psychotherapist mentor of mine once said, "We can talk about our issues until the cows come home but, until we include the body, nothing is really going to change."

Very little of psychotherapy focuses on the soul. Behavioral and medical approaches increasingly look towards pharmaceuticals to treat "brain chemistry imbalance"—and get clients back to work—and alleviate symptoms of depression. Yet such reductionist methods are simply treating the symptom and generally not looking to deeper causes.

Depth psychology—with its origins in the work of Sigmund Freud, Carl Jung, and Pierre Janet—explores the relationship between the conscious and the unconscious, the dark and mysterious realms of the psyche. In all matters of the soul, it is the depths that we seek to explore, and a skilled psychodynamic or depth-oriented therapist (Jungian, etc.) will be an invaluable guide and ally.

Somatic psychology—which arguably began with Wilhelm Reich, a brilliant but controversial student of Freud who first brought body awareness into psychotherapy—is a relatively recent fusion of psychological and somatic approaches. Approaches like Hakomi, Somatic Experiencing, and Sensorimotor Psychotherapy focus primarily on the body while addressing core psychological issues or the effects of trauma. Somatic psychology views the body as our primary resource, with the perspective that has been explored throughout this book—when we get out of our heads and into the body, we can be far more effective in shifting our core patterns.

If you cannot locate a psychotherapist with a psychodynamic, depth-oriented, or somatic approach, working with a skilled bodywork therapist while pursuing traditional talk therapy sessions can yield positive results.

YOGA

As the sister science to Ayurveda, the five-thousand-year-old healing science of India, *yoga* is an ancient discipline. With its many forms, its *asanas* and breathwork, it far exceeds being simply a form of exercise. Certainly it tones the body, builds strength, and creates flexibility; yet as one surrenders to each pose and the breath, yoga becomes a form of meditation, inviting the mind to still its endless chatter. (The word *yoga* means "yoke," the harness for oxen to pull a plow.) Although in the West we embrace yoga largely as a form of fitness, its roots and purposes are more aligned with preparing one for meditation and accessing the spiritual realms.

Yoga moves an individual through a routine of set postures (*asanas*) while coordinating with the breath. In general, they are mostly static forms, poses, and responses, as opposed to a free-flowing, creative continuum of movement and sensation; yet still this is excellent for loosening our somatic holding and armor. I have noted throughout these pages that as we limber up and become more flexible, we shift in thought and attitude, as well.

While the Western perception seems to be slowly changing, apart from large cities or progressive areas, the majority of men tend to view yoga as something of a woman's pursuit. A stigma seems to still hover—macho men don't do yoga. (They simply remain rigidly inflexible, instead.) The demographics and attitudes are changing, however. At a popular yoga studio that I used to frequent in Santa Fe, New Mexico, oftentimes the Saturday morning class was nearly half men. From college to professional level, more and more athletic teams are incorporating yoga as part of their training regimen (often the focus is to improve flexibility and thus reduce injury, but the athletes discover that they actually enjoy yoga and that it's tougher than they imagined. Hardly sissy stuff, after all).

With its regimen of postures, yoga doesn't directly free the soul like authentic movement and dance, yet it is a very worthy pursuit in personal transformation, building strength and power. (That said, on a soul level, for an individual who is usually unfocused, diffuse, and fond of discharging energy, the steady focus of yoga or *tai chi* may help shift a pattern.)

MARTIAL ARTS

While we generally associate the term *martial arts* with the fighting arts of eastern Asia, these traditional combat systems also include Western approaches like boxing, fencing, and even wrestling. Their popularity endures for a variety of reasons, including self-defense, competition, and development of mental, physical, and spiritual capacities. Popular forms of martial arts include Aikido, Judo, Jujitsu, Karate, kickboxing, and Taekwondo.

Like most sports, as a form of exercise martial arts can tone the body, build strength and cardiovascular fitness, and increase flexibility. All martial arts also offer an excellent way to employ Soul Skill #1, "Rouse from Inertia."

With their kicks, lunges, varying attacks and parries, martial arts provide an effective, safe, and ritualized way to explore our more dynamic core energies. For many men, the energies of anger and aggression have no acceptable outlet in society other than sports. Lacking viable expression, often these powerful emotions are simply repressed and relegated to our unconscious (where they continue to drive us, regardless). Martial arts can be a highly effective way to explore Soul Skill #4, "Face Your Shadow," as well as discovering our patterns of engagement and response (and learning new, embodied options). For an individual who is highly contained and restricted (particularly in regard to anger), the combative quality of martial arts can prove profoundly transforming.

NATURE

Throughout this book, nature is celebrated as an effective and direct pathway to soul expansion and embodiment. It is perhaps the most effectual means that exists, for Nature and the soul are essentially the same: the embodied creativity of the Universe. Yet in our increasingly urban and suburban world, nature seems far away and disconnected from our daily lives.

In both microcosm and macrocosm, nature models openness, expansion, nonlinear expression, and interconnected relationship. Increasing our time spent in semiwild places (or true wilderness, in those rare places where it still exists) is one of the most profound things we can do for unlocking the soul and personal authenticity—allowing the forms and forces of Nature to work on us in its own mysterious way, encouraging us to open and expand.

As with everything, it is the spirit and attitude that we bring to a thing that matters. The time we spend in nature will be most transforming if we are conscious and engaged with our surroundings, senses and heart open, following our allurement (rather than blazing through on a motorized all-terrain vehicle or "camping" at a recreational campsite with a Winnebago, radio, lounge chairs, and a portable television.)

On the journey to deeper levels *ensoulment* and discovering our soul's offering to the world, each of the body-centered tools in this appendix is a golden key laid in your open palm. Each unlocks a different gate in the mysterious realm of bodysoul. As a multidimensional man—an emerging Erotic Warrior—use these methods to reconnect with your core authenticity, discovering and shifting the somatic habits that keep you too small and contained. Paired with the Soul Skills and embodiment exercises, you will be well on your way to claiming your birthright as a wild soul, and an inspiration for others seeking a larger, more authentic life to call their own.

Notes

1. Eros, Passion, and Soul
1. *Encarta World English Dictionary (1999)*, s. v. "erotic."
2. Hollis, *What Matters Most*, 45.
3. Roth, *Maps to Ecstasy*, 181.

2. The Sacred Masculine
1. *Merriam-Webster's Collegiate Dictionary (11ᵗʰ edition)*, s.v. "husband," "husbandman," "husbandry."
2. Fox, *The Hidden Spirituality of Men*
3. Hollis, *What Matters Most*, 181.
4. Plotkin, *Nature and the Human Soul*, 205.
5. Ibid.
6. Jastrab and Schaumburg, *Sacred Manhood, Sacred Earth*
7. Kirkus Reviews, 1994. (https://www.kirkusreviews.com/search/?q=s acred+manhood%2C+sacred+earth&t=all)
8. Berry, *The Great Work*, 59.

3. Ensouling the Body
1. *Merriam-Webster OnLine*, s.v. "inspire," accessed January 12, 2012, http://www.merriam-webster.com/dictionary/inspire.
2. Berry, *The Great Work*, 81.
3. Lee, *Writing from the Body*, 96.

4. Myth, Darkness, and Light
1. Plotkin, *Nature and the Human Soul*, 138.
2. Rilke, "The Man Watching," in *Selected Poems of Rainer Maria Rilke*, (bold font in original)
3. Haugen, "The Return," unpublished poem.

4. Whyte, "All The True Vows," in *House of Belonging*, 24.

5. PLEASURE, POWER, SEX, AND EROS
1. Fox, *Hidden Spirituality of Men*, 217.
2. Roth, *Maps to Ecstasy*, 49.

6. WILD SOUL, WISE HEART
1. Buhner, *Secret Teachings of Plants*, 66
2. Harman, *Shark's Paintbrush*, 8.
3. Buhner, *Secret Teachings of Plants*, 134.
4. Ibid., 97.

CONCLUSION
1. David Whyte, "The Sun," in *House of Belonging*, 90.

Bibliography

Abram, David. *The Spell of the Sensuous*. Vintage Books, 1996.

Ackerman, Diane. *Dawn Light: Dancing with Cranes and Other Ways to Start the Day*. W.W. Norton, 2009.

Alan, Eric. *Wild Grace: Nature as Spiritual Path*. White Cloud Press, 2003.

Berry, Thomas. *The Great Work*. Three Rivers Press, 1999.

Buhner, Stephen Harrod. *Ensouling Language: On the Art of Nonfiction and the Writer's Life*. Inner Traditions, 2010.

————. *The Secret Teachings of Plants: The Intelligence of the Heart in the Direct Perception of Nature*. Bear and Company, 2004.

Childre, Doc Lew. *The HeartMath Solution: The Institute of HeartMath's Revolutionary Program for Engaging the Power of the Heart's Intelligence*. HarperOne, 2000.

Corbin, Henry. *Mundus Imaginalis, or the Imaginary and the Imaginal*. Translated by Ruth Horine. Golgonooza Press, 1976.

Deardorff, Daniel. *The Other Within: The Genius of Deformity in Myth, Culture and Psyche*. White Cloud Press, 2004.

De La Huenta, Christian. *Coming Out Spiritually*. Tarcher/Putnam 1999.

Fox, Matthew. *The Hidden Spirituality of Men: Ten Metaphors to Awaken the Sacred Masculine*. New World Library, 2008.

Grossman, Warren. *To Be Healed by the Earth*. Seven Stories Press, 1998.

Harding, Stephan. *Animate Earth: Science, Intuition and Gaia*. Green Books, 2009.

Harvey, Andrew. *The Essential Gay Mystics*. Harper Collins, 1997.

Helminski, Kabir. *The Knowing Heart: A Sufi Path of Transformation*. Shambhala, 2000.

Hollis, James. *The Eden Project: In Search of the Magical Other.* Inner City Books, 1998.

———. *The Middle Passage: From Misery to Meaning in Mid-life.* Inner City Books, 1993.

———. *What Matters Most: Living a More Considered Life.* Gotham, 2009.

Houston, Jean. *The Possible Human: A Course in Discovering Your Physical, Mental and Creative Abilities.* Tarcher/Putnam 1982.

Jastrab, Joseph and Ron Schaumburg. *Sacred Manhood, Sacred Earth: A Vision Quest into the Wilderness of A Man's Heart.* Harper Collins, 1994.

Johnson, Trebbe. *The World Is a Waiting Lover: Desire and the Quest for the Beloved.* New World Library, 2005.

Lee, John. *Writing from the Body.* St. Martin's Press, 1994.

Markova, Dawna. *I Will Not Die an Unlived Life.* Conari Press, 2000.

Montgomery, Pam. *Plant Spirit Healing.* Bear and Company, 2008.

Ober, Clinton, Stephen T. Sinatra, and Martin Zucker. *Earthing: The Most Important Health Discovery Ever?* Basic Health Publications, 2010.

O'Donohue, John. *Anam Cara: A Book of Celtic Wisdom.* Harper Collins, 1997.

———. *Divine Beauty: The Invisible Embrace.* Bantam Press, 2003.

Osbon, Dianne K. *A Joseph Campbell Companion.* Harper Collins, 1991.

Phipps, Carter. *Evolutionaries: Unlocking the Spiritual and Cultural Potential of Science's Greatest Idea.* Harper Perennial, 2012.

Plotkin, Bill. *Soulcraft: Crossing into the Mysteries of Nature and Psyche.* New World Library, 2003.

———. *Nature and the Human Soul: Cultivating Wholeness and Community in a Fragmented World.* New World Library, 2008.

Prechtel, Martin. *Long Life, Honey in the Heart.* North Atlantic Books, 1999.

Rilke, Rainer Maria. *Selected Poems of Rainer Maria Rilke.* Translated by Robert Bly. Harper Perennial, 1981.

———. *Sonnets to Orpheus.* North Point Press, 2005.

Roth, Gabrielle. *Maps to Ecstasy: A Journey for the Untamed Spirit.* New World Library, 1998.

———. *Sweat Your Prayers.* Tarcher/Putnam, 1997.

Swimme, Brian, and Thomas Berry. *The Universe Story.* Harper One, 1992.

Whyte, David. *The Heart Aroused: Poetry and the Preservation of the Soul in Corporate America.* Currency Doubleday, 1994.

———. *Crossing the Unknown Sea: Work as a Pilgrimage of Identity.* Riverhead Books, 2001.

———. *The House of Belonging.* Many Rivers Press, 1997.

Wilber, Ken. *Integral Psychology.* Shambhala, 2000.

ABOUT THE AUTHOR

 L. R. HEARTSONG teaches a sensual connec-
tion with life, nature, and the Soul of the World.
A body-centered therapist and longtime instructor
of the healing arts, he has worked with men for
over twenty years. He guides others to open their
senses and heart to embrace the deep mysteries
of soul—celebrating the body as ecstatic resource
while exploring what it means to be fully *human*.
A French-trained chef and a backyard beekeeper, he pens the weekly
Soul Artist Journal and hosts the *Riverspeak* podcast (available on iTunes).
Look for him barefoot on the earth, tending the hearth fire at the threshold between worlds. Or perhaps at www.soulquests.com.